FIGHTING FOR THE EMPIRE

An Irish doctor's adventures through imperial campaigns and two World Wars

FIGHTING FOR THE EMPIRE

An Irish doctor's adventures through imperial campaigns and two World Wars

The life and times of Thomas Bernard Kelly (1870 -1949)

David Worsfold

SABRESTORM

Designed and typeset by Philip Clucas MSIAD

British Library Cataloguing in Publication Data

A catalogue record for this book is available from the British Library

Published by Sabrestorm Publishing,
90 Lennard Road, Dunton Green, Sevenoaks,
Kent TN13 2UX

Website: www.sabrestorm.com
Email: books@sabrestorm.com

Printed in Malaysia by Tien Wah Press

ISBN 9 781781 220061

Contents

Foreword

Why write a book about an Irish doctor who few people outside of his own family remember today?

First, because I married into that family: he is my wife's maternal grandfather and her schoolgirl research with her grandmother has provided an inspirational background to this project. That is by no means the only reason.

His is a story that can be told, at least in part, many times over in thousands of British and Irish families. His story may have many more chapters than most but it will, hopefully, have a resonance with many readers.

The service those past generations gave to Britain and its Empire is part of our national and cultural legacy and it is by telling these personal stories that we gain fresh insight into how complex those legacies are. There are aspects of Kelly's story that focus on episodes of British history that are not told as frequently as they might be. Indeed, episodes that are hardly told at all and must leave many people wondering why not.

The most obvious is the sensitive subject of an Irishman proudly serving the British crown. There were thousands like him who did that without question and I hope the story of one man's service gives people the confidence to tell their own family stories when previously they may have been reticent to do so.

As I have been researching and writing this book we have been commemorating the events of the First World War but almost inevitably with a relentless focus on the Western Front. When the contribution of the Empire forces is mentioned it is nearly always in the context of the Western front, perhaps with a passing acknowledgement to the massive sacrifices of Australian and New Zealand forces at Gallipoli. There has been a paucity of coverage of the other theatres of war where tens of thousands of lives were lost, such as Egypt, Aden and Mesopotamia where Kelly served. Or of the huge contribution of Indian troops who Kelly administered to. There is a part of this book that aims to make a modest contribution to redressing that balance.

Similarly, there are many sources that cover the contribution of doctors in the Royal Army Medical Corps in supporting the British Army through two world wars and many other 19th and 20th century conflicts but very little

On March 10th 1870 Col. Thomas Bernard kelly was born. He was youngest of a family of ten. His father was Denis T. c. kelly from Galway but all that is remembered of his mother is that she came from County Mayo. The Kelly family lived in Galway City and it is interesting to note that the family of Grace kelly came from that part of Ireland, but there is no evidence that she is related. Three of his sisters became nuns Anne Kelly in 1889 became fully professed at the Presentation Convent Galway and in 1949 she celebrated her diamond Jubilee. She also was the Reverend mother and the family archivist. It was she who kept everything on the Tibetan invasion. The other two one became a sister of Charity in Paris and the other nobody has any real recollection. Maggy was the only girl who married and she had a son, Denis Moris, who became the professor of Obstitrics at the Galway University. His brother James went to Australia and was followed by Denis, who was next to him, but he was later killed in the First World War.

Thomas went to school called Clongowes and he excelled in sport especially as a sculler. Not much else is known about his early life except for one incident in 1880, when he was ten. He and his brother Dennis decided to go out in a boat for a while. Unfortunatly when they were way out from shore a strong freak storm blew. Luckily they managed to struggle to Aran Island and were unable to get to main shore for days. Meanwhile back at home the family had plunged themselves into deep mourning. Requiems, rosarys everything infact had been said for the repose of their souls. When they eventually returned all thought they had returned from the dead but once again prayers were offered but in thanksgiving. But something

The school history project by Mariette Mason from 1973
that provided the inspiration for this book.

that brings the immense contribution of the Indian Medical Service to the fore.

Finally, in terms of stories that deserve to be told more fully, there is the largely forgotten evacuation from France after the fall of Dunkirk.

Kelly's path through all these episodes of British history offers an opportunity to start peeling back the dusty blankets that have hidden these stories from view.

Researching and writing this book has been a remarkable journey taking in nearly forty countries across four continents, not literally of course as many of them are currently almost impossible to visit safely but as places and events that needed researching and understanding. Kelly's life of adventure took him around the world to places that were troublespots then and many of which remain so today and to follow his life through endless archive resources has been a huge challenge. I am sure there are many sources I have overlooked just as there were many others where my search for answers led to dead ends. I hope these haven't left awkward gaps or left too many questions unanswered.

Kelly may have been my wife's grandfather but this is much more than a family history book, although family and his Galway roots remained important to him throughout his adventurous life. There was much about his life story that the family didn't know. I have been constantly surprised how often he appears in newspaper reports, other people's accounts of events and in official records, almost like one of Alfred Hitchcock's characters quietly in the background, unnoticed until you look for him.

Many people have helped with the research, not least Rosemary his surviving daughter, my three brothers-in-law: Alastair who read various drafts and helped ensure the structure was clear and logical; Rupert who was frequently called upon to explain medical terminology; and Patrick who's insight into the Irish dimension was invaluable. Debbie Mather, his other daughter's eldest child ensured a sensitive balance was maintained in my interpretations of the family life. Unfortunately, her mother, Brigid, died before I commenced this project.

My daughter Benedicta diligently typed up all the references for the bibliography, a daunting task as I had accumulated a vast amount of source material almost unknowingly as I attempted to piece together Kelly's remarkable life.

Researchers at the main sources of official records have been diligent, polite and helpful every time I have called on their assistance, especially at the National Archives, British Library, Imperial War Museum, Liddell Hart Military Archive, Diocese of Galway, James Hardiman Library at NUI Galway, National Library of Ireland, Royal College of Surgeons of Edinburgh, the Maritime History Archive at the Memorial University of Newfoundland and the London Gazette

Many others have been helpful and welcoming especially Sister Helen Hyland and the sisters at the Presentation Convent, Galway, Manimugdha S Sharma of *The Times of India* whose knowledge of Skinner's Horse answered important questions, Julie Hempenstall from the Bendigo Historical Society for invaluable information on his family's life in Australia and the Families in British India Society for its wonderfully eclectic repository of information and pictures.

Above all, I owe a huge debt to Jane Neely, my wife's history teacher at the Brentwood Ursuline Convent High School who encouraged her in the summer of 1973 to sit down with her 86 year grandmother and capture her story which she did in great detail and had the immense good sense to keep. Four decades later that schoolgirl project proved an invaluable resource and inspiration.

Place names have been a constant challenge as spellings vary across the span of 150 years and many have been changed as countries move on from their Imperial past. For the sake of some sort of consistency and authenticity I have used the place names and spellings as Kelly would have known them, putting in modern references where there might be any doubt or confusion. This hasn't been done through any stubborn rejection of political correctness but rather to create an authentic feeling of time and place as the reader follows his life.

Of course any omissions, errors of fact or interpretation are all mine.

David Worsfold
Shenfield, Essex
April 2016

Introduction

This is the story of a remarkable Irishman, Thomas Bernard Kelly, a staunch Catholic from Galway who served the British Crown and its Empire for almost 50 years. His extraordinary life took in two World Wars, Imperial adventures, acts of heroism and encounters with royalty. It seems very strange to us today that someone from the west of Ireland – and who had no special connections with the 19th century British landowners who were still an important feature in that part of Ireland when he was born in 1870 – should spend the majority of his life in a British uniform. But that is just what he did.

There is nothing commonplace about Kelly's life. In 1880, at the age of 10, he and his brother were swept out to sea in Galway Bay during a freak storm and feared drowned, only to be found alive on one of the remote Aran Islands days later. He was academically gifted and qualified as a doctor at just 21.

The real story begins when he joined the Indian Medical Service in 1896. Over the next 30 years his life seems to 21st century eyes to have been one long adventure, full of incident and touching many of the most significant moments in the history of the British Empire. Like many of his contemporaries, he took this in his stride. There are many others like Thomas Kelly and elements of his story will be familiar to many people who have looked into the lives of their relatives who served the British Empire. Where his story differs is that it unfolds into chapter after chapter of adventure as Kelly walks across the pages of British history in the first half of the 20th century.

One of the striking features of Kelly's story is how many of the places and incidents are familiar to the modern reader as he treads through Afghanistan, Pakistan, India, Iraq and Iran. There are many distant echoes of British involvement in those unsettled parts of the world that still have a powerful resonance today.

He was posted to the turbulent North West Frontier soon after he arrived in India, living with constant danger of attack by tribesmen. His first great adventure came as a medical officer on the Tibet-Sikkim Mission of 1904, often referred to as the Younghusband Expedition, although never by Kelly. He was one of the first Westerners to set foot in the mysterious mountain city of Lhasa, winning a

Kelly as a Lieutenant Colonel wearing his dress uniform – with his DSO –
at Simla in February 1923 when he was appointed as an Hon Surgeon to
The Viceroy, Lord Reading.

commendation for bravery along the way and featuring on the front cover of the *London Illustrated News* lunging with rifle and bayonet at an assassin.

Hardly had he shaken the Tibetan snow off his boots than he was dispatched to the disputed province of Seistan in Persia to fight an outbreak of the pneumonic plague. There he faced such hostility that he and his fellow officers in the British consulate had to be saved from a rioting mob by Russian Cossacks. A few months later the famous, and controversial, Swedish Explorer Sven Hedin stayed with him and recorded his ultimately successful fight to control the plague in his book, *Overland to India*.

His first encounter with royalty came in 1911 when he was surgeon to the Bengal Lancers – the famous Skinner's Horse – which acted as the Royal bodyguard at the massive Delhi Durbar attended by George V and Queen Mary. A decade later he was to have a less happy encounter with royalty when he had to accompany the Prince of Wales (later Edward VIII) when he was sent to India to appear useful as part of the Palace's attempts to rehabilitate his poor public image. For the rest of his life, Kelly was to despise the Prince as a drunk and a womaniser. This harsh judgement came from the perspective of his Roman Catholic morality and his life-long teetotallism.

In the First World War he served with the Indian Medical Service in Aden, Egypt and Mesopotamia (covering present-day Iraq, Syria, Iran and parts of Turkey), collecting the Distinguished Service Order as well as being commended in dispatches four more times, including for his role in the aftermath of the failed attempts to relieve the infamous siege of Kut. He also returned a married man, having wed one of the volunteer Queen Alexandra nurses sent to help run the hospitals Kelly by then commanded.

The frontline beckoned almost immediately on his return to India at the end of the First World War as he was pitched into the brief but bloody 3rd Afghan War that raged across the notorious North West Frontier in 1919. The savagery Kelly witnessed during that war is painfully prescient of the shocking brutality of Islamic State and Al-Qaida today.

Retirement from the Indian Medical Service – with the rank of Colonel – in the mid-20s did not quell this restless soul. He took his family – two daughters were born in India – to live in Jersey where he believed the sea air would ease his malaria but he could never stay still for long. He disappeared to sea for three to four months every year as a ship's surgeon with the Royal Mail Lines, visiting South America and the USA. On one voyage he grabbed the headlines around the world as an early 'radio doctor', conducting an operation 300 miles away over the airwaves.

At the outbreak of the Second World War he instantly volunteered for active service but was turned down on the grounds of age – he was by then 69. Undeterred, he became a ship's surgeon in the Merchant Navy. In this capacity he took part in the evacuation of the remains of the British

Expeditionary Force and British civilians from Bordeaux (after Dunkirk), bringing home on the *SS Madura* a famous passenger list that included Hugh Carleton Greene, other journalists including Sefton Delmer, a Rothschild, Marie Curie's daughter and French and Czech government ministers.

By now firmly signed up to the war effort he went with the 8th Army to Egypt and served on Atlantic convoys. This service came to an end towards the end of 1944 when at the age of 74 he was sent home protesting that he was more than fit enough to remain at sea.

He had to return to London and rejoin his family, which had left Jersey as the storm clouds of WW2 gathered, and sit out the rest of the war.

This is just the merest outline of Thomas Bernard Kelly's remarkable life.

David Worsfold

Thomas Bernard Kelly – Immediate Family

Thomas Bernard
Born Galway 11 March 1870
Married Gertrude Agnes
  Fenn, Bombay 29 April
  1918
Died Paddington 29 January
  1949

Father
Denis Michael Kelly
Born Galway c.1826
Married Galway 2 October
  1844
Died Galway 12 May 1883

Mother
Bridget Considine
Born Clare 8 January 1828
Married Galway 2 October
  1844
Died Galway 21 December
  1894

Brothers and Sisters
James
Born Galway 1844
Died Galway 27 February
  1889

Patrick
Born Galway 1846
Death unknown

Catherine
Born Galway 1848
Joined Sisters of Charity, Paris
Death unknown

Margaret Josephine
Born Galway 1849
Emigrated to Australia,
  probably 1870-71
Married O L Randell in
  Australia 1884
Died Bendigo 1924

Denis
Born Galway 1851
Died Galway 1853

Michael Peter
Born Galway 1853
Emigrated to Australia
  1870-71
Married Margaret Carr in
  Bendigo 1887 (died 25
  August 1912)
Four children:
  Doris (1888-1967),
  Robert (1890-1943),
  Margaret (1892-1963) and
  Rita (1896-98)
Died Bendigo 22 September
  1929

Maria
Born Galway 1863
Married James Morris in
  Galway 1885
One son Denis Valentine
  born March 1887, died 3
  July 1941
Died Galway 19 November
  1890

Anne Josephine
Born Galway 22 October 1864
Entered Presentation
  Convent, Galway 21
  November 1889
Died Galway 7 October 1954

Denis Joseph
Born Galway 13 May 1867
Emigrated to Australia 1885
Died Passchendaele 4
  October 1917

John Philip
Born Galway 12 February
  1872
Died Galway 1873

**Children of Thomas
Bernard Kelly and
Gertrude Agnes Fenn**
Christine Brigid Margaret
Born Naini Tal 30 July 1919
Married (Herbert) Thomas
  Foot in London July 1942
Died Bournemouth 20
  August 2010

Rosemary Anne Josephine
Born Rawalpindi 14 January
  1921
Married Adair Stuart Mason in
  London, January 1943

Above: 2 High Street where Kelly was born. The downstairs was his father's wine, spirit and tea merchants and the large family lived above. The premises may have included all or part of the adjacent properties as High Street was re-numbered after 1870.

CHAPTER 1

Early years in Galway
Family, political turmoil and education

No 2 High Street, Galway in 1870 was at the heart of the town's bustling commercial district, with shops running up the hill to the town centre one way and a short walk the other way to the quayside looking out across Galway Bay and, beyond that, the Atlantic Ocean: an ideal position for Denis Kelly's expanding tea, wine and spirit merchant business.

It was also home to his growing household. The downstairs rooms and the courtyard behind were occupied by the merchant business, while a steep, narrow internal staircase on one side of the property led upstairs to the two floors of small rooms where his wife Bridget looked after the family.

But on 11 March that year it would have been one of her daughters who would have been administering to the everyone's needs as Bridget was giving birth to her tenth child and another son, Thomas Bernard Kelly.

Denis Michael Kelly and Bridget Considine had married almost 26 years earlier in October 1844 at Galway's Pro-Cathedral when she was just 16 and Denis approaching 20. They almost immediately embarked on having family with the first son, James, arriving the following year. These were difficult years to have children in the west of Ireland as the autumn of 1845 saw a new fungus blight the Irish potato crop before it could be harvested, triggering four years of desperate poverty, hunger, malnutrition, disease and death that became known as the Great Famine. The blight tightened its grip the following year before receding slightly in 1847, only to return with a vengeance in 1848 and 1849. The potato was the staple diet of the poor, rural communities that dominated County Galway, along with much of the rest of rural Ireland.

Estimates of the total number of deaths through the famine years vary enormously but the consensus suggests more than a million died, over 12% of Ireland's population. Another 1.5 million people are estimated to have emigrated during the Famine years, a combination of factors that led to a massive depopulation with many counties, Galway included, losing up to a third of their population between 1840 and 1850.

It left a painful scar on Irish society, one that shaped its politics and subsequent history. The decades that followed were turbulent and deeply troubled, often setting Irishman against Irishman, a legacy that would wash across the Kelly family more than once during Thomas Bernard's life.

Very few households were unaffected by the Famine, although none of Bridget Considine's immediate and very large family died during the peak years of the crisis from 1845-49. However, in the wake of the Famine, five of her seven brothers and sisters packed their bags and left for Western Australia, in particular the small town of Bendigo in the prosperous and growing mining belt. Several of her closest cousins also headed for a new life in Australia while at least two others settled in the United States.

Denis and Bridget Kelly stayed put in Galway as they waved brothers, sisters and cousins off, never to see many of them again.

By 1853, with the Great Famine still casting its long, grim shadow over the west of Ireland, there were four sons – James, Patrick, Denis and Michael – and two daughters – Catherine and Margaret. Denis senior was laying the foundations of his business that was soon to be providing tea from around the world to some of the great estates that were such a contentious feature of Ireland in the second half of the 19th century.

Then tragedy struck as the third son, Denis born in 1851, died at the age of two towards the end of 1853.

The death of a child was all too common in those days, but it seems to have had a significant impact on the Kelly household as there was then a 10-year gap before the next child, Maria, was born in 1863. There could be several explanations for this: Bridget could have suffered some miscarriages or been ill for a long period, perhaps even suffering depression with the death of Denis and birth of Michael happening within a few months of each other, soon followed by the death of her widowed father at the beginning of December 1854.

Whatever the reason, Maria's arrival heralded a rapid late expansion of the family, as her birth was quickly followed by Anne in 1864 and Denis Joseph in 1867, before Thomas Bernard's arrival three years later. There was another son, John Philip born in early 1872 – when Bridget was almost 44 years old – but he died before he reached his first birthday.

Thus, Thomas became the youngest surviving child and, not surprisingly, remained closer to his siblings born in the few years before him than to the five older siblings surviving from the earlier years of his parents' marriage. Indeed, as if to underline the age differences between the two halves of the family, soon after Thomas's birth his eldest sister Catherine joined the Sisters of Charity as she turned 20 and left for Paris, never, as far as we can tell, to return to Galway again. The second son Michael also decided to leave the now very crowded family home. He headed to Bendigo where the news from

Above: Kelly sitting with his older brother Denis, taken about 1883, around the time of his father's death.

his mother's relatives about the success they were enjoying in making a new lives for themselves Down Under must have sounded appealing. This dispersal of the family was to be a major feature of Thomas's childhood and teenage years.

Relatively little is known about Denis Kelly's family and background before he married Bridget Considine in 1844. All the evidence points to a man from a merchant family with businesses based in Galway but with a powerful drive to make something of his life. This he did, initially in business and later on in the turbulent world of Galway politics. His father rented properties in High Street and Middle Street in Galway city from the Blake of Ballyglunnin Estate and these appear to have passed to Denis Kelly sometime in the late 1840s. Martin Joseph Blake was MP for Galway and a significant landowner.

Bridget Considine came from a large and well-established family spread out across County Galway and County Clare, where she was born. They were well-educated for an Irish Catholic family in the middle of the 19th century: among her closer cousins were at least two priests, a trend that continued into the next generation with one, Monsignor Anthony Considine, born in Liscannor, Co Clare just a few months before Thomas, serving as Dean of Galway Cathedral from 1921 until his death in 1939.

Bridget's branch of the family moved from rural Clare to the centre of Galway, most likely soon after her mother Margaret died in 1840, and that is where she presumably met Denis Kelly as they married in the old Pro-Cathedral of St Nicholas, just two streets away from the High Street where they were to spend most of their married life. Whether they moved in there straight away we don't know for certain, but as it was already occupied by Denis Kelly's family they were probably found a room there, although it is also possible that they may have started their married life living with Bridget's family.

They were definitely well established at 2 High Street 10 years later. The property is listed in Griffith's Valuation of 1855 with Denis Kelly as the occupier and the Court of Chancery as the immediate lessors. Its rateable value of £21 is among the higher values for the properties in the immediate area (the average for the other High Street properties listed is just under £16), reflecting the larger – extensive would be overstating it – ground floor area with a courtyard and storage space.

Certainly by the time Thomas arrived his parents were already key figures among the aspiring Galway middle class with his father soon to join the ranks of Town Commissioners.

Town Commissions were part of the local government structure in Ireland gradually developed during the middle of the 19th century. Galway's was established by special Act of Parliament in 1836 and had 24 members elected triennially. Initially, its responsibilities were limited but it represented an important, if modest, step towards greater self-government in the eyes of many Irishmen. The Commissions were an important platform for that emerging Irish middle class to demonstrate that they were capable of managing the affairs of their countrymen.

In 1860 the Galway Town Commission recorded its powers and responsibilities in its minutes:

> "to have charge of the property of the town arising from tolls, and valued at about £2000 yearly, besides harbour dues, which in 1845 amounted to £2100 which is chiefly applied to the repair of the pier, dock-gates, buoys and mooring posts".

Denis Kelly put himself forward for election in Galway's North Ward, covering the area around High Street, in September 1873. Most of the wards were uncontested with 20 of the 24 com-missioners being re-elected unopposed that year but in North Ward there were four candidates for the two available seats with both of the sitting members – Lewis Ferdinand, proprietor of one of the local newspapers, the *Galway Vindicator*, and N McNamara re-standing.

Galway was unique in Ireland as it allowed plural voting where those people who owned a property with a rateable value of £50 entitled to one vote, those with properties rated up to £100 two votes

Right: A modern view of the former Pro-Cathedral, where his parents were married.

Above: Shop Street, Galway, in the late 19th century, looking towards High Street.

up to a maximum of six votes for properties rated at £250 or more, a system that was a constant source of friction in the often febrile atmosphere of Galway politics.

At the poll on 6 September 1873 the results were:
L L Ferdinand   100
Denis M Kelly   88
Robert Black   66
N McNamara   59

Kelly had unseated McNamara, a well-established local solicitor who had been a member for several years and was a typical representative of the professional classes who made up the majority of commissioners. Kelly's merchant background was often rather patronisingly used against him both during the election campaign and his time as a commissioner, especially by McNamara's former colleagues. Unseating a long-standing sitting member was an unusual achievement as Galway Town Commission seats rarely changed hands, perhaps unsurprising given that large numbers of votes were obviously controlled by relatively few people. There were calls for an enquiry after the election, hardly a novelty in that part of Ireland given that Galway was still reeling from a major electoral scandal in the wake of a Parliamentary by-election held in February 1872. Kelly's result was allowed to stand but he was now part of the colourful and frequently nasty Galway political scene.

A flavour of the sort of accusations being thrown around in Galway politics in the early 1870s can be found in the judgement of Mr Justice Keogh delivered to the Westminster Parliament in which he overturned the substantial Parliamentary by-election majority of the Catholic Home Rule candidate John Nolan in favour of his challenger from 1872, Captain William Tench.

"And I have further to report that a system of intimidation prevailed throughout said County, for many weeks preceding said Election, to prevent voters recording their votes for the said William le Poer Trench, and that such intimidation was exercised, amongst other ways, by means of nocturnal visits to the houses of voters, and threats there uttered, and by the posting, and sending through the post office, threatening notices and letters to voters, and wives of voters, with a view to intimidate such

Above: St Ignatius College, Galway, the Jesuit school Kelly and his brother attended.

voters from voting, as they had previously promised and intended, for the said William le Poer Trench. And I further report to Mr. Speaker that on the day of the polling, at some of the polling places in said County, especially in the towns of Tuam, Oughterard, and Ballinasloe, violent mobs were organised and did attack voters who were proceeding to the poll, to vote for the said William le Poer Trench, and returning there from, and that the lives of voters and agents for the said William le Poer Trench were endangered by such mobs, and that in one part of such County the high road was cut across to prevent voters reaching the poll."

Bitterness, violence and electoral antagonism were ever-present in Galway through the closing decades of the 19th century and were eventually to leave a deep mark on the Kelly family.

During the 1870s the responsibilities and revenue of the Town Commission expanded considerably with the income from tolls alone reaching £7935 a year in 1878. Among the additional powers given to the Commission during this period were those of the sanitary authority – including running water – and responsibility for street lighting, a gas company, the Corrib navigation canal and for establishing a tramway in the town, a project that attracted the enthusiastic support of newly elected Denis Kelly.

Above: A horse drawn tram on the waterfront at Salthill, a project Kelly's father helped to bring to fruition when he was a Town Commissioner

Galway was an expanding town in the 1870s and suburbs started to spring up around the town centre, especially in Salthill, across the other side of the quay that lay at the bottom of High Street. Plans to connect this new suburb to the town centre by tram were keenly promoted by the Town Commission and Kelly quickly joined the sub-committee that was formed to help oversee this project. This led to the creation of the Galway and Salthill Tramway Company in 1877 and the first trams ran along the two-and-a-quarter mile route on 1 October 1879, the whole project having cost £13,000 (over £1.2m at today's values). Of course, the first trams were horse-drawn as it was another 12 years before Galway was to get electricity and a few years more until electric trams were introduced.

Kelly never made a major impact as a town commissioner, although he was a diligent attender of its meetings. He was, by any standards, a modest backbencher of a type found serving on local authorities everywhere in every age. Judging from local newspaper reports and the Town Commission minutes his interventions were of a very parochial nature, especially focused on improving the basic amenities of the town's commercial and retail district, which he represented.

He was also a frequent visitor to the Petty Sessions in Galway from the late 1860s onwards, initially as a witness and later as a complainant, pursuing a variety of people who obviously did not share his aspirations for the High

Street area. Offences that he pursued included begging, "cause a nuisance on the public street by leaving dung thereon" and "breaking the surface of the public footpath without the permission of the County Surveyor". His pursuit of these cases reinforces the image of a man for whom self-improvement was a virtue and who resented anything that detracted from his image of himself, his position in the town and his desire to improve the High Street area.

On more than one occasion his rather proud and stubborn nature almost ended up with him appearing before the Galway courts himself. Throughout the 1870s he frequently fell out with the Blake Estate over the rent and various local rates on the properties in High Street and Middle Street (which was sub-let). His practice of deducting all charges from the rent so he submitted a net amount did not go down well with Walter M Blake who inherited the Estate on the death of his father in 1861. These disputes twice resulted in the Estate issuing a summons against Kelly, one being served on Bridget when her husband was away. Whenever the disputes got to this stage he paid up promptly and the cases never went to court.

When not arguing with the Blakes, he extended his desire for municipal improvement to the town's sanitary arrangements which he clearly did not consider to be adequate for the up-and-coming Irish middle class he represented and an inhibition to creation of a proper environment for the commercial sector, at the heart of which was his High Street business and home. His concern did, however, also extend to the Claddagh, the self-contained community of fishermen, mostly Irish speakers, living along one side of the bay, some of it probably visible from the upper floors of his home at 2 High Street.

This community was exceptionally poor, living in cramped basic accommodation, little more than huts, often with animals sharing a family's one internal room. The abject poverty of the Claddagh became ever more obvious as the rest of the town slowly emerged from the ravages of the Famine and started to establish itself, modestly, as one of the larger commercial centres in the west of Ireland. Kelly wanted the improved sanitary arrangements the rest of the town was enjoying by the mid-1870s to be extended to the Claddagh, an issue he raised from time to time without much success, alongside the need to deal with certain persistent "nuisances" in the town itself.

An opportunity to press this demand arrived in the form of a Parliamentary Commission.

Life was far from plain sailing for the Galway Town Commission during the 1870s as it tried to prove itself capable of running the town's affairs and it incurred several large debts. In May 1877 the Taxation of Towns Inquiry Commission, established by the London Parliament, arrived in Galway wanting to know why, in particular, it was so in debt to the gas company.

Both bove: Two views of the Claddagh, the poor fishing community Kelly's father campaigned to extend modern sanitation to.

During this inquiry it became clear that there were several loose ends in the town's finances and most of the town commissioners appeared before the Inquiry Commission.

Kelly found himself giving evidence on several points to the Inquiry. Initially his contributions were fairly inconsequential but, slowly, the Inquiry became more interested in the terrible conditions that were allowed to persist in the Claddagh. Kelly was called back to explain allegations he had made of bullying to prevent one of the sanitary inspectors completing some work, Kelly having urged the Galway Town Commission on several occasions to carry out a complete sanitary inspection of the town.

What he didn't expect was to find himself the subject of suggestions of cronyism because his eldest son, James, who owned at least two horses and carts, was doing some work for the Commission, transporting road materials. The suggestion was that this was being done under a contract from the Commission, something the Inquiry would have taken a dim view of, as it did when it found out that fellow member for North Ward and newspaper proprietor Ferdinand's son had a printing contract from the Commission.

Kelly, was quick to defend himself and his son:

"I am not in the slightest way interested, directly or indirectly, in my son's contract. My son is of age, working immediately for his own benefit independently of me."

The chairman quickly picked up his slip in mentioning a contract and he was forced to clarify this:

"No my son doesn't have a contract. His horses are employed simply for the day, at 5s a day."

This was a rather crude attempt to discredit Kelly as a witness but his reassurance was enough for the members of the Inquiry, although they left the town without resolving any of the major issues it faced, including the failure to carry out a full sanitary inspection. It does confirm the deeply divisive nature of Galway politics and the extent to which Kelly had alienated some important interests through his surprise election. They may have failed to nail their target this time but they were not inclined to give up easily.

Kelly's interest in the town's sanitary arrangements may seem rather strange for a tea, wine and spirit merchant. It was clearly partially driven by self-interest as he wanted to improve the environment for himself and his fellow merchants, retailers and traders in and around the High Street. Strangely, it was an interest – even obsession – his son was to share. Thomas Kelly's war diaries from Egypt and Mesopotamia in the First World War are littered with references to his inspections of latrines and constant demands that sanitary arrangements, especially for the Indian troops, be improved. Perhaps this, and his interest in health and medicine, has its roots in his father's time on the Galway Town Commission as he watched him struggle to improve the sanitation of the Claddagh.

By the time his opponents attempted to use the Parliamentary Inquiry to tarnish his reputation, Denis Kelly had already successfully defended his seat in another contested election in September 1876. He finally enjoyed the luxury of being returned unopposed with the long-serving Ferdinand in 1879, their scrape with the earlier Inquiry clearly not having damaged their reputations in the town too much. This was to be his last term on the Commission, however.

As the new decade arrived politics in Ireland was becoming more volatile as the nationalist cause began to find its voice, in particular through the Irish National Land League's campaign to abolish landlordism and give tenant farmers the land they rented. The Land League was launched in October 1879 with the controversial Charles Stewart Parnell as its President and a series of protests, including rent strikes, followed over the next few years. Galway's Town Commission was soon sucked into the maelstrom Parnell's Land League created as it stirred the nationalist passions that were never far below the surface in Irish politics.

In 1882 the Commission, including Kelly, declined to support a petition for the release of Parnell who had been imprisoned along with other nationalist leaders in the notorious Kilmainham Gaol in Dublin the previous October on the grounds that it was too political. It subsequently changed its mind when local protests highlighted the plight of a Galway man held with Parnell. Kelly was absent from this crucial re-run of the vote. Whether this was by accident or design we don't know but it appears that he wasn't sympathetic to Parnell's cause.

In that September's Commission elections he faced opposition from the Land League and, although he was re-elected, once again behind Ferdinand, vigorous protests by the Land League about the eligibility of voters in North Ward (and East Ward) and the manipulation of the unique plural voting system in Galway led to the Queen's Bench in Dublin ordering the election to be re-run.

Kelly, along with the other previously successful candidates in North and East Wards, found himself on the receiving end of some savage criticism over their attempts to wriggle out of paying the costs of the case. The *Galway Express* of 20 January 1883 accused them of "ungentlemanly conduct" over a last-minute manoeuvre to employ counsel to ensure they didn't have to meet the complainants' costs once they knew they were going to lose the case. "This piece of trickery was as unkind and ungenerous as it was uncalled for and contemptible," raged an editorial in the paper.

Against this bitter background the new election took place a month later on 22 February 1883. As polling day approached, the *Galway Express* once again turned its fire on Kelly, patronisingly dismissing his credentials as a town commissioner by pointedly commenting favourably on the suitable professional, educational and social backgrounds of many of the other candidates. This must have hurt a proud man who aspired to better himself and, at the same time, make a contribution to Galway civic society.

In the run-up to the election Kelly wasn't well and his eldest son, James, canvassed every voter in the ward on his behalf. It was to no avail. When the results were announced he had lost his seat to L A Lynch, a candidate with the backing of the relaunched Irish National League:

Lynch   89
Ferdinand   85
Kelly   71
Fahy   66

The result was not universally welcomed in the town and even Ferdinand's nationalist-leaning *Galway Vindicator* turned on the successful Mr Lynch the week after the election:

"The energy used by members of the Land League in favour of Lynch and Fahy amounted almost to intimidation. It was wholly incompatible with the freedom of election supposed to be conferred by the Ballot Act. Seizing upon voters when approaching the courthouse, guarding them up to the Deputy President, Mr Kirwin, and absolutely preventing them from being spoken to by anyone but themselves was a course of action as reprehensible as it was unfair".

The *Galway Express*, which had so savaged Kelly in the run-up to the election took an altogether calmer view of the conduct of the election:

"There was a pretty fair share of excitement during portions of the day but not in any degree equal to that of former elections".

Kelly may have had good grounds for contesting this election but he was by now quite sick; the illness that had prevented him campaigning on his own behalf obviously progressing rapidly. He died of kidney disease less than three months after the election on 12 May 1883 with his wife and family by his bedside at 2 High Street.

It is not hard to imagine just what a serious blow losing his seat to Parnell's Land League in such circumstances must have been to a man for whom the respectability of his position meant so much. His father's death just a short time after losing his seat in the wake of such a high-profile controversy must have made a deep impact on the 13-year-old Thomas. It is probably here that the seeds of his life-long hostility to Irish nationalism were planted.

Denis Kelly was the first to be buried in the newly acquired family plot in Forthill Cemetery, a further expression of the higher status the family sought and now enjoyed. But his passing was not reported with the flourish and long list of mourners and family usually accorded to respected citizens. The *Galway Vindicator* managed to get the news into its evening edition on the day of his death but it didn't report on the funeral:

> "This day, quite unexpectedly at his residence in High-Street in this City Mr Denis Kelly, Merchant. Deceased had been some time in delicate health but his illness was not considered serious."

The *Galway Express* the following week noted that the funeral had taken place at the Pro-Cathedral – where Denis Kelly had married Bridget nearly 40 years earlier – with a "respectable gathering". These minimal reports in the main newspapers are surprising and provide a telling commentary on how the Kelly family was viewed in the wake of months of political controversy.

The eldest son, James – by now 39 – took over the running of the business with some help from the rest of the family, most of whom were still living at 2 High Street. Thomas was the only one still at school, having followed his brother Denis Joseph to St Ignatius College in Galway, which was run by the Jesuits.

Unsurprisingly, he was close to Denis, who was almost three years older than him. On at least one occasion, these two brothers got themselves into serious trouble. When Thomas was about 10 he was taken off in a small boat in Galway Bay with Denis and some of his older friends. The story he related years later was that a sudden storm blew up – not unusual in Galway Bay – and that the boat was swept out to sea, eventually landing them on one of the Aran islands where all they could find to drink was potcheen, a notoriously powerful spirit often illegally distilled from potatoes or barley. It was a few days before they sobered up enough to make it safely back to the mainland to the relief of their distraught mother who had arranged for prayers to be said for their safe return. Whether it was by accident or design that the older boys found a convenient supply of potcheen on this adventure we shall never know; what we do know is that this experience of being marooned on a remote island with drunk and presumably very incapable older boys turned the 10-year-old Kelly into a strict teetotaller for the rest of his life.

It is possible that other factors contributed to his dislike of alcohol. He always described his father's business as merely a tea merchants, never referring to the wine and spirit trade he carried on as well, although that is how the business is clearly described on all the headed paper and invoices that survive. Is it possible that some of the clientele and other associations that grew up around the wine and spirit trade conducted from 2 High Street were disagreeable in some way to young Thomas?

Alternatively, it maybe that his status-conscious father used headed paper that made the business sound rather bigger and more important than it was. He certainly wouldn't be the first or last person to do that.

A rather more useful skill the young Thomas acquired from his older brothers was horse riding. His father owned horses as part of the tea merchant business and it is quite likely that the young Thomas joined him – or more likely one of his older brothers – on deliveries to some of the larger estates surrounding Galway that his father counted among his clients. Thomas was a natural and very capable horseman, something that was to help shape his career in the Indian Medical Service.

He was clearly a well-above average pupil because in early 1886 he was enrolled at the Jesuits' top boarding school in Ireland, Clongowes Wood College, with his fees of £5 paid in cash, almost certainly by the church, not uncommon in the late 19th century. This was for two terms of cramming to help him fulfil his dream of getting into medical college and it clearly worked as in October of that year he sat the preliminary examination for entry to the relatively new Triple Licentiate qualification offered by the Scottish medical and surgical colleges at the Royal University in Dublin.

He passed and on 18 November 1886 – not yet 17 – he was registered as a medical student studying for the Joint Qualifications in Medicine and Surgery at the rapidly expanding medical school in Queen's College, Galway, part of the Dublin Royal University.

Why did he want to be a doctor? There is nothing obvious in his family background or the career choices of his siblings that points to this as a career, beyond his father's desire to serve the public and, maybe, his father's concern for the town's sanitary arrangements. He may even have gazed out towards the mouth of the River Corrib and across to the Claddagh from his room at the top of 2 High Street and wondered what he could do to help improve the lot of the impoverished fisherman. Certainly, wherever his subsequent career took him he always strove to help the least fortunate and most vulnerable, even in the most trying of circumstances, often starting with a concern for their sanitary arrangements and general hygiene.

The Jesuits, of course, have always had a reputation for ensuring that bright boys from whatever background have a chance to realise their talents, often within the context of the church and priesthood. This was a route that clearly didn't appeal to Thomas. Once the Jesuits who ran his school in Galway realised the vocation of this obviously gifted child lay elsewhere, probably through his aptitude for science and biology at school, they would have seen it as their duty to nurture it. This they did by finding and paying for a place at their top school in Ireland. Thomas spoke fondly of his time at

Clongowes Wood, often making it sound as if he spent longer than two terms there. Unfortunately, nothing remains of his school record.

Thomas was loyal to the Catholic Church throughout his life, as was his sister Annie, to whom he remained very close as his life of adventure took him far from Galway. When, towards the end of her life, Annie reflected on this period she often remarked that young Tom had been rather spoilt and that everything was done to help him.

With the church's support and the backing of his family, Thomas was now ready, a few weeks before his 17th birthday, to lay the academic foundations of the great adventure that was to be his life for the next 60 years.

Above: The Kelly family plot in Forthill Cemetery, Galway.

CHAPTER 2

Leaving Galway
The family departs

As the teenage Thomas Kelly started to focus on his ambition to become a doctor, 2 High Street became a much quieter place after the death of his father.

Not only did the constant bustle and demands of Town Commission business suddenly stop, but also the family fragmented quickly in the years after his father's death. Perhaps the legacy of the bitter political battles he fought cast a dark shadow over the household and the business: it would be surprising if they didn't given the extent and tone of the coverage of his father's final election campaign in the local press. Galway was a small place and all the family's associates would have known the various accusations that were thrown around over the two elections in 1882 and 1883.

The eldest brother James appears not to have been such an astute businessman as his father so the ability of one business to support his siblings may have become strained, especially with Thomas's college fees to pay from the end of 1886 onwards. Maybe just the loss of the dominant figure in the family forced them to re-assess their commitment to the family, the business and to Galway. It was the start of a decade-and-a-half in which this large family virtually disappeared from the Galway scene.

The early 1880s were tough times in the west of Ireland with poor harvests and constant hardship caused by falling commodity prices and rising farm rents. This period, referred to as the Distress in heart-rending stories in newspapers of the time, was another period of mass emigration and the Kellys and Considines joined that exodus in search of a new and better life elsewhere.

Within a few months of their father's death, Margaret, now in her mid 30s, left Galway for Australia. She joined her older brother Michael who had left a decade earlier and members of the Considine family who had emigrated in the 1850s and 1860s and successfully established themselves in Bendigo, Victoria, one of Australia's boom towns of the gold rush era.

Michael was already well on his way to becoming a successful businessman. He clearly had more of his father's business acumen than his

Above: Michael Kelly (1853-1929), Kelly's second oldest brother who left Galway in the early 1870s and established himself as a successful businessman and stockbroker in Bendigo.

older brother James. It was probably the prospect of playing second fiddle to James back in Galway that drove the obviously ambitious Michael to head for Australia so he could carve out his own path to success. One of their Considine cousins was running the main hotel in the town – the Niagara Hotel – so there would have been plenty of work for any family members heading out to join them, either at the hotel, Michael's shops and other businesses or in one of the expanding mining enterprises that provided the bulk of the region's employment.

None ever returned to Galway.

Margaret married towards the end of 1884 and died in Bendigo in 1924, aged 74, while her brother Michael married Margaret Carr, daughter of an earlier generation of Irish emigrees who left during the Great Famine. They, too, settled in Bendigo where they brought up three children, none of whom married, in a fashionable house called Norwood which is still there today. A fourth child died as a baby. He become a prominent citizen in the town, serving as chairman of the Bendigo stock exchange, and lived until 1929, although his wife died in 1912 at the age of 51.

The next to leave Galway was Denis Joseph, who also headed for Bendigo soon after finishing his schooling, most likely departing in early 1885 as he approached his 15th birthday.

The departure of Denis must have left a big gap in Thomas's life. Years later he would still talk affectionately about his nearest sibling and he must have had some inkling when waving him goodbye in 1885 that their paths might not cross many more times, if at all. He was right. Denis and Thomas never saw each other again but remained in touch across the continents, especially through their sister Anne – self-appointed family historian and focus of family communication over the next 50 years. The news of Denis's death near Ypres when serving with the Australian Imperial Force in 1917 hit Thomas hard: an indication of the extent to which, as far as Galway was concerned, the family vanished, is that Denis's name does not appear in any of the records of Galway's war dead.

Although Denis initially settled with the rest of the family in Western Australia he later joined the army and served as a sergeant with the Western Australian Mounted Rifles in the Boer War at the end of the 1890s, obviously sharing his younger brother's proficiency as a horseman as this was a cavalry regiment.

The state of Victoria went through a severe economic slump in the early 1890s caused by the crash of Baring Brothers, a bank that was still causing more than its fair share of economic turmoil a hundred years later. Denis's decision to join the army may well have been prompted by the economic depression that hit Victoria.

There was also a huge exodus of Considine first cousins to Western Australia during the 1870s and 1880s with virtually entire branches of Thomas's mother's family making new lives for themselves Down Under, although a few headed off to the United States, probably encouraged by the British Government incentives being offered to people in Galway to emigrate to the USA.

Maria, now 21, was the next to leave the family home. She married James Morris in 1885 in a ceremony at the Pro-Cathedral that was conducted by the Bishop of Galway, a rare privilege and an indication of where the Kelly family stood at least in the eyes of the Catholic Church in Galway, helped by the new link with the already well-established Morris family. Morris's father was Barony Constable and a member of the Galway Board of Guardians, duties that his son was to take over after his death in 1888. It was a marriage of which Maria's late father would have almost certainly approved.

Initially they lived at 2 High Street and their only child, Denis Valentine Morris, was born there on St Valentine's Day 1887. He became a key figure in Thomas Kelly's life, ensuring that he retained a strong connection with Galway, long after most of the rest of the family had left or died. Soon after the baby's arrival Maria and her husband moved to a place of their own in nearby Eyre Street.

There were to be no more Morris nieces and nephews. Maria died, just aged 27, on 19 November 1890. Her death and funeral were extensively reported in the local papers, giving a flavour of the status of the two families, the controversy over Denis Kelly's election defeat clearly mellowing with the passing of time, even for the once hostile *Galway Vindicator*:

> "It is with sincere regret that we have to record the death of Mrs. Morris, the beloved wife of our respected citizen, J. Morris, Esq., Eyre Street. The deceased was a daughter of the late Denis Kelly Esq., T.C., P.L.G. She married very young and had only been married for about five years, but during her short life she earned for herself the esteem and affection of everyone with whom she came into contact. Of a bright, cheerful and pleasing disposition, she made herself generally agreeable, yet of deep religious feeling and kind good nature. She was a member of the Ladies' Association of the Children of Mary at the Pro-Cathedral, and so high was the esteem entertained for her by the late Bishop of Galway, Dr Carr, the present Archbishop of Melbourne, that his Grace specially officiated at her marriage".

Her Requiem Mass at the Pro-Cathedral was celebrated by Fr T B Considine, one of her cousins, and the final absolution was said by Dr McCormack, Dr Carr's successor as Bishop of Galway, who had already become quite close to the remaining Kelly family. Thomas was listed as one of the three principal mourners, as he was by then already the oldest man in her close family still living in Galway. She was buried alongside her father in the family plot at Forthill.

Above: The Presentation Convent, Galway where Kelly's sister spent her entire long adult life. It still looks the same today.

Maria's marriage and subsequent move to Eyre Street after the birth of her son wasn't the only departure from the family home in High Street in 1887.

Just as Thomas Kelly was settling into the second year of his medical studies at Queen's College, his sister Anne was making important decisions about her life.

On 26 April 1887 she entered the Presentation Convent in Galway to start life as a nun and was to remain there until her death in 1954, serving for several years between the two World Wars as Mother Superior as well as a teacher at the school attached to the convent and later as Novice Mistress. The Bishop of Galway, Dr McCormack, recorded both ceremonies on Anne's way to becoming a fully professed nun – as Sister Columba – in his personal diary.

> "Ceremony of Reception at Pres Con (G). Gave Habit to Sr M Columba Kelly; gave a short address" – 24 October 1887

> "Officiated at religious Profession of Sr M Columba Kelly & Sr M Joseph Brady, Pres Con, Galway" – 21 November 1889.

Annie, as she was always affectionately known in the family, was to become the main focus of Thomas Kelly's continuing relationship with Galway, along with his nephew Denis Valentine Morris. He corresponded with her regularly (of which only a few examples survive) and always visited the Presentation Convent when he was able to return to Galway.

This left just Thomas and his eldest brother James, now in his early 40s and unmarried, still living with their widowed mother at 2 High Street as 1887 drew to a close. What a contrast that must have seemed to the hustle and bustle of a packed house of just five years earlier. This wasn't the end of the story of the shrinking Kelly presence in Galway.

In February 1889 his brother James died a few months short of his 45th birthday, leaving the family without anyone to run the business. It isn't clear what happened to it after James's death although the property remained in the family's hands and Thomas's and his mother Bridget's home for a few more years.

Thus in just a six short years after his father's death, Thomas's widowed mother found herself living with just her youngest surviving son – out of 11 children – at 2 High Street. It is hard to imagine a more dramatic disintegration of a large family.

Of course, by this time Thomas was well into his studies, his two terms at Clongowes Wood College in 1886 – of which he was very proud – having been a success. By early 1887 he was studying for the relatively new triple Licentiateship created in 1884 by the Scottish medical and surgical colleges. The 1880s was thus a decade of extraordinary contrasts for him: huge personal success on one hand but marred with family tragedy and departure on the other. This must have been hard for a teenage boy to handle and must have contributed to his inability to show his family any emotion in later life, although that wasn't an uncommon trait in men of his generation.

The future, however, must have looked exciting as his medical education gathered pace, especially as he was part of the new generation of doctors being trained at the medical school in Queen's College, Galway, an institution rapidly expanding and growing in prestige during this period. The course he was studying was part of those developments, although it was for an external qualification as it was to be some years before the College could grant its own degrees.

Before 1858 and the passing of the Medical Act, the Royal College of Surgeons of Edinburgh and the Royal College of Physicians of Edinburgh offered completely separate licentiate qualifications. While these continued after 1858, those students looking to become Army doctors in particular had to have both a surgical and a medical qualification. The Edinburgh colleges therefore created a "Double Qualification" for those set on a military career. In 1884 this was further extended when the Faculty (later the Royal College) of Physicians and Surgeons of Glasgow came in and a new "Triple Qualification" was created. This became the main route for students registered with those colleges to obtain an initial medical qualification and was equivalent to a university degree. This qualification was taught at the medical school at Queen's College and was the course Thomas chose to follow, being the most extensive and demanding.

Thomas's decision to take this qualification suggests that he may already have had an eye on the possibility of a career in military medicine. It wouldn't be surprising if he was already casting his eyes far beyond the west of Ireland as he embarked on his studies with so many of his siblings already settled in Australia and emigration and overseas adventure such a major feature of Irish society as the 19th century drew to a close.

CHAPTER 3
_____

Medical education and training

Setting sights on new horizons

Thomas's training for the Triple Licentiate followed the conventional programme prescribed by the Scottish colleges, starting with six-month long courses in anatomy and chemistry which were examined by professors at Queen's College under a scheme they had set up to teach the Triple Licentiate in the west of Ireland. He also studied natural history and natural philosophy during his first year at Queen's College, Galway.

In the latter part of 1887 he had his first experiences on a ward when he started his first course in clinical medicine at the Galway County Infirmary and other hospitals in the town. All of these courses he successfully passed first time before moving onto surgery during 1888 and 1889 – throughout his life he considered himself a surgeon first so these would have been key courses for him.

The next two years must have been an emotional roller-coaster for him. The excitement of his studies and his steady progress towards becoming a doctor was cruelly contrasted with the sadness of losing two of his siblings unexpectedly.

In July 1889, just six months after his eldest brother James died aged 44, he had to head off to Glasgow to sit the Second Examination of the Joint Qualification, again passing first time. On his return to Galway, he was thrown into midwifery as well as continuing with the second part of his clinical surgery course before turning to medical jurisprudence, pathology and practical pharmacy the following year. 1890 was a year of sadness too as at the end of that year his married sister, Maria, died of meningitis.

Thomas's finances were improved considerably by the award of scholarships. As well as the prestige that went with achieving such academic distinction there were significant financial advantages. As one of two fourth-year scholars in 1889 he received £25 (£2750 at today's values) and many of his course and examination fees were reduced by 50%. The following year as Senior Scholar he received £40 (£4400), which must have been a very

Above: Queen's College, Galway in the 1880s at the time Kelly studied medicine there.

welcome contribution to the costs of travelling to Edinburgh and staying there for the final examinations and interviews, as well as useful supplement to whatever income or savings his mother was living off.

His senior scholarship was specifically in anatomy and physiology and it required him to take on additional responsibilities at Queen's College under the guidance of Professor Joseph Pye as clearly set out in the college calendar and regulations:

> "The Scholar will be required to act as Demonstrator in these subjects, and the Examination will be directed to ascertaining his fitness for the position, and will include, in addition to the usual Course in Human Anatomy and Physiology, the preparation and recognition of specimens and the description of Museum preparations. Candidates are recommended to practise diagram work. An Examination will be held in the Physiological Laboratory at which Candidates will be required to show a practical acquaintance with the physiological apparatus."

This appetite for scholarship and learning never left him. All through his life he made strenuous efforts to keep up-to-date with the latest medical research, not always the easiest task in some of the remote and dangerous regions he was to serve. He also developed a rigorous and methodical approach to the many hugely varied challenges he faced during his long

Right: Kelly as Senior Scholar in 1890 recorded in the Queen's College yearbook.

career in India and the Middle East which must, at times, have set him apart from his peers. It was a characteristic that was to benefit many thousands of patients over his long career.

His final studies in Galway in early 1891 were for his Vaccination Certificate at the Galway (Town) Dispensary. The focus following that was all on the final examinations that summer and in order to prepare for these he moved to Edinburgh, taking a room in the city centre at 28 Forrest Road.

His final assessment took place at the Royal College of Surgeons of Edinburgh on 14 July 1891 in front of an august panel as the College's register records:

CXXVI   QUEEN'S COLLEGE, GALWAY.

SESSION 1890–91.

FACULTY OF ARTS.
SENIOR SCHOLARSHIPS.

Greek and Latin Languages   Denis Mangan, B.A.
and Literature.
Modern   Languages   and   John Moran.
Modern History.
Mathematics,   .   .   John Paul, B.A.
Natural Philosophy,   :   .   William Gannon, B.A.
Metaphysical and Economic   Thomas Downard, B.A.
Science.
Chemistry,   :   .   Mortimer Hynes.
Natural History, .   :   .   Thomas J. Connolly.

JUNIOR SCHOLARSHIPS.
SECOND YEAR.
Literary Division.

Charles H. O'Hara. | John Beatty.
David M. Keegan. | James Stuart.

Science Division.

John A. M'Clelland. | Daniel M'Cay.
John C. Hayes. | Joseph Lundie.
Andrew Rutledge,

FIRST YEAR.
Literary Division.

William M'Gregor. | Robert M'Ilwaine.
Richard T. Barniville. | Andrew J. Walker.
John Sloane.

Science Division.

Henry Anderson. | John Henry.
William Burke. | William H. Ewing.
John Stewart.

FACULTY OF MEDICINE.
SENIOR SCHOLARSHIP
(*in Anatomy and Physiology*).
Thomas B. Kelly.

FOURTH YEAR.
Michael J. B. Costello. | Charles H. Foley.

THIRD YEAR.
Robert Allen. | Richard Baile.

SECOND YEAR.
Robert W. Clements. | Edward De M. M'Donnell.

FIRST YEAR.
Literary Division. | *Science Division.*
Humphrey Turkington. | John J. Daly.

"In presence of Messrs Wylie, Douglas, Muirhead, Andrew (Physicians), Duncan, Miller, Bell (Edin. Surgeons) Patterson & Sloan (Glasg. Faculty): appeared Thomas Bernard Kelly, Galway, being examined on his skill in Medicine, Surgery & Midwifery, found duly qualified to practise these arts and received the Joint Diploma of the Triple Qualification Scheme."

So, at the age of 21 years and four months, he returned to Galway as a fully qualified doctor.

He immediately took a position as a demonstrator in anatomy at Queen's College, also teaching students, many of whom must have been his own age.

This was a young man with a thirst for further knowledge, however, and teaching and working in the college laboratories in Galway was never going to satisfy him for long. He soon set about studying ophthalmology and towards the end of 1893 he started applying for positions as a house surgeon in this discipline. This eventually took him to the Eye Hospital in Bristol (long since absorbed into the Bristol Royal Infirmary) and while there he started studying for the fellowship of the Royal College of Surgeons of Edinburgh.

This wasn't a requirement for entry into any of the military medical services. Indeed, he was among a minority of those recruited to the Indian

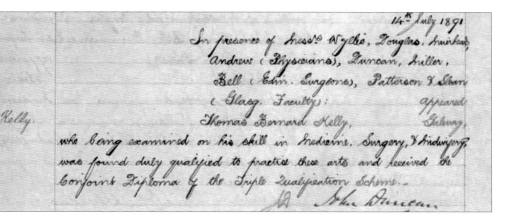

Above: Entry in the Royal College of Surgeons of Edinburgh's register recording Kelly's success in 1891.

Medical Service to hold a fellowship from one of the royal colleges. He was, perhaps, still unsure of the precise direction he wanted his career to take and felt that obtaining a higher-level qualification in the form of a fellowship would give him more options.

Before he completed his fellowship studies, however, family tragedy intervened once more. As Christmas 1894 approached his mother died on 21 December. She had been suffering from a heart condition for some time so her death may not have come as a surprise to Thomas, but it must have been a big blow to receive the news while working on the other side of the Irish Sea.

He completed his fellowship a year later, at the end of 1895 and the *Galway Express* reported the event in glowing terms.

"ANOTHER SUCCESSFUL GALWAYMAN.

It will be pleasing to the very many friends and acquaintances of our young fellow-townsman, Mr Thomas B Kelly, to learn that he has successfully passed through the recent medical examination at Edinburgh, obtaining all the necessary qualifications in his honorable profession. Dr Kelly held the responsible position of Demonstrator of Anatomy in Galway's Queen's College, and had shown himself a gentleman of more than ordinary ability during his entire College career. He is the youngest son of our late highly respected and much-esteemed fellow townsman, Denis Kelly, Esq, TC, of High Street. We congratulate Dr Kelly on the success he has achieved, and feel confident he will reflect credit on his native town and prove an ornament to the noble profession to which he now belongs."

FINAL EXAMINATION.

SCHEDULE

OF THE COURSE OF STUDY FOR THE

JOINT QUALIFICATIONS IN MEDICINE AND SURGERY

OF THE

ROYAL COLLEGES OF PHYSICIANS AND SURGEONS OF EDINBURGH, AND
THE FACULTY OF PHYSICIANS AND SURGEONS OF GLASGOW.

1150

N.B.—Every Candidate must deliver to the Inspector of Certificates before he is admitted to the Final Examination, this Schedule carefully filled up with the particulars of his Course of Study, dated and attested in the last page by his Signature. (See Chap. V. § 25.)

1. Name of Candidate in full ...... *Thomas Bernard Kelly*
2. Date and place of Birth, as certified ...... *11th of March 1870. Galway (Town)*
3. Date of Registration as a Medical Student ...... *18th of November 1886*
4. *Preliminary Examination.*—Name of the Board under which it was passed ...... *Royal University (Dublin) October 1888*
5. Date of passing Second Examination ...... *July 1889 (Glasgow.)*

6. Courses of Study prescribed.	Year.	Place and duration of the Instruction given, with Names of Teachers.	Certified by.*
Practical Pharmacy (3 Months),	1889	*Medical Hall (Greatys) Galway (3 mth)*	
Practical Midwifery, or Attendance on Labour Cases (not less than six),	1890	*Clonbur No. 2. Westport No. 2 Lanesborough No. 2. Dispensary Districts. Seven cases.*	
Hospital, Medical and Surgical, of not less than 80 Patients (24 months),	1887 -1890	*County Infirmary or Town Hospitals (Galway) 24 months.*	
Attendance at a Dispensary, or as an Assistant to a Registered Practitioner (6 months),	18	*Clinical Clerk to Co. Infirmary Jan 1st March 31st 1890 Out Patient Practice at " April 1st July 1st 1890 (Vide Regulation Ch III Sec 3 (d))*	
Vaccination Certificate by a Public Vaccinator, or Registered Practitioner,	1891	*Galway (Town) Dispensary*	

* In Schools or Hospitals where separate Certificates are not issued by the Teachers, the Dean or other official of the School, or Hospital accredited to sign on behalf of the Teachers will certify the Courses by their or his signature in this column, but where separate Certificates are issued, this is not necessary.

Above: Detail of Kelly's successful completion of the Triple Diploma.

Whether Thomas felt this completed the rehabilitation of the Kelly family reputation just 12 years after the electoral disputes had, to put it mildly, tarnished it we don't know, but it certainly resonated with his sister Annie as it is the earliest of many newspaper cuttings included in the scrapbooks she built up over the next 30 years recording her younger brother's travels and exploits.

He didn't return to work in Galway after obtaining his fellowship but took the opportunity to further his studies in ophthalmology by becoming a house surgeon to Argyll Robertson in Edinburgh, the pre-eminent ophthalmologist of his day and who identified a condition where unusually constricted pupils do not react to light and which is still known as Argyll's Pupil. Like many medical students who studied under Argyll Robertson, Kelly was always proud to label himself one of "Argyll's Pupils". His pride was fully justified as the achievement of a young Roman Catholic doctor from the west of Ireland in securing a post with one of the top surgeons of the day was quite considerable.

This appointment only lasted six months before he moved to London in June 1896 to pursue by what was now his clear ambition to join the Indian Medical Service (IMS), a life-changing decision.

The IMS was founded in the late 18th century and was a part-military, part-civil organisation. Its military role was to provide medical services to many and very diverse Indian army regiments, the British regiments being served by the Army Medical Service which became the Royal Army Medical Corps (RAMC) after 1898. Most IMS appointments carried a mixture of military and civilian responsibilities and up until a re-organisation just before Kelly applied it was usual for officers to opt after an initial three years' service for either civilian or military ranks, depending on their preference for future postings. This distinction was abolished at the end of 1886 along with the administrative division of the Service into the three traditional Presidencies of British India – Bengal, Bombay and Madras. Thus Kelly was in the very first batch of applicants to be examined for the new national and fully unified IMS.

How long had this been his objective? It could date back to his original application to study for the Triple Licentiate, which was specifically designed for those who wanted to enter military service, or he could have merely seen that as a way of keeping open a wider range of options for when he qualified. The Edinburgh medical colleges were among the principal sources of recruits for the IMS towards the end of the 19th century and of the 12 who passed the IMS entry examinations and were accepted at the same time as Kelly, four had Edinburgh connections.

With few close family to return to in Galway perhaps he finally settled on the idea of a life away from Ireland as he watched many of his colleagues in Edinburgh look to military service as the next step in their careers. The turmoil that enveloped Ireland in the wake of the Easter Rising in 1916 and the civil war in the early 1920s, leading to the eventual emergence of an independent republic, has obscured the fact that many Irishmen were proud to join the British armed forces in the late 19th and early 20th centuries. With his father's background as a Town Commissioner and therefore playing a modest part in the apparatus of British rule in Ireland, a career as a doctor in part-military IMS would not have seemed such an unusual choice.

It is probably easier to understand why he opted for the IMS over the Army Medical Service which was embroiled in controversy about pay, ranks and promotions in the late 1880s and early 1890s.

It would have been hard for an Irish Catholic from a relatively modest background to prosper in the AMS of the 1890s, dominated as it was by former pupils of the British public schools and traditional universities. The idea of a purely military career that could take him anywhere in the world at short notice may also not have appealed to him. At least in the IMS he would have had an expectation of serving largely in one country for several years.

Also, the prospect of working in civilian roles, in charge of local hospitals and medical services could have been significant factor in the appeal of the IMS. It would ensure he dealt with a wide range of medical conditions and keep him close to ordinary people. He certainly served those people well throughout his career.

A *History of the Indian Medical Service* published in 1914 explains the advantages and disadvantages of the reformed twin-streamed service that Kelly was anticipating joining:

"Every officer of the IMS is posted to Military duty on first entering the service and must do two years Military duty before he is eligible for civil employ. The majority apply for civil employment sooner or later but some officers spend their whole service doing regimental duty; and others, after a longer or shorter trial of civil work, revert of their own choice to military employment.

"The advantages of Military employ are obvious, and are especially attractive to the younger members of the service. The work is usually not too hard, except in times of war or epidemic; the pay is somewhat higher than in civil employ; there is always congenial society. For the regimental medical system is still in force in the Indian Army, the medical officer is one of the officers of the regiment to which he is posted, as much as any other officer in it, not a member of a separate department of his own, standing entirely outside regimental life. And, while there may be two opinions as to the relative efficiency of the departmental and the regimental system of medical administration, there can be only one as to which is socially the most pleasant for the officers concerned. Against these advantages, however, various drawbacks must be set. The military medical officer is not likely to get anything more than his pay. In some cases, it is true, he may get charge of a cantonment hospital or a small civil surgeoncy or jail in addition to his military duties, with extra pay for the extra work; but he cannot count upon such with any certainty.

"Again the work in the hospital of a native regiment, while light, is often very uninteresting. There is next to no surgery, and the whole professional work sometimes resolves itself into the treatment of a few cases of fever, dysentery, blistered feet, or rheumatism. In such cases the medical officer is apt to become rusty and lose interest in his pro-fession. And even in regimental employment, life may be deadly dull if stationed in a small outpost with only one or two other European officers."

He applied on 5 June 1896, listing his place of residence as 3 Lansdowne Place, Brunswick Square WC, most likely rooms he had taken for the short duration of his stay in London while he took the IMS examinations and attended the interviews. This application stated his intention to take the optional examination in French. It also included two references, one from Lord Morris who had been MP for Galway in the 1860s, serving for a period as Attorney General for Ireland, and was in 1896 Lord Chief Justice of Ireland. He later became the 1st Lord Killanin.

The references were brief but fulsome.

Above: Lord Morris of Galway, later the1st Lord Killanin, who acted a personal referee to Kelly's application to the Indian Medical Service.

26 Grosvenor Place
I recommend Dr T B Kelly as a candidate for the Indian Medical Service. I have known him several years long. He is I believe of regular steady habits and is, in my opinion, likely in every respect to discharge the duties of service with understanding of the public expectations.
Morris

Kelly's other referee was the Bishop of Galway, Dr McCormack, who was close to the family and wrote a suitably supportive reference.

Mount St Mary's, Galway
27 April 1896
I have had ample opportunity of knowing Doctor Thomas Kelly, who is a native of Galway, and a member of a most respected Galway family. I am able to bear testimony to Dr Kelly's character as that of a young gentleman of superior intelligence and steady habits, honourable in all his ways, and highly esteemed by all his acquaintances.
F J McCormack
Bishop of Galway

The provision of two references was a bit of overkill on his part as the regulations for applying to the IMS only required one to be submitted "from a magistrate, or a minister of the religious denomination to which the candidate belongs, who has personally know him for at least two years". With a peer and a bishop he clearly wasn't taking any chances.

The examinations took place in London and at the Army Medical School at Netley Hospital, just outside Southampton. Kelly's results were good enough to put him near the top of the list of candidates who qualified in that session. This would have given him some say as to where in India he wanted

Above: Netley Hospital – the Royal Victoria Hospital in Hampshire – where Kelly completed his examination and training for the Indian Medical Service in 1896.

to be posted, at least in terms of the three main administrative regions derived from the recently abolished Presidencies.

He came third in "Marks obtained at Netley by Surgeons on Probation for the Indian Medical Service".

Out of 900 possible marks in each subject he obtained:
Military surgery 547
Military medicine 663
Hygiene 475
Pathology 750
Total 2435/3600

In the London examinations he was fifth overall in the examinations that started on 7 August 1896.

Out of 1150 possible marks in each subject he obtained.
Medicine 615
Surgery 770
Anatomy and physiology 660
Chemistry, pharmacy and drugs 550
Total in compulsory examinations 2595/4600

Grand total 5030/8200
Top was 5626, bottom 4269

Oddly, considering his later constant attention to the sanitary and hygiene arrangements of the units he was attached to, his weakest paper was hygiene.

The combined results of the London and Netley examinations are recorded in the Register of the Service and placed him fourth in 'Grand Total of Marks Gained by Surgeons on Probation for the Indian Medical Service at both Examinations and their final Order of Merit'.

He had passed. Within a few months this 26-year-old Galwayman would be setting sail for India.

CHAPTER 4

To India
Defending the Raj

Thomas Kelly returned to Galway in the autumn of 1896 to say farewell to his sister Annie – now Sister Columba and living in the Presentation Convent in Galway where she was to spend the rest of her long life – as well as the Morris family and his other acquaintances. He may also have disposed of the tea, wine and spirit merchant business or just wound it up – if that hadn't been done after his brother James's death five years earlier – and terminated the lease on the family home above the business at 2 High Street.

It was to be 11 years before he returned to Galway, although at the time he would have anticipated his first long home leave being granted after about seven years in India; still a very long absence from his home town by modern-day standards in the age of jet travel and instant global communication, but part of a standard pattern for people serving the British Crown overseas in its then vast Empire.

Above: The Oceana, the ship on which Kelly sailed for India in 1897.

SCHEDULE B.

FORM OF PASSENGER LIST.

25

SHIP'S NAME	MASTER'S NAME	Tons per Register	Aggregate number of superficial feet in the several compartments set apart for Passengers, other than Cabin Passengers	Total number of Statute Adults, exclusive of Master, Crew, and Cabin Passengers, which the Ship can legally carry	WHERE BOUND
Oceana	Stewart	3573			Sydney

I hereby Certify that the Provisions actually laden on Board this Ship are sufficient, according to the requirements of the Passengers' Act,

for _____ Statute Adults, for a voyage of _____ days.

(Signature) *C. Stewart* Master.

Date 25 / 3 / 189 7 .

Names and Descriptions of Passengers.

N.B.—Cabin Passengers must also be included in this Schedule, after the other Passengers. See. 6 of 26 and 27 Vict., Cap. 51.

Port of Embarkation	No. of Contract Ticket	Names of Passengers	Profession, Occupation, or Calling of Passengers	ENGLISH				Port at which Passengers have contracted to Land
London		Billey, Master Earle			1			Bombay
"		Clark M.A.		1				"
"		Sutton M.		1				"
"		McArdle Sub Lt AAF		1				"
"		Cooley " Ch.		1				"
"		Law " CA		1				"
"		Kilby " J.B.		1				"
"		Hugo " JA.		1				"
"		Straich " W.H.		1				"
"		Leakin " CH.		1				"
"		Lincoln " CHE.		1				"
"		Rice " RH.		1				"
"		Barnes Surg Lt SMS		1				"
"		Sealy " St.		1				"
"		March M Zij		1				"
"		Frederickson M.A.D.		1				"
"		Wilson Lt WH.		1				"
"		Franklin Min		1				"
"		Walker M Geo F.		1 1				Colombo
"		Ambrose M Mr G.		1 1				"
"		Mrley M.A.2		1				"
"		Carson's M Mr Scot				1		"
"		Heymman M		1				"
"		Davidson M J WB.		1				"
"		Hobson Brig J'nl				1		"
"		Bowran M.D.						"
"		Bruce M Ernest		1				"
"		Victor Capt M.		1				"
"		Seal M.D.		1				"
"		McNiven M Mr			1 1			Calcutta
"		Hayley M Mr		1 1				Penang
"		& 2 child		2 1				"
"		McGregorM Mr			1 1			Singapore
"		Aitken Min		1				"
"		Wills		1				"
"		Spink M Mr		1 1				"
"		Young M Geo		1				"

ST27 243 1

His initial training was at Netley where, among other things, Kelly was, according to his own accounts, tested in horsemanship, although this isn't recorded in the official papers. Tests of physical fitness were obligatory so it may have formed part of those. It is likely that proficiency on a horse influenced what postings he and his fellow successful applicants would receive once they arrived in India, as travelling around the more remote and often mountainous areas required considerable skill and experience on horseback.

His commission as a second lieutenant was confirmed on 28 January 1897 and he set sail from London with the other new IMS officers who had qualified with him the previous summer on the *Oceana* on the 25 March 1897, arriving in Bombay after a voyage of around two weeks. This took him through the Bay of Biscay and down the Suez Canal with a refuelling stop at Aden, places that were to feature large in his life in the two world wars that he would serve in during the next century.

What would a 27-year-old Irishman have made of India, the Jewel in the Crown of the British Empire? Another Irishman, Eugene O'Meara, who made the same journey as a fresh-faced second lieutenant in the IMS a year later gave a vivid account of his arrival in Bombay in his book about his experiences *I'd Live It Again*:

"Splash! And a loud rattling of anchor-chains disturbs the lazy humid air, and we are at anchor in Bombay harbour. A breathless haze blots out everything save the ghostly shadows of other ships lapped by the colourless water, but away to starboard a rosy tint, growing every minute more intense, throws into relief the emerging coastline of India. Later, as the launch bears us swiftly to the shore, we glance back at the great white vessel with its tier upon tier of burnished yellow portholes blinking at the rising sun. How wonderful the graceful line of hull! A symbol of power, too, and the link that connects us with our native land, so that we have a feeling of appreciation and sadness at this moment of good-bye.

"The first sight of India is amazing, intoxicating, bewildering, stupefying. You have strayed suddenly into a new world unlike anything known to you before in its whirl of complexity and infinite variety. The play and wealth of colour. The crowds of strange faces, the babble of unknown tongues, the new religions, new clothes, new food, new everything. Even the flora and fauna are all different, new trees, shrubs and flowers, new animals and birds. After a time things begin gradually to sift and sort themselves, and you awake from this elaborately staged dream with the smell of the East in your nostrils, that wonderful blend of spice and garlic, goats and dust.

"The mass of incongruities unfolds itself. From the high-caste wealthy rajah in his elaborately gold-embroidered clothes, with ropes of priceless pearls, to the untouchable thin-legged sweeper in his single cotton garment diligently sweeping the street. The great public buildings resplendent with cool colonnades, towering cupolas and pinnacles, side by side with the most miserable insanitary huts with walls of filthy matting and roofs thatched with leaves.

"Gradually rousing from this dream, you are drawn into the whirlpool, and the call of the East begins. Much as you may grumble and try to resist, it grips you. Few can resist its fascination."

Kelly was posted to the Bengal command, which covered the whole of Northern India from the border with Afghanistan in the north-west, Tibet in the north and Burma to the east, as was the next person on the new IMS General List who qualified with him, James Hugo. While Hugo was sent to the North West Frontier to serve with the Malakand Field Force and a young Winston Churchill, Kelly was sent to the other corner of the Bengal command to serve under Capt H B Vaughan with the 7th (The Duke of Connaught's Own) Bengal Infantry with a range of additional civilian responsibilities across Bhutan and in the towns of Baxa and Jalpaiguru, all set in the foothills of the Himalayas.

The journey from Bombay on India's west coast to the Himalayas in the north east of Bengal entailed a train journey of two or three days across central India (the famed Indian railway network was extensive by the mid-1890s). He changed trains at Allahabad for the last leg of the journey to Gorakphore where there was a major Indian army base. From there Kelly would have made the final leg of the journey by tonga, a small cart drawn by relays of galloping ponies before arriving at the infantry base and reporting to Capt Vaughan, the senior IMS officer there. The tonga was a form of transport that he would become very familiar with during his time in India and in the Middle East during the Great War where tongas were still in service as ambulances.

Servicing the far-flung military outposts along the frontier with Nepal and the many small civilian medical stations would have entailed a lot of travelling, all on horseback and often in long, overnight journeys to avoid the heat of the day. He was exposed to extreme variations in climate and temperature as he moved from the stifling humidity of the valleys to exposed, rugged mountainous areas. Kelly had Indian orderlies to look after him and his horses as he travelled across the region but would often have been the only European medical officer at some of the smaller, more remote stations.

He dealt with a wide range of military personnel and civilians – all Indian. He would have had to quickly familiarise himself with tropical diseases and many conditions peculiar to that part of the world that he would have previously only encountered in text books. His mixture of military and civilian responsibilities would have at least ensured he did not suffer the sort of tedium associated with purely regimental appointments. It also earned him more than the basic pay of a new second lieutenant.

IMS officers were expected to learn Hindu and this would have been a high priority for Kelly if he wasn't to rely on Indian medical orderlies constantly to translate for him. India is a country of many languages and, by the end of 1899, he was listed as being proficient in Urdu as well as Hindu, making communication with his patients much easier. During that autumn he was sent to the major recruiting depot at Gorakphore for three months and would have encountered at least one of the large Mohammedan regiments based there around that time. They would have been Urdu speakers and would have provided him with the incentive to learn their language.

One of the responsibilities that went with the civilian duties was that of pathologist, occasionally helping with criminal investigations, giving evidence in court and, for capital crimes, officiating as the medical officer at executions. He also had the authority to sentence Indian orderlies under his command to flogging, something he would almost certainly have had to do as it was an established part of the culture and military discipline as his fellow Irishman O'Meara explained in his recollections:

> "Jail is no punishment for many criminals, certainly not for the habitual offender in India. I do not advocate flogging for a number of offences, but there are crimes for which it should be more frequently given, such as brutal assaults and robbery with violence. Never once have I had to sentence a man to be flogged a second time, and I know this is the experience of many."

Flogging was still permitted in the Indian Army during World War One and Kelly on at least one occasion in Mesopotamia imposed such a sentence after a summary court martial. Later in life he never expressed any qualms about capital or corporal punishment: in that respect he was very much a man of conventional views for his generation.

Life was far from all work, however. IMS officers enjoyed many of the pastimes indulged in by the British Raj – big game hunting, pig sticking – a substitute for fox hunting – and polo being among the most common. Kelly was an enthusiastic participant in all of these, no doubt showing off his excellent horsemanship whenever the opportunity arose. His skill at polo would have helped him integrate with the British officers – both military and medical – at the many bases and stations he visited. The IMS was looked down on by some British officers – especially those in the newly formed

Royal Army Medical Corps – but a good polo player was always in demand whatever officer's uniform they wore.

While he readily fitted in with any outdoor pursuit involving horses, Kelly probably found the culture of the mess a little jarring at times as he was a committed teetotaller following his childhood experiences with his brother and potcheen while holed up on one of the Aran islands in a storm. The regimental officers' mess in India – especially when a large number of younger officers were present – was a place notable for heavy drinking and, not infrequently, riotous behaviour. It isn't hard to imagine him excusing himself and retreating to his quarters to catch up on the latest medical books and journals and to write letters to his relatives in Ireland and Australia. He was a prodigious letter writer, although only a handful have survived, and never let his knowledge of the latest medical techniques and breakthroughs get behind.

On the whole, the final years of the 19th century were quiet in that part of northern India, although there were flare-ups from time-to-time elsewhere, and much of his time would have been spent with routine cases. That was soon to change.

Below: The Taj Mahal in 1903 when Kelly was posted to Agra.

Above: Decorative detail from the interior of the Taj Mahal, 1903.

In January 1900 he was promoted to Captain after the standard three years' service and appointed to the 2nd Regiment Central India Horse, the first of several postings to cavalry regiments. They were based at Agra, south of Delhi, and a frequent scene of bitter clashes between Hindus and Muslims.

Agra, of course, is the home of the Taj Mahal and Kelly was soon sending photographs of this most famous of Indian buildings home to Galway for Annie (now firmly settled in her new life as Sister Columba in the Presentation Convent) to stick into one of the many scrapbooks she kept of her younger brother's exploits, some of which have survived and are still in the family.

Kelly didn't stay at Agra for long as he was quickly re-posted to the Chitral Field Force on the notorious North West Frontier where, five years earlier, one of the heroic battles of the British Empire had been fought and won with the relief of a besieged British force in the fort at Chitral. 1900 was a period of considerable upheaval for the Indian Army with sudden demands for military manpower in South Africa to fight the Boers and from China to quell the Boxer Rebellion. Added to this was growing unrest among the Mahsud tribesmen in Waziristan, a few hundred miles south of the northernmost outpost of Chitral and part of that almost permanently unsettled region that remains one of the world's most violent troublespots today.

Its reputation meant that postings to the North West Frontier held a heroic glamour for the British army in India and Kelly was now set to experience that himself.

In the late autumn of 1900, in a tough mountainous region where much of the terrain is covered by snow all year round, the new Capt Kelly found himself in charge of one of two sections of the 33rd Native Field Hospital, and for the first time officially on active service. The 33rd NFH was based in Calcutta where the A and B sections remained while the C and D sections where sent to Chitral. There they were split between the two forts in the region, Chitral and Drosh with Kelly taking command of the unit at Chitral. The senior IMS officer, Capt Sydney Browning Smith was seven years Kelly's senior and a veteran of the siege of Chitral, having been mentioned in Dispatches for his part in the relief in July 1895.

Above: Approaching the fort at Chitral on the NW Frontier 1900-01.

Above: A key bridge on the route between the forts at Drosh and Chitral
on the NW Frontier 1900-01.

Kelly spent a year in that remote but strategically important region with forces protecting the notorious Khyber Pass, one of the few mountain passes from Afghanistan to India.

He dealt with casualties from occasional skirmishes across the region, although it was relatively quiet there during 1900 and 1901. When Capt Smith was sent to Waziristan in the middle of 1901, Kelly became the Senior Medical Officer of the force. His units were small, mobile forward hospitals and he had a lieutenant to assist him with Indian NCOs, medical orderlies and stretcher-bearers attached to each section. He would have seen at first hand the sort of indiscriminate, often sudden attacks that rebel tribesmen launched on British and Indian forces and would have lived with the occasional threat of sniper fire, especially when travelling on horseback between Drosh and Chitral, a day's journey. Even medical officers were armed on the North West Frontier.

While it is almost certain that during the previous three years he would have heard tales in the officers' mess of the savagery of the many warring tribes spread out across the NW Frontier, he was now facing the possibility of being confronted with it first hand as a young Winston Churchill had been just three years earlier when serving with the Malakand Field Force and which he recalled in *My Early Life*:

> "It is a point of honour on the Indian Frontier not to leave wounded men behind. Death by inches and hideous mutilation are the invariable measure meted out to all who fall into the hands of the Pashtun tribesmen."

Rudyard Kipling put the danger rather more vividly in his poem *The Young British Soldier*:

> "When you're wounded and left on Afghanistan's plains,
> And the women come out to cut up what remains,
> Jest roll to your rifle and blow out your brains,
> An' go to your Gawd like a soldier."

He would also have seen something of the British policy of retaliation in action and probably heard a lot more about it from Capt Smith and some of the other hardened North West Frontier veterans serving with him at Chitral.

Since the early 19th century the British had periodically pursued a policy of "Butcher and Bolt" when trying to suppress trouble in the North West Frontier. It meant launching well-targeted and resourced attacks on suspected rebel strongholds, killing as many as possible, razing them – whole villages sometimes – to the ground and leaving. It was seen as a more practicable and effective solution than trying to occupy large swathes of mountainous terrain with massive numbers of troops.

Above: The fort at Drosh on the NW Frontier 1900-01 during the time Kelly was posted there.

Atrocities and retaliation still blight that part of the world today. Execution of civilian hostages is nothing new and the 21st century equivalent of the Butcher and Bolt policy is now carried out largely from the air often with remote-controlled drones, although the outstanding example of it being deployed in recent years was the assassination of Osama bin-Laden by American special forces in 2011 in Abbottabad in those same tribal territories of the North West Frontier.

By the turn of the 19th century the policy had mellowed slightly from its earlier ferocity but was still frequently employed. Villages suspected of harbouring troublemakers were evacuated and then burnt down. These were routine actions as Lt (later Lt Colonel) Henry Tyndall recorded almost nonchalantly in his diary for September 1897:

> "On the 16th it was determined to punish the Mahmunds who were found to be the chief offenders in the attack at Markhannai by burning as many villages as possible and it was not expected that we should

meet with much opposition in the daytime…We burnt two villages and had a pleasant lunch under some shady trees in the second village without seeing any opposition, and then advanced towards the next village". [There the tribesmen were waiting for them and they had to retreat].

These experiences left Kelly in no doubt about what he thought of the warring tribes of the North West Frontier: he despised them for the rest of his life. His exception was the Pathans whom he held in high regard, admiring their bravery and loyalty. There were several large Pathan regiments in the Indian Army, whom he was to serve alongside on many occasions.

Although not required to do so, and the IMS not offering any tuition or examination in it, he learnt their language – Pashto. The relative peace of most of 1901 in Chitral would have afforded the ideal opportunity for Kelly to expand his linguistic skills by mastering his third native language.

While he may not have taken to the inhabitants, he was attracted to the spectacular scenery of the region sending dozens of photographs back to Annie for her scrapbook and probably using them as an opportunity to reassure her that it was an idyllic and peaceful part of India despite what she may have been reading in the newspapers.

The disbandment of the Chitral Field Force at the end of 1901 brought a complete change of scene and pace for Kelly as he now took up his first, and as it turned out his only completely civilian appointment with the IMS.

He was moved to the Medical College at Calcutta, a city of several million people that then enjoyed the status as the capital of India. There he became Professor of Physiology with a huge workload that consisted of rather more than the gentle teaching responsibilities the job title suggests. He was also the one qualified surgeon serving the Indian population for the whole of central Calcutta, clocking up a staggering 5000 operations in the 18 months he was there. Years later he still reflected on this as the most stressful time of his career in India, quite a claim considering some of the places he was to serve in over the next 20 years.

It was part of the usual pattern of service for IMS officers to be given a purely civilian appointment after a period of active service early in their careers. Many stayed in these largely civilian roles for long periods only returning to military service when wars broke out. Others returned to appointments with Indian regiments quite quickly. Kelly was firmly in the latter camp.

While in Calcutta he decided to buy a dress sword, presumably with one eye on the ceremonial occasions celebrating the Coronation of Edward VII that were due to take place in Calcutta in the summer of 1902. An IMS Captain would have been expected to attend many of these events and a dress sword was an essential part of the dress uniform even for a doctor. He bought a good-quality inscribed sword from Wilkinson that strangely captures the transition from the Victorian to the Edwardian eras with an Edward VII hilt and an elaborately decorated Victorian blade.

By the turn of the year Kelly was back in a military role with a new posting as the mid-ranking of three medical officers with the 9th Gurkha Rifles, just in time to accompany them to the January 1903 Coronation Durbar at Delhi which was attended by the new king's brother, the Duke of Connaught. This spectacular event would have been a foretaste of the even grander Durbar for the Coronation of George V eight years later at which Kelly was to find himself almost literally at the right hand of the new King.

After the Durbar the 9th Gurkha Rifles moved back to their base in the foothills of the Himalayas at Landsdowne, north east of Delhi, but he was quickly on the move again by the summer to take over as medical officer for the 17th Infantry (The Loyal Regiment) back in Agra.

These brief interludes took him on a whistlestop tour of the country and gave him a broad insight into to the diversity of the Indian Army but contained no hint of what was in store for him over the next few years. He was about to be appointed as one of the medical officers supporting the Tibet-Sikkim Mission, nowadays often known as the Younghusband expedition and the last great expansionist imperial adventure of the British Empire. He was soon to be marching across the Himalayan mountains that he had seen in the distance many times during his postings in his first seven years in India.

CLIMATE AND METEOROLOGY

Date.	Place.	Elevation in feet above sea-level.	Minimum temperature in Fahrenheit degrees.	Maximum temperature in Fahrenheit degrees.	Remarks.
1904 Feb. 17	Tuna	14,950	+13 (+8)	32	Half-gale, S., and clouds.
,, 18	,,	,,	+9 (+3)	34	Wind and clouds; snow all round, but none at Tuna.
,, 19	,,	,,	+6 (+2)	35	,, ,,
,, 20	,,	,,	+6 (−2)	43	Calm, clear; clouds later.
,, 21	,,	,,	+11 (+3)	46	Cloudy, moderate wind, slight snow.
,, 22	,,	,,	+6 (0)	49	Calm, clear; clouds, S.W.
,, 23	,,	,,	+10 (+4)	50	Slight snow at night. Wind after 3 P.M.
,, 24	,,	,,	+8 (+2)	56	Calm, clouds to S.W.
,, 25	,,	,,	+15(+10½)	53	Calm.
,, 26	,,	,,	+25 (+21)	54	Cloudy, S.W. (warmest night).
,, 27	,,	,,	+15 (+8)	46	Windy and cloudy. Slight earthquake at 11.20 A.M. Snow to W. afterwards.
,, 28	,,	,,	+14 (+8)	49	N.E. wind. S.W., snowy clouds.
,, 29	,,	,,	+14 (+8)	51	Calm, clear morning. Windy afternoon.
Mar. 1	,,	,,	16 (−8½)	50	Fine, calm, clear morning. Cloudy afternoon and light snow.
,, 2	,,	,,	+15 (−5)·	43	Calm, clear morning. Wind S. afternoon.
,, 3	,,	,,	+12 (−5)	46	Calm, clear morning, wind and clouds.
,, 4	,,	,,	+17 (−12)	46	Calm, clear morning and day; 2 in. snow during night.
,, 5	,,	,,	+14 (−8)	38	Calm, clear morning and day.
,, 6	,,	,,	+16 (−11½)	45	Clear but windy (S.W.) and dusty.
,, 7	,,	,,	+19 (−14)	46	Half-gale, S. all day.
,, 8	,,	,,	+14 (−8)	44	Calm and clear morning. Strong S. wind afternoon.
,, 9	,,	,,	+15 (−9½)	45	Light snow fell early morning, later calm and clear. Snow again 7.10 P.M.
,, 10	,,	,,	+10 (−5⅘)	34	Cloudy and windy, snow early morning, and a little during day.

Above: Kelly's meticulous temperature record included as an appendix to Waddell's book 'Lhasa and its Mysteries'.

CHAPTER 5

Trapped at Tuna
Tibet: the first six months

The story of the year-long trek across the Himalayas to be the first Western force to reach the forbidden city of Lhasa has been told many times. It was part of The Great Game played out over the last decades of the 19th century and the first decade of the 20th century between the British Empire and Imperial Russia.

Russia harboured ill-defined ambitions to snatch India from British rule and periodically pushed its military might southwards and tried to enlist the support of the various tribes and countries that were adjacent to India's long northern border; one of the reasons Britain kept constant vigilance at the passes of the North West Frontier. The possibility of Tibet falling under Russian influence had been high on Britain's foreign policy agenda for some years when news of Russian attempts to elicit the support of the Dalai Lama, Tibet's spiritual and temporal ruler, reached British ears in the early 1900s. How to respond to this threat – real or perceived – struck right at the heart of the fault line in British foreign policy.

The British government of the time was a Conservative administration under the cautious third time Prime Minister Lord Salisbury who summed up his approach to world affairs in a single sentence: "English policy is to float lazily downstream, occasionally putting out a diplomatic boathook to avoid collisions." Caution was in ample supply following the expensive and controversial wars in South Africa with the prevailing foreign policy being to consolidate and protect the borders of the world's largest empire, not to set them "Wider still and wider", in the words of Arthur C Benson made famous by Edward Elgar as "Land of Hope and Glory".

In India, however, they had a Viceroy (the effective ruler of India) in Lord Curzon who was firmly in the 'Forward Policy' camp, forever seeking ways of protecting the Indian Empire by extending its influence and its borders. Since his appointment in 1898, Curzon had been making efforts to bring Tibet, a vast, mysterious country running for thousands of miles along India's northern borders, under British influence. Initially, he aimed his efforts at establishing trade links through the Chinese, the only external power to maintain any representation in Tibet with a permanent official – the Amban – based in the Tibetan capital Lhasa. These approaches were rebuffed by the Dalai Lama, who started making tentative overtures to the Russians instead. This was his big mistake as it gave Curzon and his Forward Policy allies the excuse they were looking for to urge the cautious British Cabinet to move on Tibet.

In November 1902 Curzon was emphatic about his concerns over Russian ambitions in one of his many missives submitted to the Secretary of State for India, Lord George Hamilton, in London:

> "I am myself a firm believer in the existence of a secret understanding, if not a secret treaty, between Russia and China about Tibet: and, as I have said before, I regard it as a duty to frustrate their little game, while there is still time".

By then Salisbury had retired and Arthur Balfour, a long-standing friend of Curzon's, had succeeded him as Prime Minister and a more sympathetic hearing was forthcoming, vociferously supported by the new Commander-in-Chief of the Indian Army, Lord Kitchener, the greatest living British military commander. Curzon suddenly had powerful allies.

By April 1903, the Cabinet relented and authorised a limited excursion into Tibet but only as far as Khamba Jong, just over the border – and across the mighty Himalayas – from Sikkim a small, independent province effectively controlled by the British through India. This was the starting signal for a year-long campaign that was to far exceed this modest brief and end in the Tibetan capital of Lhasa in September 1904.

Curzon set about assembling a force that was vastly more than would have been required to secure a trading post at Khamba Jong, an objective the expedition paid only cursory attention to as it set its sights on reaching deep into the heart of Tibet from the moment it left India to start its journey through Sikkim in November 1903.

By that time a huge force had been assembled with 3000 fighting troops, many from the Gurkha and Pathan units that were accustomed to high altitudes, and around 7000 supporting sherpas, porters and other staff essential for hauling such a large force over the highest mountain range in the world. The commanding officer was an engineer, Brigadier-General Leslie Macdonald who although only in his mid-40s had extensive experience on the North West Frontier, in East Africa and China. He was instinctively cautious, frequently worrying that the supply lines across the mountains were being stretched too far and often reluctant to commit large numbers of fighting men too far forward. This brought him into conflict with the senior political officer on the expedition, Colonel Francis Younghusband, a passionately committed advocate of the Forward Policy. The Indian Political

Service was very influential and Younghusband had the ear of Lord Curzon. His almost blinkered belief that the Russians were exerting great influence in Lhasa and were in league with the Chinese became the driving force of the expedition.

A third senior officer attached to the expedition was a doctor, the 50-year-old (Laurence) Austine Waddell who had a well-established reputation as an orientalist, naturalist, archaeologist and, crucially, the nearest the British had to an expert on Tibet. Waddell had been in India with the Indian Medical Service since 1880 and had served on the North West Frontier as one of the medical officers in the Relief of Chitral in 1895. By 1903 he was a Lieutenant Colonel in the IMS and was appointed as the Principal Medical Officer to the expedition and Commanding Officer of the 71st Native Field Hospital that was the principal medical resource for the expedition.

Captain Kelly was part of the team of 14 doctors assembled by Waddell to travel with the expedition. These were mainly drawn from the IMS as most of the troops and supporting workers were Indian or from other mountain tribes and races, although there were a couple of RAMC officers among the medical staff. He was one of a team of seven captains, two majors and five lieutenants who had responsibility for the health of the entire party, a daunting prospect as no-one since Alexander the Great had attempted to take such a large fighting force through such high altitudes. It was because of the unknown consequences of asking men to carry their kit, and possibly fight, in the Himalayas that Kelly was selected for the expedition. It was well known that many people who spent time at high altitudes suffered severe eye problems, not least through snow-blindness, so including a skilled ophthalmic surgeon in the team was essential and Waddell acknowledged his contribution in his account of the expedition:

> "Snow blindness caused very little trouble, as all the men were provided with green and smoked glass goggles. As this affliction is due to an intense congestion of the conjunctiva or membrane over the eyeball, the treatment practised by Captain T. B. Kelly of the Indian Medical Service is worth recording, namely, by the application of adrenaline, which is so constringent as to blanch at once the most congested surface".

This wasn't the only ailment that came as a consequence of the long trek over the Himalayas. Frostbite was a major problem. Although only two men died from it many others had problems, not least, according to Waddell when they got too close to fires in an attempt to relieve it. A wide range of throat and chest complaints, especially pneumonia, accounted for several deaths and for many men invalided back to India as the expedition progressed. In addition Waddell noted: "Mountain sickness was experienced by nearly everyone more or less at the high altitudes, in the form of headache and nausea, with occasional retching and vomiting".

Those unpleasant experiences lay ahead of them when the force gathered for departure from the railhead at Siliguri on 6 November 1903. Kelly and the medical team had already been there for some weeks, as they had to check the medical fitness of all of the men for the demanding conditions expected. This task completed and all the troops, their supplies and supporting staff ready they left for their journey into the unknown, a scene vividly recorded by Waddell:

> "From the base at Silliguri, where the shrieking locomotives dumped down their hundreds of tons of food and other stores daily from Calcutta, some camels and thousands of bullock-carts with their yoke-oxen, brought all the way from Bombay and Madras, carried the loads along the cart-road winding up the Tista Valley for 45 miles, and when the road became too steep for the oxen, draught-mules replaced the bullocks in the carts. Where the cart-road ended, pack-bullocks carried the stores up the goat tracks, which the sappers and pioneers had enlarged into mule paths in surprisingly quick time. When the track became steeper, pack-mules and ponies were used, and when too steep for laden mules, several thousands of coolies 'humped' the loads on their backs".

The men carried a carefully prepared field kit supplemented by special winter clothing that weighed just 40lbs (18kg). Officers, who travelled on horseback whenever possible, were permitted 80lbs of kit, most of it carried for them by orderlies. Of course, the field hospitals had a vast array of additional equipment and supplies that must have required a small army to man-handle over the mountains.

From the moment the expedition departed from Siliguri Kelly kept a daily record of the altitude, weather conditions and, crucially, the temperatures they were exposed to until the whole party had completed its return journey at the end of September the following year. This record was reproduced as an appendix by Waddell in his book *Lhasa and Its Mysteries With a Record of the British Tibetan Expedition of 1903-1904*.

> "I am indebted for the following records of temperature to Captain T. B. Kelly, IMS. They were taken with the utmost care inside a double-fly Cabul tent, with the door-flap half open in order to show the actual temperature to which the men were subjected to. Other observations out of doors at the same time and in the same locality, taken by myself and others… showed that the tent temperatures differed from the outside ones by an average of 4° Fahrenheit only."

On the day they left Siliguri the temperature ranged between 64°F and 78°F (18°C to 25.6°C), nothing unusual for India at that time of year. Within three months they were to be exposed to sub-zero temperatures the like of which most of them had never experienced as Waddell observed:

"In the Tibetan expedition the men, who were mostly natives of the tropics had to be out in the open air, and marching under these rigorous temperatures, so that it is a matter of congratulation that they entirely escaped any disaster such as befell the Russians in the Turkish War of 1877, when the 24th Division lost over 6000 men in a snowstorm in crossing the Skipka Pass". [Shipka Pass in the Balkan mountains]

The first stages of the expedition took them into British Sikkim and the Sivok Gorge through which the Tista river flowed and which was partially swamp. This made it very humid, often covered in a thick mist, and a notorious breeding ground for malaria-carrying mosquitoes. Later in life Kelly suffered frequent bouts of malaria and, although no-one knows when he first contracted it, the days spent slowly marching through this region in temperatures reaching 30°C are as likely a culprit as any.

The first major staging post was established at Rangpo, after which the cart tracks turned into winding mountain passes as they moved towards Pakyong, already 4450ft above sea level and which they reached just a week into their march.

The supply depot established at Rangpo was a huge enterprise as it was where all the winter equipment for the expedition had been stockpiled ready for distribution as the 3000 troops and 7000 supporting men passed through. It is here that you get a sense of how well resourced this Imperial adventure was.

Often troops and the native workers had to pay for extra equipment: not for this expedition as Waddell records:

"Warm clothing was issued free to the men, both troops and followers, on a most generous scale, to protect against the cold and frostbite. In addition to the usual winter scale of clothing, which included a Balaclava cap, heavy flannel-lined warm coat, woolen drawers, thick boots, waterproof sheet each man also received –
1 sheepskin coat (Poshtin) with long sleeves.
1 thick quilted cotton rug
1 pair thick woolen gloves
1 pair fur-lined bag gloves
2 thick lambswool vests
1 pair quilted cotton overalls

1 heavy woolen comforter
1 pair felt knee boots ("Gilgit-boots")
1 pair woolen socks
1 pair of goggles against snow-blindness."

This generous issue of kit had to be carried by the enlisted men and by the 7000 native supporters. The soldiers additionally had to carry their weapons, 20 rounds of ammunition and four days' rations. Officers like Kelly would have been able to put most of it on their horses or other animal transport or, when that wasn't available, pass it to one of the native bearers to carry. The bearers – known as the Coolie Corps – were drawn from a wide range of hill tribes from all over British India – Kashmir, Bhutan, Nepal, Garhwal and Sikkim, among others – and, according to one British officer Lt Mark Synge, took to their work with remarkable forbearance:

"The cooli [sic]…was as merry a soul as you meet on a day's march. Some were quite boys, not more than sixteen, yet the way they shouldered their loads was wonderful. The regulation load was eighty pounds, but I have often seen quite a youngster with a hundred pounds on his back, taking it steadily up thousands of feet, and taking it as a matter of course, and giving you a grinning greeting as you passed him."

The heavy equipment was carried by around 10,000 mules, although the death rate among these animals was horrendous as the mountain paths became more treacherous, altitude took its toil and the aconite plants lining the paths proved to be poisonous to them. Within weeks 5000 had to be replaced. A plan to supplement them with 8500 yaks backfired when the herd contracted anthrax and the animals proved less reliable than hoped.

Edward Candler, a *Daily Mail* journalist, one of four reporters travelling with the expedition was not impressed with the yaks when they did arrive as he told the readers of the *Daily Mail*:

"The yak is the most extraordinary animal Nature has provided the transport officer in his need. He carries 160 pounds, and consumes nothing. He subsists solely on stray blades of grass, tamarisk, and tufts of lichen, that he picks up on the road. He moves slowly, and wears a look of ineffable resignation. He is the most melancholy disillusioned beast I have ever seen, and dies on the least provocation. If only he were dependable, our transport difficulties would be reduced to a minimum. But he is not"

There were three other correspondents travelling with the expedition – embedded in modern terminology, although not subject to the full rigours of modern censorship: Perceval Landon of The Times, Henry Newman from Reuters and C B Bailey from the *Daily Telegraph*. One of the remarkable achievements of the expedition was the efficiency of the communications back down the line as it advanced, in large part a consequence of placing an experienced engineer in overall charge. The British public and Kelly's sister Annie back in the Presentation Convent in Galway were able to follow every step en route to Lhasa through their daily newspapers within days of the events happening.

Alongside the latest telegraphic technology, General Macdonald established a hugely efficient postal system so that letters to and from his troops were delivered and collected almost daily wherever they found themselves in Tibet. Kelly, a prodigious but not especially descriptive letter writer, took full advantage of this, writing dozens of letters to his sister. Very few of his letters from his decades of service survive. The handful that do are from the latter stages of his time in Tibet.

The field hospital paused for nearly three weeks at Pakyong in relatively benign conditions, save for the occasional thunderstorm, before making its first major ascent to Gnatong (Gangtok), an old frontier outpost just short of the nominal border with Tibet and sitting high up in the Himalayas at 12,000ft. Kelly's unit arrived there on 5 December, just a month after departing from Siliguri and quickly set about adapting some of the buildings for use as a hospital as they were starting to get a regular influx of casualties, not from battle but from the increasingly harsh weather conditions as the Tibetan winter approached. Daytime temperatures were only a few degrees above freezing and at night they dropped to as low as 14°F (-10°C) according to Kelly's readings, taken just inside the tent flaps. As firewood was in short supply it was limited to cooking so the men, officers included, had to rely on the many layers of winter clothing they had been issued to keep warm, much of it not removed for days on end. Just about every man abandoned shaving, prompting General Macdonald to jokingly offer a prize for the best beard by Christmas.

Altitude sickness, throat infections and frostbite, alongside digestive disorders caused by cooking at the much-lowered boiling point of water at altitude formed the regular daily list the expedition's doctors had to deal with. Most patients were temporarily hospitalised but the worst were sent back to India. In his final dispatch, General Macdonald recorded that, excluding war casualties, 411 men died during the year-long trek and another 671 were sent back to India unfit for further service. Of these, he stated that 202 deaths and 405 of the medical repatriations were "more or less due to the special climatic conditions". Put another way, at least one man died every day and another two were invalided out of the expedition force, a rate of attrition unthinkable nowadays.

The main force, including General Macdonald, meanwhile established its winter headquarters at Chumbi in a valley at 9780ft and christened the greatly extended base New Chumbi. The long struggle to establish an efficient supply line began while the political negotiations ebbed back and forth with Younghusband getting ever more impatient at having to wait for Macdonald to be satisfied that he could support an extended line.

Between Gnotong and the new base at Chumbi stood the Jelap La pass, marking the rough and imprecise border between Sikkim and Tibet at an intimidating 14,390ft. It was steep going up and just as steep going down, vividly described by Alan Fleming in *Bayonets to Lhasa*:

> "It was undefended, and this was fortunate for the expedition, as it clambered painfully up the southern face of the mountain range and slithered down the far side where, after the leading troops had trampled the snow, the track, 'as steep as the side of a house, became a regular slide, as slippery as glass … I believe [wrote an officer afterwards] there was not a single load that was not thrown at least once. Some body said that it reminded them more of the retreat from Moscow than the advance of the British army'. Because of the height, animals as well as men found themselves distressingly short of breath".

Kelly's medical unit was moved up to Chumbi at the end of December, arriving on Christmas Day 1903, just in time to enjoy the one break he was going to have from the monotonous diet of porridge, mutton stew, biscuits, jam and chapatis with the occasional ration of butter. The officers at Chumbi sat down to a Christmas dinner of turkey, ham, plum pudding, mincemeat, cake and champagne, which must have tested the supply lines to the limit. The champagne arrived almost frozen, however, not something that would have bothered Kelly as a teetotaller. This was to be the last culinary treat for a long time as Charles Allen comments in *Duel in the Snows*: "Almost ten months passed before any of those present enjoyed another meal even half as good".

By this time, the relationship between the cautious Macdonald and the pushy Younghusband was very strained. Macdonald was not keen on advancing further into Tibet, pleading concerns about his supply lines, while Younghusband was convinced that the Russians were about to out-manouvre the British force and suddenly appear in Lhasa. Apart from the odd Russian rifle, no evidence of Russian incursion into Tibet was subsequently found. In the first week of January Younghusband finally got the better of Macdonald, having played Curzon and Kitchener back in India for all he was worth with his dire warnings of the consequences of delay.

Macdonald and Younghusband agreed that the main target was now to be Gyantse Jong (fort), which the British saw as the major impediment

Above: Crossing the Tang La Pass from 'India and Tibet'
by Francis Younghusband.

Above: 110th Indian Field Hospital in convoy.

Above: Officers at Tuna with Kelly sitting on the ground on the left.

standing between them and Lhasa. It was a classic case of what has come to be known nowadays as "mission creep". Macdonald, however, wanted to keep his force at Chumbi until the spring, while Younghusband wanted to take up a position much closer to Gyantse as soon as possible: "Just over the Tang-la we knew there was a small place called Tuna, and there I wished the Mission established with a good escort and plenty of ammunition and supplies, while all the arrangements were being completed for the further advance on Gyantse," the latter wrote afterwards acknowledging that it was risky as they would effectively be surrounded by Tibetans.

It was this advance with around 300 troops and nearly 700 supporting units and coolies that was given the green light on 4 January 1904 and the force with Kelly set off just two days later. Later in life he always described himself as a "Macdonald man" when people asked him about his experience in Tibet. Quite likely it was this three-month phase of the expedition that cemented his dislike of Younghusband.

Tuna was at the end of a barren plain, well illustrated by one of the hundreds of pictures taken Lieutenant Frederick Marshman Bailey, a prolific photographer during and long after the expedition (see page 67). It captures Kelly's Field Ambulance strung out across the hard, icy track making its way across the frozen plain to Tuna, 14,950ft above sea level. It looks inhospitable and the thought that this might be home for several weeks, even months must have weighed heavily on the minds of Kelly and his unit as they approached the scruffy, unwelcoming village.

They left Phari, the main depot serving Chumbi, on 6 January and immediately found themselves faced with the most ferocious cold weather conditions as the first day's march ended and camp was set up at Chugya where the overnight air temperature collapsed to a staggering -26°F (-31°C). Bailey's picture was probably taken the next day as the column approached Tuna, having successfully crossed the Tang-la peak at 15,200ft.

The many accounts and letters from officers and men who found themselves dragged by Younghusband to Tuna all speak of how bleak and depressing it was, everyone except Younghusband, that is, who wrote almost lyrically to his wife about the great feat of taking an Indian army over the Tang-la peak and about the first sunset at Tuna: "My dear mountains took on every shade of purple & blue & delicate pink on the snows. Then the wind eased as the light faded away & a calm still night set in with the stars shining out more brilliantly than you ever imagine them". He was alone in his enthusiasm for the place.

Even the passionate Tibetologist Waddell who had travelled with the advanced units despised the place: "With nothing to relieve the dullness but herds of roving kyang [wild asses] and the encircling hills beyond, the eye wearies of the stretches of loose gravel with its stunted tufts of withered grass, and the monotony of it all oppresses the spirits. The wind, which we had all fortunately escaped on the pass by getting over it so early, now began, and even at midday pierced through our clothes." The wind, according to Kelly's records, rarely abated over the next three months and frequently reached gale force, although when it swung in from the south west it at least brought some respite from the otherwise freezing conditions and frequent snowstorms.

General Macdonald arrived in Tuna two days after Younghusband's force and immediately ordered its withdrawal as he felt it was too vulnerable, not capable of supporting itself and almost impossible to supply: Younghusband refused. This juncture marked the complete breakdown in the relationship between the two men. Younghusband won the argument and Macdonald withdrew back to Chumbi taking some of the force with him, including Waddell. This left the small medical unit in the charge of Major C Wimberley with Captain Kelly as his second-in-command, although Waddell did subsequently return to Tuna to offer them some support.

Macdonald's fears were well grounded as forces of Tibetan troops amounting to several thousand men were soon advancing on Tuna. The place was turned into a fort, surrounded by barbed wire and with loop holes for the rifles cut out of every wall. Sentry rosters were doubled from the normal levels for such an encampment and the whole company had to stand ready for attack at the most vulnerable moments an hour after dusk and an hour before dawn every day. The Maxim machine guns, meant to give the British and Indian forces a huge advantage in firepower frequently froze in the sub-zero temperatures and even the ordinary rifles were so vulnerable to the freezing conditions that the soldiers took the bolts out of them and put them in their sleeping bags where they frequently slept in full kit, including their boots.

To say this small, isolated force was vulnerable would be a spectacular understatement. For three months the officers and men compelled to stay at Tuna had to live with the constant fear of attack and, very likely, death, eloquently summed up by Charles Allen:

> "Had the Tibetans launched a night attack on the Mission at Tuna the garrison would almost certainly have been overwhelmed – and Colonel Younghusband would no doubt have found a place in the same pantheon of lost military heroes as Generals Custer and Gordon. But the attack never came. It was later learned that the Tibetans had gone so far as to begin a night attack – only for it to fall apart as the men refused to advance. The British view was that they had lost heart, but it is more likely that it was halted because it went against the Dalai Lama's orders that no violence be shown to the intruders. Whatever the reason, it cost the Tibetans dear, for here at Tuna they lost their best chance of removing Younghusband and his Mission from Tibet".

For three long months, Kelly endured the hardships of Tuna, no doubt frequently inundated with men suffering from frostbite and various altitude-related conditions, always under pressure to return them to the fighting strength as quickly as possible. Needless to say this wasn't always possible and Lt Bailey, the photographer, recorded in his diary how he had to hold down the Assistant Post Master sent with the Tuna detachment while the two doctors amputated both his frostbitten legs. When Kelly was learning his surgery back in Galway he could hardly have envisaged he would be practising it in such harsh, unforgiving conditions a decade later.

When the weather eased, supplies along with fresh troops and coolies could be sent from Chumbi but this didn't always ease the load of the medical staff. One batch of 200 coolies arrived without goggles and suffered from snow blindness as a result, making Kelly rather busy with his adrenaline-based remedy so liked by Waddell. Another batch arrived without winter boots and suffered severe frostbite. This was repeated many times.

Above: The exposed fort at Tuna.

If this wasn't bad enough Younghusband turned on the handful of medical staff as conditions worsened. His private secretary and the Tibetan translator, Captain Frank O'Connor wrote to Mrs Younghusband as her husband succumbed to one of the many bronchial conditions that sooner or later afflicts most people spending long periods at high altitudes unless they are born and live there permanently. It was unjust in its criticism of the medical team struggling with the appalling conditions his boss had led the advance party into against Macdonald's advice:

> "The Col I am sorry to say is not himself at all. It is nothing serious but a nasty cough & cold & subsequent weakness. Would you believe it the Doctors & field hospitals have come up to these windy conditions unprovided with medicines for coughs & colds of any sort, kind or description! One just coughs until one gets well – or doesn't! They can find literally nothing – except quinine".

In reality what most of the men were suffering from was altitude sickness, which only a return to lower altitudes will cure, certainly not a selection of early 20th century cough and cold remedies as the ill-informed O'Connor and his boss thought. It seems very unlikely that the forceful and opinionated Younghusband didn't express this dissatisfaction directly to the doctors struggling to keep his force healthy, further reinforcing Kelly's dislike of him.

As the winter eased during March and Younghusband recovered the force began to prepare for the next stage of its advance despite continuing bitter arguments between Macdonald and Younghusband about the level of supplies

Above: The forces eventually leave Tuna and head for Guru, the site of the massacre of Tibetans.

and the security of a supply line now stretched out over another high mountain pass. Reinforcements were moved up but these didn't bring any relief to the medical team's workload as they arrived in a sorry state, according the *Daily Mail's* correspondent, Edward Candler:

> "In mid-March a convoy of the 12th Mule Corps, escorted by two companies of the 23rd Pioneers, were overtaken by a blizzard on their march between Phari and Tuna and camped in two feet of snow with the thermometer 18° below zero. A driving hurricane made it impossible to light a fire or cook food. The officers were reduced to frozen bully beef and neat spirits, while the sepoys went without food for thirty-six hours … The drivers arrived at Tuna frozen to the waist. Twenty men of the 12th Mule Corps were frost-bitten, and thirty men of the 23rd Pioneers were so incapacitated that they had to be carried in on mules. On the same day there were   seventy cases of snow-blindness among the 8th Gurkhas".

Slowly but surely fresh troops were moved up to Tuna and at the end of March the advance on the next objective – the fort at Gyantse – began. This soon brought the expedition into its first serious contact with Tibetan forces and the most controversial – and for many the most shameful – moment of the year-long adventure. Kelly found himself at the centre of events as they unfolded across the Tibetan mountains and plains.

CHAPTER 6

Tibet
The advance to Lhasa

Younghusband, with at least the tacit backing of the Viceroy Lord Curzon and the Commander of the Indian Army Lord Kitchener, was now determined to reach Lhasa despite this still not being the publicly stated objective of the Tibet-Sikkim Mission. As soon as sufficient troops had been moved forward and General Macdonald reluctantly acknowledged that adequate supplies were available to support a further advance, the British forces moved out of Tuna.

Just 50 miles ahead was another mountain pass at Guru and here on 31 March 1904 the British were confronted by around 3000 Tibetan troops, poorly organised and equipped only with old matchlock rifles with a handful of sangars (old cannons) on the hills above. Their troops were mainly lined up behind a five-feet high rock wall at Chumik Shenko constructed specifically to block the pass to the British.

What happened next is surrounded by controversy. The Tibetans asked the British to turn back, a request predictably rejected by Younghusband. Neither side wanted to fire the first shot but, as so often in tense situations, it appears a minor incident turned into just the spark needed to ignite it.

As the British delegation was negotiating with the Tibetan generals a scuffle broke out between Sikh troops escorting the British officers and the Tibetan guards. This provoked one of the Tibetans, known as the Lhasa General, to fire his pistol. Whether this was meant just as a warning to calm the situation down or a deliberate shot we shall never know but the bullet hit one of the Sikhs in the face. The situation quickly escalated as the Sikhs turned on the Tibetan guards. The Tibetans for their part surged forward and attacked the British negotiating party, which included the journalists accompanying the expedition. The *Daily Mail* correspondent Edmund Candler bore the brunt of this attack and was badly injured.

While the negotiations were being conducted the British troops had spread out around the pass, effectively surrounding the Tibetans on three sides. They were now ordered to open fire by General Macdonald. It was a brutal non-contest as the superior British weapons, including the Maxim machine guns, sent an almost unanswered hail of bullets into the Tibetan ranks. It was a massacre by any reasonable yardstick.

Waddell said it was all over in just 10 minutes as the British forces: "poured a withering fire into the enemy, which, with the quick firing Maxims, mowed down the Tibetans in a few minutes with a terrific slaughter". The commander of the Maxim guns, Lieutenant Arthur Haddow, stopped firing so appalled was he by what he saw in front of him: "I got so sick of the slaughter that I ceased fire, though the general's order was to make as big a bag as possible. I hope I shall never again have to shoot down men walking away."

Eventually the Tibetans were allowed to withdraw, leaving an estimated 600 to 700 dead behind with another 168 wounded. It was a sight, said Waddell, that "deeply engraved itself on the memory of all who saw it".

Above: Kelly treating the Tibetan wounded after the massacre at Guru.

"Near the wall, and from 20 to 30 yards from it, the dead and dying lay in heaps one over the other amidst their weapons, while a long trail of piles of bodies marked the line of the retreat for half a mile or more; and cringing under every rock lay gory, wounded men, who had dragged themselves there to hide. The ground was strewn with swords and matchlocks, also several rifles, mostly of Lhasa manufacture, but at a distance many of the slain looked as though they were sleeping quietly by their arms.

"It was especially pathetic to see the wounded Tibetans expecting us to kill them outright, as they frankly said they would have done to us."

The British suffered 13 wounded, including the *Daily Mail's* Edmund Candler who had his left hand amputated.

The British now turned into the magnanimous and humane victor, a feature of so many British military campaigns through the centuries, vividly recorded by Waddell.

"As soon as our own wounded had been attended to, a party of our medical officers went over to the battlefield, rendering assistance to the enemy's wounded and dying, and alleviating their pain and suffering. Many of the dying received water or brandy, or had their pain eased by morphia, or their bleeding stopped, or their wounds bound up with the field dressings of our men. I had several of the cleaner Tibetan tents torn up as bandages and dressings for these wounded, and the poles, scabbards and muskets served as splints. Afterwards these wounded Tibetans, to the number of about 200, were carried in our ambulance litters and on the backs of the prisoners into Tuna and Guru, where hospitals were improvised for their treatment. Many of the wounds were in the back, received in flight, yet many of the enemy stood their ground till the last, showing great personal bravery".

The decision to treat the Tibetans was credited by Younghusband in his book *India and Tibet*, published in 1910, to Macdonald.

"After the action, General Macdonald ordered the whole of the medical staff to attend the wounded Tibetans. Everything that was within our limited means we could do for them was done. Captains Davies [sic Davys], Walton, Baird, Franklin and Kelly, devoted themselves to their care. A rough hospital was set up at Tuna. And the Tibetans showed great gratitude for what we did, though they failed to understand why we should try to take their lives one day and try to save them the next". [Davys and Franklin were, in fact, Lieutenants]

What is remarkable is that of the 168 recorded Tibetan casualties admitted to those makeshift hospitals, 148 survived. Many of these decided to stay with the British forces as part of the Coolie Corps.

The presence of the journalists at the sharp end of this incident ensured it was widely reported around the world. Perceival Landon didn't mince his words when telling the story to readers of *The Times*.

"Men dropped at every yard. Here and there an ugly heap of dead and wounded was concentrated, but not a space of twenty yards was without its stricken and shapeless burden. The slowness of their escape was horrible and loathsome to us".

Controversy swirled around the incident but in his book Younghusband was unapologetic.

"It was a terrible and ghastly business; but it was not fair for an English statesman to call it a massacre of 'unarmed' men, for photographs testify that the Tibetans were all armed; and looking back now, I do not see how it could possibly have been avoided".

For Macdonald and Younghusband in early April 1904 there was no time for analysis of what might or might not have been, they were for once united in their determination to press on to Gyantse.

The force moved on quickly but found that the Tibetans were far from totally demoralised after the Massacre of Chumik Shenko. On 9 April they found themselves confronted by another large Tibetan force at Red Idol Gorge. A day-long battle ensued before a combination of being outflanked by Gurkhas and a full-frontal assault by the Sikh regiment forced the Tibetans into another retreat, having lost another 200 men with minimal British casualties. Kelly's field ambulance had been moved up from Tuna to support this push.

Two days later the British forces reached Gyantse and to their surprise found the town, which sits at 13,200ft, and the fort overlooking it open. Younghusband quickly established a headquarters in the town and set about negotiating with the Tibetan rulers representing the Dalai Lama, who was on a lengthy retreat throughout these events although sufficiently in touch to pass orders to his officials and frontline generals. However, the brief sense of unity between Younghusband and Macdonald quickly evaporated.

The ever-cautious and thorough Macdonald withdrew the main force – and Kelly with it – back to the main base at Chumbi in order to secure and protect what was by now, at least in his view, a precarious supply line. Younghusband wanted to press on to Lhasa and tried to bypass Macdonald by telegraphing the India Office in London. He found that the widespread reporting of the massacre had suddenly dimmed the support for the mission and his pleas for support fell on deaf ears.

In early May, he took matters into his own hands using reports of a large Tibetan force at Karo La, about 50 miles east of Gyantse as an excuse to authorise an attack. With Macdonald conveniently two days' hard riding away at Chumbi a force led by Lt Colonel Herbert Brander attacked and defeated the Tibetans at Karo La on 5-6 May, Macdonald's orders prohibiting the attack arriving too late.

The British now suffered their first – and only – major setback of the campaign. While Brander's force was being successful at Karo La, 800 Tibetans attacked Younghusband's base, retaking the jong at Gyantse but failing to capture the town below. This left the town under constant threat of bombardment from the Tibetan artillery high above it and thwarted all Younghusband's attempts to break out of the town during the rest of May.

This turned the mood in India against Younghusband. Kitchener rallied to the cause of General Macdonald and insisted that he should have the final say in all military matters, leaving Younghusband to deal with the political negotiations, the more limited task he had been charged with in the first place.

This news reached Macdonald at Chumbi where he was already busily strengthening his forces and where Kelly was, for once, out of the firing line as he awaited the arrival of two additional field hospitals with the reinforcements. Macdonald made the IMS doctors feel considerably more

Above: The Mission forces camped at Karo La. Kelly's is the white tent at the front, seventh from the left.

welcome than Younghusband had at Tuna. One of the most published pictures at the time and in most of the books on the expedition since was taken while the force was being consolidated at Chumbi that May. It is frequently described as 'Macdonald and his staff' showing the Brigadier-General seated in the centre with four officers on either side and another four standing behind him, with Kelly on the far right, very definitely a 'Macdonald man'.

A frustrated Younghusband made his own way back to Chumbi arriving on 10 June full of unsubstantiated stories about the significant Russian support the Tibetans were receiving. He received only limited support from India and London and was told to keep negotiating with the Tibetans while the main military force, now firmly under Macdonald's control, was

Above: The imposing Gyantse Jong, site of the fiercest battle during the Mission.

assembled. The need to relieve the force Younghusband had left under a state of semi-siege in the town below Gyantse Jong was high on the British agenda, although a company of Sikh Pioneers had reached it at the end of May, sufficiently strengthening the garrison to make its capture by the Tibetans unlikely. The daily bombardments continued, however.

This enlarged, and by now properly resourced, force left Chumbi on 12 June for Gyantse, a march that would take the 2000 fighting men and supporting units around two weeks. With it was Kelly, destined for another six months of frontline action after his brief rest at Chumbi.

Its first major obstacle, a fortified monastery at Niani, was reached on 26 June and was overcome by Gurkhas and Pathans in house-to-house fighting with the loss of one British officer and five men with another six wounded. Two days later two smaller fortified monasteries protecting Gyantse were also successfully overcome with minimal British casualties.

There was now a brief pause in the fighting while the Tibetans were invited to surrender the fort at Gyantse, probably the best fortified and imposing of all the Tibetan military establishments. All attempts to negotiate a surrender failed and so on 6 July a force of around 2000 Indian and British troops launched an assault on the Jong, defended by over twice as many Tibetan troops. Waddell was in little doubt about what he witnessed that day: "The capture by a comparative handful of British and Indian soldiers of this almost impregnable fortress, held by 7000 of the enemy, must rank as one of the most heroic achievements in the annals of frontier warfare".

The complex and well-planned assault was launched at 5am. It first of all involved retaking all of the buildings around the foot of the fort while artillery started bombarding the main fortifications and Tibetan gun emplacements above. Once this first objective was achieved Major C Wimberley was sent forward with a medical team to establish a forward dressing station in one of the buildings armed with a Red Cross flag. It was, he wrote back to his wife, a hair-raising task: "The bullets were kicking up the dust all around us. How we escaped Lord only knows."

For 11 long hours the battle raged as repeated attempts to break through the thicker than anticipated walls failed until two men, Lt John Grant and Halvidar [Sergeant] Karbir Pun, both wounded, broke through and established a foothold into which the Gurkhas rapidly advanced. This broke the resistance of the defenders and the Jong quickly surrendered. Grant was awarded the Victoria Cross and Pun the Indian Order of Merit First Class, the equivalent of the Victoria Cross, which wasn't awarded to colonial troops until the First World War.

Despite nearly 12 hours of fighting in temperatures that reached 100°F(38°C), British and Indian casualties were again fairly light with one officer and three men killed and seven officers and 30 men wounded. The Tibetan losses were numbered in the hundreds and would have been higher had Macdonald not forbidden any pursuit of their retreating columns, no doubt mindful of the awful slaughter at Chumik Shenko three months earlier. Once again, the Tibetan wounded were recovered and treated by the expedition's medical team.

With Gyantse taken the way was clear to Lhasa, which the British had now firmly fixed as their objective with the aim of securing a trade and diplomatic treaty that would ensure Tibet stayed out of Russian influence.

Four days after the assault on Gyantse, Kelly wrote to his sister Annie, one of five letters of his that survive.

"Gyantse 10.7.04.
My dear Annie. As you see by the above I am again at the centre of operations but in a few days hope to go from here to Lhasa. We have had some fairly severe fighting here, and lost a few officers and a good number of men. We have thirty seven killed & wounded in taking the Jong or Fort here but the Tibetans lost over 400 killed alone, principally from shells bursting.
"Since we arrived on 26th June we have had three days fighting and the rest peace which they are trying to induce the Tibetans to agree to a treaty but is no use, until we show them that we can march through this benighted country whenever we please they will not believe that we are in the slightest bit serious about this.

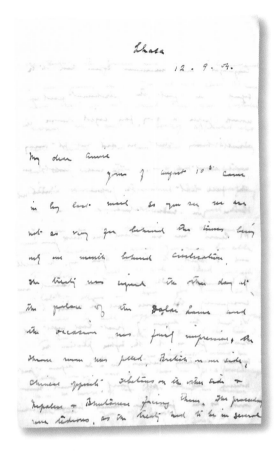

Left: One of the handful 0f letters from Kelly to his sister Annie that survive.

"It is about 145 miles from here to Lhasa and including fighting we hope to be there in three weeks from now. We shall probably be opposed at the Sampo river (upper part of the Brahmaputra) but I think we will get over alright. You will probably not get any letters for a month or so as the post-office arrangements will probably end at this place so not to worry as I have no intention of leaving my life in this part of the Indies.

"Sorry to hear about James. It certainly is trying for Denis Val. I enclose letters from Maggie and much love.

Yours aff

Tom"

This letter, along with the others, is hugely revealing, especially of his and Annie's devotion to each other. It is very clear that he had been keeping her well informed all along the way and that she had been following his progress assiduously via his letters and through the newspapers. The scrapbook the letter is stuck into contains newspaper cuttings about the expedition, pictures from the newspapers and photographs that her brother sent her.

It also shows how he kept in touch with the family, despite not having seen any of them for over seven years and in the case of his sister Margaret (the Maggie referred to in the letter), not since she emigrated to Australia in the early 1880s, more than 20 years previously. The Denis Val he refers to is Denis Valentine Morris, the now 17-year-old son of his sister Maria who died in 1890, aged just 27. He took a considerable interest in Denis Morris's education and welfare, no doubt heightened by the news that Annie must have conveyed to him that Denis's father James was ill. He actually didn't recover from that illness and died in September that year, leaving Denis an orphan and more dependent than ever on his uncle's support.

Back in Tibet, the main force, including Kelly, set off for Lhasa on 14 July, facing a trek over the highest mountain pass they had yet tackled, Karo La, where Lt Col Brander had been fighting in May when the Tibetans re-took the Gyantse fort and made Younghusband's life difficult. It stood at an intimidating 16,670ft. Fortunately, they were now well into the Tibetan summer with the daily temperatures at that altitude now hovering between freezing at night and 70°F (21°C) during the day. The day that Kelly went through the Karo La pass on 17 July he recorded it as a "Fine, clear, calm day".

Three days later he was writing to his sister again from Nakartse Jong, the postal services obviously having been extended to support the expedition all the way to Lhasa.

"My dear Annie. We have arrived so far without much incident. After leaving Gyantse we followed up a ridge which came to the Karo La and crossing this (16670ft) found ourselves again faced by the Tibetans. We flushed them out with small loss to ourselves one killed and six wounded and came along the plateau arriving here yesterday afternoon. This Jong or Fort is almost as strong as Gyantse but they did not hold it, clearing out before we arrived leaving serious quantities of grain & powder. We camped on the shores of a splendid lake (Yamdock Tso) and will push on tomorrow hoping to reach the river in five marches.

"It is very, very nice during the day, in fact abit warm at times but we have cool nights – in fact we had seven degrees of frost three nights ago.

"We have more of that beastly wind which annoyed us all in the mountains with the interruption of an occasional storm. As I am writing we are having a thunderstorm & the ground is white with hail but it will not melt before nightfall. Some of the Headmen of Lhasa came in today and requested that we return to Gyantse to negotiate but they were told the time for chat was past & now we would move on & meet them at Lhasa. I have very little faith in the promises of the Political Officers and would not be surprised if we come to them before arriving at Lhasa … The place we are in a present is splendid & we could easily spend some leave here in an excellent climate & get good sport.

"Hope you got my last letter including one from Maggie. She does not seem very cheerful but then she always brings in some lugubrious topic with her letters. Hope Denis is getting on all right with his exams. If he is at home remember me to him & much love.
Your aff brother
Tom"

The emphasis Kelly puts on the word 'home' in the final sentence of his letter is very telling. After Denis Morris's father James married Katie Rafferty in December 1891, little more than a year after Maria died, Denis was always a bit of an outsider to the new family, which was quickly extended with the birth of three more children. The 1901 census doesn't record the 13-year-old Denis as being at the family home in Eyre Street in Galway and for some years Kelly had been supporting him from afar, especially paying for anything this bright young man needed to support his education and his ambition to follow his uncle into the medical profession.

The skirmish that he refers to was really little more than that, although as it took the Gurkhas up the steep slopes either side of the pass in order to out-flank the Tibetans, it probably still ranks as one of the highest altitudes at which British forces have fought. This turned out to be the last that the expedition was to see of the Tibetans as a fighting force, although they resorted to a scorched earth policy by emptying all the villages and monasteries of food, grain and fodder for the animals.

Their only remaining obstacles in the quest to reach Lhasa now were natural ones, the most intimidating being the mighty Tsangpo river which they reached on 25 July. The recuperating Candler was inspired into a fit of lyricism when describing the sight of the river to *Daily Mail* readers:

> "We looked down on the great river that has been guarded from European eyes for nearly a century. In the heart of Tibet we had found Arcadia – not a detached oasis, but a continuous strip of verdure, where the Tsangpo cleaves the bleak hills and desert tablelands from west to east. All the valley was covered with green and yellow cornfields, with scattered homesteads surrounded by clusters of trees, not dwarfish and stunted in the struggle for existence, but stately and spreading – trees that would grace the valley of the Thames or Severn. We had come through the desert to Arcady".

At the narrowest part of the river there was an old iron suspension bridge and this was quickly secured by the advance units of the forces, which then set about locating the various small boats used as ferries – and the boatmen to manoeuvre them across the river. The whole crossing took four days but cost the expedition's chief transport officer Major George Bretherton and four of his men their lives when an improvised boat they were experimenting with overturned and they were swept away. Kelly recorded this incident in another letter to Annie on 28 July.

> "My dear Annie. I hear there is a chance of mail going off tomorrow morning so am dropping you a line as to how we are getting on. We have crossed over the plateau all night, having had a little fighting at

Above: Crossing the Tsangpo, where Major George Bretherton was killed.

the Kassha 16,700ft and are now camped in the Valley of the Chang
Chu or Tsampo, which is supposed to be the upper waters of the
Brahamputra, and getting our little army over its muddy water. When
we are crossing it is about 200 yds width but very rapid and
consequently progress is slow. Up to date we have had one officer and
three men drowned but things are proceeding more smoothly and we
hope to get all over by the 30th and then we expect to reach Lhasa in
four marches. It is pretty warm here 98°F (36.7°C) in day and 50°F
(10°C) at night, so we have no hardships to grumble about, although
the British troops who joined us recently are never happy if they don't
grumble at something [the 1st Battalion of the Royal Fusiliers had
joined the largely Indian force after the Tibetan attack on the Mission
at Gyantse]. I wish they had been with us last month then they would
have had some cause for a little discontent.
"We expect no more fighting and only a month's halt in Lhasa in which
case we expect to spend Xmas in India. If nothing unexpected turns
up I will take leave in April next and look you up in Galway but it is a
long way ahead is it not? Au revoir for a while with love.
Your aff brother
Tom"

His optimism about the relatively short stay he expected in Lhasa let alone returning to Galway for the first time in eight years the following spring is touching and misplaced. Neither was to happen.

On 31 July the final march to Lhasa commenced and just three days later they reached the outskirts of their ultimate objective with mounting excitement, as Waddell recalled.

> "The last stage of our long and toilsome journey was reached on 3rd August 1904, when we arrived at our final destination, the mysterious city which had preserved its isolation for so many centuries, and which was now for the first time in its history entered by a European force. Fired with a kindling enthusiasm, our feelings of eager anticipation as we started off that morning, when every step we took of the road might reveal the sacred city, can be imagined and must have been akin to the emotions felt by the Crusaders of old on arriving within sight of Jerusalem."

As they drew closer, Waddell and some of his medical officers rode up to a gateway that hid the city from view:

Above: 'Macdonald's Men' – Officers at Chumbi shortly before leaving for the final advance to Lhasa. Front l to r: Maj George Bretherton, Col H Read, Brig General James Macdonald, Maj H A Iggulden, Maj William Benyon; Back l to r: Maj M R E Ray, Capt C A Elliott, Lt B H Bignell, Capt Thomas Kelly. This picture also appears in 'Duel in the Snows' but incorrectly identifies Kelly as Bretherton. The caption on this picture is in Kelly's own hand.

Above: The gateway into Lhasa through which the Mission forces entered.

"On climbing the ridge alongside the gate, which was crowded with several hundred inquisitive monks and townspeople thronging out to see the white-faced foreigners, the vast panorama of the holy city in its beautiful mountain setting burst upon our view, and we gazed with awe upon the temples and palaces of the long-sealed Forbidden City, the shrines of the mystery which had so long haunted our dreams, and which is revealed before us at last".

Kelly conveyed his own thoughts on Lhasa to his sister on 8 August:

"My dear Annie. Here we are at last, camped outside this mysterious city. We arrived on the 3rd having had no opposition since leaving the river Tsampo. The whole place seems taken up with enormous Gampas or monasteries, one just below our camp called Daibury contains 7000 lama each having his own cell – not over clean and occupied principally in tending his prayer wheel. All day long groups of religious wander in the circular road round the holy city, praying at certain spots. It takes away from our respect for their piety when we learn that the circumambulating religious are paid by richer persons to perform this devotion for them by proxy.

"On the whole the city and surroundings are picturesque, situated in a broad valley. The Dalai Lama's palace is perched up on a rock 300ft high jutting out over the centre of the plain. The Medical School is on a similar rock about ¼ mile south of this & the town situated east from these points.

"The gilt roofs show up well against a background of bare mountains, but on closer inspection the streets are filthy, the Tibetan idea of sanitation being primitive.

"I was very pleased to hear from Denis that he had passed his 1st year It is a great result his being able to get to the UC [University College] & start straight off at medical work. He says that you have arranged with his step mother about his room and board & that he is rather pleased that they have moved in elsewhere so I presume it is all right. He seems to want a bicycle, so I think you might spend £14 or £15 and get him a decent one as a reward for passing. King will send you any money you may require.

Your aff brother

Tom"

Above: The Mission quarters in Lhasa, near to where Kelly and Cooke-Young were attacked.

This letter gives a glimpse of the generosity of his financial support of Denis Morris as £15 in 1904 would be worth around £1600 today, although bicycles were still something of a novelty then.

Waddell took Kelly and a group of medical officers to visit the Medical School not long after arriving in Lhasa and was, predictably, not particularly impressed:

"The temple carried us back to the early ages of the Greeks when Medicine had its home in the sacred shrines. Here the Lamas combine the duties of doctor of the body with those of priest. At present there are fifty-four priests and three teachers ... The treatment of disease, though based in some measure upon the judicious use of the commoner simple drugs of the country, is, as was inevitable amongst so superstitious a people, saturated with absurdity. The Lamas follow the ancient Romans and Arabs in employing such things as fox's liver and hot blood. They believe that all poisons are neutralised and rendered innocuous when placed upon vessels of mussel shells or mother-of-pearl ... They teach a crude sort of anatomy, not by dissection, but by means of a fantastic chart of the body ruled into minute squares in which the positions of the internal organs are marked."

Above: All the officers of the Mission at Lhasa with Kelly sitting in the front row, seventh from the right.

The talks between the Tibetans and Younghusband and his political staff progressed at snail's pace, not helped by the absence of the Dalai Lama who had left Lhasa well in advance of the British arrival. On the British side, delays occurred in the communications with the Viceroy's office at its summer headquarters in Simla. It was also the cue for more disagreements between Younghusband and Macdonald.

As the military phase of the expedition had finished control passed to the political department headed by Younghusband. He was determined to take as long as necessary to get the Tibetans to sign the treaty he had drawn up, which went much further in its demands than anything he had been authorised to seek by Simla and London. Macdonald was concerned about the prospect of his vast force having to make the 400-mile return journey through a rapidly deteriorating Tibetan winter. He had seen the hardships his men had endured the previous winter and had no desire to expose them to the same thing again and urged the Indian government to set a time limit on the negotiations. Macdonald sought the opinions of the medical staff and it isn't hard to imagine Kelly's meticulous records of the weather conditions they endured during the long march to Lhasa – and which Waddell reproduced in full in his account – being a key element in the evidence they presented to Macdonald. This produced a spiteful response from the self-obsessed Younghusband in a letter to his father on 30 August.

"Macdonald has done the most mean-spirited and almost traitorous act I have heard of for many a long day. He first told a committee of doctors to say the latest day we could stay here on the existing scale of clothing. Then he called together Commanding Officers and made the boss doctor [Waddell] – a miserable old woman whom he had tutored to say what he wanted – tell them his opinion that September 1st was the latest date. Then he asked the COs their opinion and they, knowing nothing about conditions here in October or of the vital importance of staying here as long as possible, said September 15th. Then Macdonald comes to me and tells me it is the opinion of the medical officers and the COs and his own opinion as well that we cannot stay here after 15th September and that he his telegraphing this to Government".

This provoked a furious row between Macdonald and Younghusband that was never satisfactorily resolved. It marked the final, irrevocable split between the two men but Younghusband got his way through a determined campaign to undermine Macdonald with Curzon and Kitchener. The negotiations had to be concluded and a treaty signed before leaving Lhasa, no matter how long it took.

The British and Indian forces made themselves as comfortable as they could while the negotiations dragged on, helped by the plentiful supply of grain, barely, vegetables, fish and game in the surrounding area. The officers commandeered one of the buildings, christened Lhalu Mansion, as their mess. This was to be the focus of the most serious incident involving the occupying force while it was in Lhasa. On the morning of 18 August Kelly was making his way over to the mess for breakfast with another IMS officer, Capt Andrew Cooke-Young, when they were attacked by a well-built monk wielding a large sword, an incident that was to catapult Kelly into the world's newspapers, including in a dramatic drawing on the front cover of *The Illustrated London News*.

One of the witnesses to the attack was Lt Col Herbert Brander. "He rushed at them from behind and cut Capt Cooke-Young on the back of the head with his sword. Luckily, the blow fell on that officer's forage-cap which, although it was cut through, served to protect his head from serious damage. Capt Cooke-Young, however, fell forward on his face, and Capt Kelly, seeing a man of the 23rd [Sikh Pioneers] with a rifle and a fixed bayonet, seized it and went for the Lama. He drove the bayonet through the man's arm. Bringing him to his knees, and with a second thrust, directed at his face, he pinned him by the cheek to the ground. Capt Kelly then withdrew the bayonet, whereupon the lama charged, head downward, and brought

Above: The front cover of the Illustrated London News 1 October 1904
capturing the moment Kelly fended off the Tibetan assailant who had felled
his fellow IMS officer Capt Cooke-Young.

Above: The assailant under guard awaiting execution the day after the attack.

him down. Seizing the rifle, the Lama made for the camp, with it in one hand and his sword in the other. Capt Cooke-Young now rushed at him again, only to receive a second, and severer sword-cut on the side of his head. Immediately after this our men closed on the fanatic, and Havildar Buta Singh brought him down with a blow with a stick aimed at his knees".

News of the incident was quickly relayed to the Viceroy, Lord Curzon, in Simla and Sir John Broderick, the Secretary of State for India, in London by telegram:

"Tibet. Macdonald reports Captains T. B. Kelly and A. W. C. Young, Indian Medical Service, attacked 18th August at Camp entrance by a lama - Kelly wounded slightly in hand, and Young wounded severely in head, sword cuts. Macdonald considers only isolated case of fanaticism. Assailant captured and hanged; four hostages demanded by Younghusband from monasteries, and fine of Rupees 5,000 inflicted."

Thanks to the robust telegraphic communication lines set-up the news also very quickly found its way into the newspapers. Back in Galway Kelly's sister was cutting out a Press Association report just three days later that must have alarmed her:

> "Two officers of the Indian Medical Service – Captains Young and Kelly – were standing near the outskirts of the camp, close to two sentries, when suddenly a Lama, who had a sword hidden beneath his robes, rushed from a place of concealment and before the officers could defend themselves, struck Captain Young on the back of the head, knocking him down. He then attacked Captain Kelly, who threw his hat into the fanatic's face, and, seizing the sentry's rifle, bayonetted him in the arm and face. The man fell, but not before he had inflicted a severe wound upon Captain Kelly's hand. Having regained his feet, the Lama butted Captain Kelly with his head, knocking him down, and then turned on Captain Young, who by this time had got up. The officer attacked the Lama with the empty scabbard, which the latter had thrown away. This weapon, however, proved to be useless and Captain Young, being unable to defend himself, received another wound, six inches long, in the head".

Annie's concern is shown by her underlining of the words at the end of the report: "The wounded officers are doing well, and are not in any danger".

Kelly's wound to his right hand initially caused him serious concern as he was worried that it was sufficiently deep to cause permanent damage to his tendons, a potentially career-ending injury for surgeon. Fortunately, it turned out not to be as bad as he first feared, although he bore a very visible scar on his hand for the rest of his life.

Captain Cook-Young was more severely wounded and was sent back to England on a medical certificate but returned to India in late 1906. He went on to serve in Russia 1914, Gallipoli 1915, Egypt 1916, and Iraq 1916-17 and eventually retired from the IMS in 1928.

One extraordinary footnote to this incident comes in a letter from Capt Cecil Mainprise, one of the few Royal Army Medical Corps doctors on the expedition. There was often a tension between the RAMC and the IMS with the former feeling themselves very much superior and only there to treat the small number of British officers and soldiers while the thousands of Indian troops and coolies were left to the IMS doctors. In a letter of 1 September 1904 Mainprise mentions the attack on Cooke-Young and Kelly in remarkably dismissive language:

> "Everything is quiet except that we had an attack by a Lama on two Sikh fellows in the Bazaar the other morning. One fellow was badly slashed over the head with a sword – the other – Kelly – carried only slightly in the head".

The obvious absurdity of calling someone named Kelly a 'Sikh fellow' shows how many RAMC officers viewed the IMS despite months of close contact on the expedition.

The attack was clearly premeditated as the captured lama was found to be wearing chain mail under his monk's habit. When questioned he revealed that he was avenging his brother who was killed at Gyantse and was a member of a fighting order of monks who guarded the larger monasteries in Tibet. He was tried the next day by a special commission and hanged at 4pm that afternoon, as Mainprise recorded in that letter of 1 September: "Next day we publicly hung the Lama and left him hanging for 24 hours as a warning to others". A huge fine was also levied on the Tibetans and four monks taken as hostages to deter future attackers. Kelly and Cooke-Young were the last wounded casualties of the expedition.

Kelly also wrote to his sister on 1 September, obviously not his first letter since the attack nearly two weeks previously.

Above: Lhasa – a view constructed from three panels from a panoramic photo of the city seen by only a handful of Westerners before the Mission arrived.

"My dear Annie. Here we are still waiting for the treaties & communications to be signed, sealed and delivered but no one knows when these will be completed as the Dalai Lama has gone into retreat and will not send his seals of state to be applied to the necessary documents. I suspect nevertheless that we shall be able to get away from here before winter sets in and arrive in Chumbi by November. By that time most of us will have had enough of the hills for a time but in a short period everyone will wish to get back again to them.

"We are having quite a lot of rain here [something Mainprise also mentioned] upsetting all the preconceived ideas of the rainless country of Tibet, all the hills are usually covered with snow. This snow line now being about 17,000ft [Lhasa was at just over 12,000ft]. It gets

quite hot in the day but has not fallen to freezing point here yet. Next month I suspect the streams will be frozen pretty hard & we will have all the chill we want. My hand is all right again now and we have had no more trouble with fanatical lamas since, the prompt hanging of the last gentleman & the fine of R5000 [Rupees] seems to have convinced them it is a game that does not have much profit. I have been able to get some skins. I do not know whether they are very good or not but as soon as we get within reach of India I shall send them on so you and Sister Aloysius can share them if they are any good by the time they reach you. "There are very few decent souvenirs to be got here so I am not taking home many. Now au revoir with love.
Your affectionate brother.
Tom"

Left: One of the handful of souvenirs Kelly brought back from Tibet, a gilt bronze White Tara Buddha with turquoise inlays on a Lotus plinth.

Kelly sent back quite a few gifts and souvenirs to his sister over the years, most of which were sold to help support the work of the nuns or fund his nephew's education.

The treaty was eventually signed on 4 September in a day-long ceremony in the Potala Palace. It established extensive trading rights for the British in Tibet and recognised the Sikkim-Tibet border. These two elements survived a major revision in 1906: the others did not. A huge indemnity of R7.5m was slashed by two-thirds and the condition that Tibet should have no relations with any other foreign powers was relaxed in a fresh Convention with the Chinese – who had long exerted considerable influence in Tibet – so that the British agreed "not to annex Tibetan territory or to interfere in the administration of Tibet", while the Chinese undertook "not to permit any other foreign state to interfere with the territory or internal administration of Tibet". This, at least, delivered the original principal objective of the expedition, which was to prevent the Russians developing a significant presence in Tibet and using that to threaten India.

Kelly, along with most of the British officers, attended the protracted, multi-lingual signing ceremony as he recorded in the final letter of his that has survived, written on 12 September.

"My dear Annie. Yours of August 10th came by last mail so you see we are not as very far behind the times, despite being so far beyond civilisation.

"The treaty was signed the other day at the palace of the Dalai Lama and the occasion was fairly impressive. The Throne room was filled, British on one side, Chinese opposite, Tibetans on the other side & Nepalese & Bhutanese facing them. The proceedings were tedious, as the treaty had to be in several languages and numerous copies had to be signed, In fact the parchment used up could paper a very fair sized room, the result being that we did not get away until about 6pm. They will publish the full text in the papers so I will not bother you with the details.

"We leave here in about one week from now and I expect to be in Agra by the middle of November. The rains have ceased and consequently the river will be easier to cross.

"We had six degrees of frost last night and when we get onto the higher plateau we expect anything between 10 and 20 degrees of frost. However, we are all fairly hardened now and as our faces are turned towards the country we know, the journey will be a trifle compared to our journey up. You do not seem to have read that at one period there was a Catholic Mission here and a Bishop appointed who was joined by some nuns. That was about the 15th Century and even now there are a good number of Catholic Christians resident here. Some pray using rosary beads. I will send you one as a specimen. There are some fine jade beads in it which you may be able to utilise. I will be able to send you back a lot of skins in time for Xmas, so you will be well supplied with presents. I expect you will have got my letters to Denis by this time. I trust you will have no difficulties about his College Course and if he does not get a scholarship he is no worse off than before. Now au revoir with love.

Your aff brother

Tom"

The weeks after the treaty signing were taken up with a wide range of celebrations, including race meetings, football matches and hunting trips, as well as extensive sightseeing and souvenir hunting. Kelly left Lhasa on 23 September with the main column, now in a race to make it back to India ahead of the rapidly gathering Tibetan winter.

They almost succeeded and were only a day's march away from reaching the tree line beyond the Himalayan pass at Tang La when the weather took a sudden turn for the worse. The temperature plunged and a combination of snow and ice buried the tents that night and obliterated the road, which was

Above: The silver Tibet medal awarded to Kelly showing the Potola at Lhasa. He also had the Gyantse clasp awarded to those who took part in the battle for the fort.

by now well made thanks to Macdonald's engineers.

The next day they attempted to move off but progress was extremely slow, made worse, according to Waddell, because many soldiers had lost their snow goggles thinking they wouldn't need them any more. This suddenly presented the medical team with around 200 cases of snow-blindness to be treated with Kelly's adrenaline-based remedy. Hardly anyone escaped some consequences of being caught in this sudden severe weather, as Waddell noted: "Everyone of us had his face severely blistered and burned by the terrible glare from the snow, so much so that it peeled and was painful and tender for a week or more". It would seem that Macdonald's earlier warnings, based on the medical team's advice, that to delay departure from Lhasa anything beyond 15 September risked encountering bad weather weren't so cautious after all. That extra week spent celebrating the treaty signing was the difference between escaping this final, painful reminder of the force of a Tibetan winter and making it back over Tang La unscathed.

Younghusband had raced off ahead of the main army with just a small escort so he could bask in what he imagined was his great triumph and so escaped this savage conclusion to the expedition. He was instead finding that the British government was furious with him for so exceeding his brief and already planning to water down the treaty he had delayed so long in Lhasa to negotiate.

It took until early November for the field ambulances carrying the sick and wounded to reach the original starting point at Siliguri, almost exactly a year since their departure. From there, the casualties were loaded onto hospital trains, and the doctors bid each other farewell as they headed back to their bases, Kelly's being at Agra.

In General Macdonald's final dispatch published in *The London Gazette* on 13 December Kelly found himself in select company as he was Mentioned in Dispatches for the first time in his career, along with Lt Colonel Waddell and Major Wimberley of the IMS and Major Aldridge of the RAMC, the only doctors singled out by Macdonald.

Having arrived back in India, he turned his thoughts to applying for his first leave back home since arriving in India in 1897 and spending Easter with Annie in Galway. His superiors had other ideas.

CHAPTER 7

'The angel of death'
Persia and the plague

Kelly's first surprise was that he wasn't rejoining the infantry brigade he left at Agra the year before but instead heading for Jhansi, about 100 miles south of Agra in Uttar Pradesh, and the base for the 1st Bengal Lancers, the famous Skinner's Horse, also known as the Duke of York's Own. The regiment was raised by Colonel James Skinner in 1814 in the days of the East India Company and its loyalty to the British Raj during the Indian Mutiny of 1857 had earned it a place as one of the elite regiments of the Indian Army.

Kelly arrived in Jhansi on 29 November 1904 as cover for Major George Mould, a New Zealander who had been in the Indian Medical Service for nearly 20 years and was on eight months' home leave. Kelly was the only medical officer with the Lancers and must have spent Christmas 1904 at Jhansi anticipating the possibility that the next Christmas he might be at home in Galway.

In Jhansi he had additional responsibilities, not all of which were entirely to his taste.

There was a general hospital for the local Indian population that kept him busy with a range of medical conditions and operations and which provided a welcome change from the routine of the small garrison. There was also a brothel.

Sexually transmitted diseases are a constant problem for large armies serving a long way from home and the British army in India was no exception. In the bazaar at Jhansi there was a brothel that had achieved a semi-official status on condition that the prostitutes who worked there submitted to a monthly medical examination. Kelly was on this monthly rota when Lord Kitchener, Commander-in-Chief of the Indian Army, arrived for an inspection of the troops at Jhansi. He also inspected the brothel and said the women there were unattractive and ordered the hospital assistants to find some "younger blood". As soon as Kitchener left Kelly stepped in and told them they would do nothing of the sort. He didn't approve of the arrangement with the brothel and certainly wasn't going to do anything to promote it. It was the first of many instances where Kelly's principles led him to a different conclusion to his superiors – and he wasn't afraid to articulate or, as in this case, act upon them.

1905 came and his application for home leave was on the table but deferred while the regiment's senior medical officer Major Mould was still away on leave. When he returned as autumn beckoned Kelly's hopes of getting back to Galway must have risen once again.

However, his exploits in Tibet had brought him to the attention of the Viceroy, Lord Curzon, as well as the senior echelons of the IMS who identified him as the man to resolve a dangerous threat to public health: an outbreak of pneumonic plague on the important trade routes through Persia. This was ringing alarm bells in the Viceroy's office as all attempts to control it and prevent its spread seemed to be failing.

The Indian authorities were extremely vigilant when it came to deadly infectious diseases such as cholera and the plague. Two severe outbreaks of the plague in India in the mid-1890s were still fresh in the memory and the Viceroy's Council received regular and very detailed reports of the number of cases across India. It had been monitoring the rapid increase in the number of cases and the geographic spread of an outbreak in Persia that probably started in November 1904. It spread rapidly during the following winter and the authorities in Tehran had imposed strict quarantine regulations on the infected areas. These were of limited effect, however, and by the end of 1905 appeared to have broken down. The political background in Persia didn't help as the Iranian constitutional movement was gathering force and destabilising the increasing unpopular autocratic rule under the Shah.

The British grew steadily more nervous of the threat of the plague continuing its spread southwards and into India. It decided to act by sending a small medical team of its own into the heart of the infected region.

Thus in February 1906 Kelly found himself on the way to the remote Persian province of Seistan, accompanied by an Indian assistant with a brief to do whatever he could to halt the spread of this feared disease.

Seistan, now largely part of present-day Iran along with most of Persia, remains an isolated and remote region. It sits in the south-east of the country with a border with Afghanistan along the Helmund river. In 1906 part of the administrative region of Seistan was in present-day Afghanistan and the border was being still being argued over in the Second Seistan Boundary Commission (1903-1905) headed by Colonel (later Sir) Arthur MacMahon, with a further overlay of competing claims from the Russians, a very real presence in this part of the world, and the Belgians who had a strong influence on trade through the region.

Right: A contemporary map of Persia showing the province of Seistan jutting out into Afghanistan in the south east of Persia.

Mikhailovsk · Old bed of the · Baly laju · Dash-adalu · Kara · Bokhara · B

Khiva Bay · Kizil Arvat · Kara kum Desert · Chardjui · Chardji mihor · Karch

Ft. Choitsha · Ft. Pultawskoje · Black Sands · Charwak-tube · Burdalyk

Geok-tepe · Askabad · Anau · Merv · Kara Turkomans · Andkho

Astrabad · Bujnurd · Shirwan · Chauchü · Iabad · Meana · Kurjukli · Charwakh · Dasht-i-Chul · Daolata

Shahrud · Abbasabad · Farudsh · Kuchan · Meshed · Sarakhs · Rukhnabad · Old Sarakhs · Panjdeh · Maruchak · Maimana

Damgan · Nishapur · KHORASSAN · Shahr · Zulfikar · Chaman-i-bed · Bala Murghab

Great Salt · Faizabad · Khaf · Herat · Kushk · Kala Nao · Meshhed

Desert · Bajistan · Jumam · Kakhk · Ghurian · Obeh · Paropamisus

Khur · Tabbas · Tun · Bushruyeh · Kain · Sabzawar · AFGH · Zarni · Kala Musa

SISTA · Duhuk · Birjand · Tabbas · Anardara · Diadia · Farah · Bakwa · Garishk

Yezd · Khusf · Gustan · Bistan · Neh · Lash · Jewain · Kash · Kala Bist

Lut Desert · Balahaus · Seistan · Chakansur · Kaleh-i-Fath · Kala Jahar

Kerman · Nasratabad · Hamun-i-Helmand · Husainabad · Helmand · Rudbar · Sand

KERMAN · Bam · Sarhad · Ladis · BALU

Bandar Abbas · Rudbar · ampur · Magas · Chodabandan · Pandjgur

Bashkerd · Kasrkand · Geh · EKRAN · Baluchistan

Above: 1906 map of Seistan showing it bounded on the east by the River Helmund.

To further complicate the picture there were several important tribes but no dominant local ruler. Some of the tribes accepted the restrictions that were imposed in order to stop the spread of the plague but others completely ignored them, meaning that the authorities could never be certain they had eliminated it from any town or village.

It was also one of the least hospitable parts of Persia and still commands its own meteorological definition, this one from the *McGraw-Hill Dictionary of Scientific and Technical Terms*:

> "**Seistan**: A strong wind of monsoon origin which blows from between the northwest and north-northwest and sets in about the end of May or early June in the historic Seistan district of eastern Iran and Afghanistan; it continues almost without cessation until about the end of September; because of its duration it is known as the wind of 120 days (bad-i-sad-o-bistroz)".

Kelly was facing a medical crisis with huge added complications from political, tribal and religious tensions and it was to prove every bit as dangerous as that year-long trek through Tibet.

As he set off northwards from Quetta that February with his new assistant he had one potentially significant advantage over others struggling to hold back the plague in Seistan – a new vaccine developed by the Indian government's specialist plague research laboratory in Bombay. This well-funded facility was established at the end of 1896 in the wake of a particularly devastating plague outbreak that came via the trade routes from China and Hong Kong. By 1902 it was already testing a newly developed vaccine with impressive results according to the *British Medical Journal* in a report in September 1904.

> "It is claimed that the number of deaths from plague has been reduced by this inoculation to less than one-sixth of what it is among the non-inoculated. In the severe epidemic in the Punjab of 1902-3 half-a-million people were inoculated by medical men specially sent out from England. According to the latest information published by the Government of India, the proportion of deaths to attacks in the inoculated was under 25 per cent, or less than one-half of that observed in the non-inoculated. From numerous observations it results that the number of attacks is less than one-third of that in the non-inoculated population. These figures refer to the Indian natives, whose susceptibility to plague is, like that of the Chinese, much higher than the susceptibility of the white races. Among inoculated European residents no fatal cases of plague have so far come to notice."

While progress was being made towards an at least partially effective vaccine, the medical experts were struggling to ascertain the principal causes of the plague, still a matter of scientific controversy today, according to the *BMJ* of the period reporting on the range of work being undertaken at the laboratory.

> "Investigations made in the laboratory into the transmissibility of plague by means of rat fleas have given so far negative results, though the hypothesis itself appears extremely plausible. A large amount of research has been done in the laboratory in various other directions in connexion with plague and other disease, such as different methods of disinfection, serum diagnosis of enteric fever, Malta fever, plague; distribution of plague bacilli in tissues and secretions of sick and convalescent; the presence or otherwise of plague microbes in dwellings, clothing, furniture, and soil, and in various species of animals, etc., as well as on cholera, relapsing fever, scurvy, epizootic lymphangitis, beri-beri, snake venom and antivenene, scorpion venom, diphtheria, leprosy, variola and vaccinia, surra, lathyriasis; on the morphology and classification of mosquitos, etc".

Kelly, as a diligent reader of medical journals and the latest scientific reports, would have been aware of the work of the Bombay laboratory and the potential of the new vaccine but, given the sensitivity and importance of his mission, he would have been given access to far more data than the Indian government was allowing into the public domain. This was a sore point with the *BMJ* correspondent in 1904.

> "Only a part of these investigations has been published, the majority being contained in laboratory records and reports to Government, which will never see the light of publicity. We understand that certain difficulties exist in the matter of publication, and this has had a deterring and paralysing effect on the laboratory's activity. M. Haffkine's [the head of the laboratory] work in India has a world-wide interest, and it is essential that any regulations which hinder the publication of his results should be removed as soon as possible."

It seems that whichever way he turned the 36-year-old Kelly faced controversy as he headed for the small, single-storey British consulate in Nasratabad, the main town in Seistan. He arrived there to find that the Russians and Belgians had been busily blaming the British for spreading the plague from India, contrary to the evidence available in early 1906. The Belgian customs authorities had made a big show of demonstrating they were fighting this threat, a singularly pointless exercise according to Angus Hamilton, a Fellow of the Royal Geographical Society who was travelling around Afghanistan at the time.

> "The Customs barrier in Seistan is reinforced by a plague cordon between Seistan and Khorassan against caravans from India, in spite of the fact that the period of any possible incubation has expired long before a caravan from Quetta [the last major trading post in India before crossing into Persia] can reach Seistan."

On top of the Belgian posturing the Russian legation in Tehran was spreading rumours that up to 99 per cent of the deaths from the plague in Seistan had been caused by spread from India. The poorly educated people daily threatened with death – over two years Nasratabad went from a town with a population of 2500 to barely 300 – were very susceptible to this sort of misinformation and one of Kelly's first challenges was to tackle this.

He set about this difficult task in two ways: one rigorously scientific, the other humanely practical.

He mounted a large-scale map in the consulate and collected as much information as possible about where cases had been reported, when they had been reported, how many people had moved across the region and when. It was a classic epidemiological study using the theories first demonstrated 50 years earlier by John Snow in London's Soho district when he proved that cholera was a water-borne disease and not an airborne one. This quickly gave him a very good idea of where the hotspots were and the principal directions of spread.

Alongside this he had to start inoculating people and get them to take basic precautions to prevent further spread. This went less well.

By now the world's press were following events in Seistan with British, Russian, American, Australian, as well as Indian papers reporting the spread of the plague and the arrival of a British doctor to tackle it. This news also spread locally.

Kelly knew that proving the effectiveness of the vaccine was going to take time and that more immediate steps to stop unnecessary and preventable spread were needed. After some difficulty, he managed to recruit two of the local Belgian customs officials to help him persuade the inhabitants to burn the clothes of the dead plague victims, their huts and household furniture. In return, they agreed to provide new clothes for the surviving family members and sufficient means to build new reed huts which was what most of the locals lived in.

This quickly backfired.

The Belgians had become unpopular among the handful of leading manufacturers of the area – almost three-quarters of the trade out of the region was in carpets – because of their role in implementing the quarantine restrictions which greatly inhibited inward and outward trade. Alongside the carpet manufacturers were a group of religious leaders, ever resentful of any outside influences. Between them they started rumours flying that the British doctor and his Belgian allies were burning the Koran, dressing the women in nice clothes so they could seduce them and using new medicines – inoculations – to spread the disease.

Fear, ignorance and religion are a potent mix and on 27 March a mob of 500 started rampaging through the streets of Nasratabad, quickly burning down a small Belgian hospital before turning on the British consulate where just six British officers, including Kelly, and 20 Indian sepoys were stationed.

Kelly and the commanding officer, Captain Macpherson, went outside in an attempt to pacify the mob but the situation was already beyond control and they were beaten and stoned, retreating, bruised and battered

Above: The British consulate in Nasratabad outside which Kelly and the consul were stoned by an angry mob.

into the main consulate building as the troops inside fired warning shots over the heads of the rioters.

The rifle shots were sufficient to alert the Russians in their consulate in the immediately adjacent sister town of Husseinabad to the seriousness of the trouble that was brewing. They were in a rather stronger position in terms of military forces as a detachment of Cossacks [Russian cavalry] had recently been posted there and they were quickly on their way to disperse the baying crowd, some of whom were by then on the roof of the besieged consulate. The Russians knew that if they burnt out the British the riot would gather momentum and numbers and attack them next: they were protecting their own interest as much as those of Kelly and his British colleagues.

News of the attack on the consulate quickly spread round the world, hitting the British papers just four days later.

"BRITISH CONSULATE MOBBED. AN OUTBREAK IN SEISTAN.

The following telegram, says Reuter, has been received in St. Petersburg from Teheran:—"A fanatical Persian doctor named Kukema incited the population of Seistan against the European doctors, who had begun to take the plague sufferers from their houses to the hospitals, destroyed the medicines and surgical appliances, and attacked the British Consulate. The Consul himself and the British doctor were beaten with sticks and the Customs-house was only saved by the timely arrival of the Russian Consul with Cossacks.

"The responsibility for the outrage rests with the Governor of Khorassan, who, acting contrary to the orders of the Persian Government, sent the fanatic to Seistan to declare that no epidemic of plague existed in the province and that the reports of its prevalence were the inventions of Europeans."

The speed with which this news travelled is quite remarkable because the Persian government had refused permission to erect a telegraph line from anywhere in Seistan so all telegrams and dispatches still had to go by horse.

Back in the Presentation Convent in Galway Annie must have by now been despairing of the ability of her younger brother to get himself caught up in danger in the world's far-flung trouble spots. Kelly wouldn't have had time to worry about Annie as he had to move quickly to get his medical operations up and running again.

The most important medicines and equipment had been stored by Kelly in the main consulate building so although the outbuildings he was using to do his laboratory work were ransacked, the most important materials were saved from the rioters.

He wasted no time in getting back to work and had a large officer's tent pitched in the courtyard in front of the consulate which he turned into a laboratory and treatment room, complete with microscope and all the equipment he needed which had quickly been sent from India together with some Indian troop reinforcements.

The speed of the return to what passed as a strained normality is best judged by the arrival on 10 April – just two weeks after the riot – of the famous Swedish explorer Sven Hedin, who was making an extended trip from the Mediterranean down to India. He chronicled this expedition to survey and map the area in his book *Overland to India*, published in English in 1910.

He had sent a messenger ahead a few days earlier and was expected at the consulate – which sent some of its reinforcements out to escort him into Nastratabad – but he was clearly impressed with the warmth of his welcome. Having described his sense of foreboding on approaching "this plague haunt" he turned to the desolation of the de-populated streets as he rode up to the British consulate:

> "A broad, open street or market-place leads up to the portal of the court of the English Consulate. In the midst of the large quadrangular court, where it is vain to try to make anything grow, stands the Consulate, a long building, in a simple, practical, Oriental style, with a verandah or a colonnade on stone pillars around it. At the principal entrance the Consul, Captain Macpherson, comes out to bid me welcome, and in a few minutes I am installed in my fine apartments, amid all the comfort it is possible to wish for in this remote corner of the world.
>
> "Six Englishmen, without ladies, were staying in Seistan, and with them I spent nine memorable days. Englishmen have a knack of making themselves at home in whatever part of the world their lot may cast them, and even here in this wretched Nasratabad they lived much as in London. They did not come unshaved to luncheon in the great saloon, and at dinner they appeared in spruce attire, with starched shirts, dinner jackets, and patent leather shoes. And then we sank into the soft armchairs, and took coffee, with prime cigars, and, while the gramophone reminded us of the divas and tenors of the great world, whisky and soda were served, and we talked of Iran, Tibet, and the plague. We were in high spirits; and it was difficult to believe that all the while the angel of death was roaming about in search of his hapless victims."

The teetotal Kelly wouldn't have been enjoying the whisky and soda but he did enjoy the opera arias. The small, wind-up gramophone and the handful of 78rpm discs that had been transported to Nasratabad were a new experience for him and the 18 months he spent listening to the very early acoustic recordings in the consulate at Nasratabad inspired a love of lyric opera that never left him. He counted Cavelleria Rusticana, Pagliacci, The Merry Widow, the Pearl Fishers and Sansom & Delilah (in particular the aria 'Softly awakes my heart') as particular favourites and would often listen to them years later when living in Jersey.

Hedin devoted a whole chapter of *Overland to India* to Kelly's battle with the plague, noting that he had already lost one assistant to the disease. He had failed to notice a small prick in his finger when cultivating a sample from a plague victim and was dead within 13 hours. He clearly admired Kelly's courage in going out to treat plague victims. The meticulous care and precautions he had to take to prevent infection could never be relaxed:

"The doctor is more exposed to danger near such a patient than anywhere. All that is necessary to give him the disease is that the patient's bubo bursts and the smallest particle of expectoration alights in the doctor's eye, where the microbes can thrive in moisture. If he has the smallest scratch in the conjunctiva caused, for example, by a minute grain of sand, the microbes enter and do their work".

The death rate across Nasratebad and Husseinabad shocked Hedin: "In these two closely-packed, insanitary, poor, dirty communities, the Angel of Death has now established its headquarters." While he was there reported plague deaths were running at between 10 and 20 people a day among the small populations that remained in the towns. Many deaths were not reported, a problem that Kelly was slowly getting on top of with a network of merchants and others who shared his determination to tackle the problem and were keeping him informed.

Getting people to bury plague victims in the properly designated sites was also a major problem, not helped by the town only having two coffins, which were constantly recycled with the bodies often just dumped beside as yet undug graves.

He was making more progress with his vaccination campaign, which was beginning to gather momentum by the time of Hedin's visit.

"Captain Kelly kept an exact record of all the inoculated. My number was considerably over 400. Of all those who had been inoculated up to that time not one had died. The natives themselves began to take note whether a man who died had been inoculated, and could draw their own conclusions. But still their distrust had not been overcome, and 400 was a trifling percentage of the whole population".

After Hedin's departure the warmer weather arrived, during which the spread of the plague is naturally slowed, and Kelly's steady progress with inoculation saw the number of cases he was reporting to the Indian and Persian governments – he had to submit regular reports to the Tehran Sanitary Committee as well as to the Indian government – fall steadily. By the end of

66

The quarantine at Bandan is still enforced, causing the greatest inconvenience to traders and travellers. This is apparently not in accordance with the terms of the Paris Convention and is obviously unnecessary; a double line of observation posts (Bandan and Birjand) should surely constitute an ample safeguard.

• • • • • •

• • • • • •

67

(*Secret.*)

Plague Supplement to the Seistan Consular Diary, No. 35, for the period 3rd to 9th September 1906.

No cases of plague have been reported in Seistan during the past week,—this being the third week the country has been entirely free from the disease.

The Mumtahin-ul-Sultana received a telegram this week from the Mushir-ed-Dowleh, telling him that, under the orders of the Shah, he was to take over charge of the anti-plague operations in Seistan. The Mumtahin sent a copy of this telegram to M. Cattersel, who replied that he could not take any action in the matter until he had heard from his chief in Tehran.

M. Cattersel now agrees to induce the Deputy Governor to send orders to the Katkhudas, informing them that they must hold the house-holders in their villages responsible for the immediate notification of the appearance of plague in their houses, and that any Katkhuda, who does not notify M. Cattersel of the appearance of plague in his village, will be severely dealt with. It is doubtful if this order will be obeyed, as the people seem very averse to notifying the Customs authorities of the presence of disease. This week, a case of supposed plague was reported, which had been concealed for 10 days; luckily it proved to be a case of venereal disease with buboes.

I have failed to induce M. Cattersel to send Doctor Fateh Ali Khan, with one of our men, on tour in the district,—he excuses himself on the grounds that he cannot spare the services of Doctor Fateh Ali as a Mirza. This is to be regretted, as at present the people are amenable to reason, and if they had the rationale of the various anti-plague measures fully explained to them, and the advantages which they might hope to gain by adopting a vigorous anti-plague propaganda, laid before them in plain language, I think it very probable that the people (who appear to be much more intelligent than the Indian peasant) would agree to the greater part of our proposed measures.

The period of quiescence is now rapidly passing away, the temperature falling steadily, and this week the ground water has begun to rise. Practically nothing has been done to prepare the people to accept isolation or segregation, in the event of plague re-appearing, and consequently we shall probably have to depend on inoculation, towards which, apparently, most of the people appear to be favourably disposed.

T. B. Kelly, *Captain, I.M.S.,*
On Plague Duty in Seistan.

Above: The official plague diary detailing some of Kelly's frustrations

August he was able to report three consecutive weeks without a single case.

However, the colder, wetter weather was approaching and he was worried and concerned about the potential for this initial success to be undone. An angry memo to the Viceroy's office in the first week of September 1906 set out the causes of his anxiety.

The Shah of Persia had informed one of the local leaders, the Mumtahin-ul-Sultana that he was to take charge of anti-plague operations in Seistan. This set alarm bells ringing for Kelly and he tried to enlist the support of Monsieur Cattersel, the senior Belgian official in the area to insist that the local village leaders take full responsibility for notification of any cases of the plague. Cattersel agreed to elicit the support of the Deputy Governor of the region but Kelly was sceptical this would have much effect: "It is doubtful if this order will be obeyed, as the people seem very averse to notifying the Customs authorities of disease. This week, a case of supposed plague was reported, which had been concealed for 10 days; luckily it proved to be a case of venereal disease with buboes".

Cattersel was less co-operative when it came to Kelly's request to send a local doctor with one of Kelly's assistants on a tour of the districts to explain the need for continuing precautions. This was potentially disastrous, Kelly warned his superiors.

"This is to be regretted, as at present the people are amenable to reason, and if they had the rationale of the various anti-plague measures fully explained to them, and the advantages which they might hope to gain by adopting a vigorous anti-plague propaganda, laid before them in plain language, I think it very probable that the people (who appear to be much more intelligent than the Indian peasant) would agree to the greater part of our proposed measures.

"The period of quiescence is now rapidly passing away, the temperature falling steadily, and this week the ground water has begun to rise. Practically nothing has been done to prepare the people to accept isolation or segregation, in the event of the plague re-appearing, and consequently we shall probably have to depend on inoculation, towards which, apparently, most of the people appear to be favourably disposed".

A toned down version of this request was passed to the authorities in Tehran but Kelly didn't wait for an answer. He produced his own literature in the local languages and visited the villages himself. Judging by the statistics reported over the subsequent months this had the desired effect, as the plague did not reassert itself during the winter of 1906-07.

He had obviously risked rebuke from his superiors by taking matters into his own hands but it appears they approved of his actions, not least because

Above: The Persian carpet Kelly brought back from Seistan in 1907 and which still adorns the floor of the visitor's lounge in the Presentation Convent, Galway.

they gave him additional authority early in 1907 by appointing him Vice-Consul for the Districts of Seistan and Kain.

Another plague-free summer and autumn was sufficient for the Indian government to recall him from his 18-month plague duty and on 21 October 1907 he was finally granted one year's leave out of India. He was on his way home for the first time in almost 11 years.

CHAPTER 8

On His Majesty's Service
Ireland, India and Royalty

The next phase of Kelly's life is neatly bookended by the only two periods of extended home leave he had before he approached retirement from the Indian Medical Service in the mid-1920s, a period of almost 30 years. Many who served in India were used to not returning home for several years at a time but events conspired to make Kelly's absences longer than most and his periods of home leave rather less frequent. On returning from Persia this time there was no doubt that he was due a break. He had just been through as tough a three years as any doctor in the IMS and was already long overdue a spell back home in Ireland. This was promptly granted and he started one year's leave on 21 October 1907.

He didn't return from Persia empty-handed and boarded the ship in Bombay with a trunk full of presents for what was left of his family in Galway. In particular, he had a fine Persian carpet – Seistan's main manufacturing industry was carpet-making – for the nuns at the Presentation Convent. Remarkably, this carpet still proudly adorns the floor of the visitors' lounge in the convent over 100 years later and is known by all the nuns as "Colonel Kelly's carpet".

His first concern on reaching Galway as Christmas 1907 approached was to find out how Denis Morris was doing with his medical studies, having been admitted to the same medical school at University College, Galway that his uncle attended 20 years earlier. By the time Kelly arrived in Galway, Morris was in his second year and progressing comfortably. The arrival of his uncle and his discovery of an aptitude for gynaecology appears to have transformed him into an outstanding scholar as he was able to start his third year as an exhibitioner and never looked back. This would have had the added bonus of easing Kelly's financial commitment, as he was Morris's only means of support by now. His father had died relatively young in 1904, while Kelly was in Lhasa, and his step-mother, by all accounts an unstable woman, had very little to do with him.

There was no family to stay with in Galway so Kelly would have installed himself in one of the city centre hotels that were accustomed to accommodating British officers and Empire civil servants on long periods of leave. The Galway he returned to was struggling economically. Its population was in decline. Across the county as a whole it fell another 5% during the first decade of the 20th century taking it to a low of 182,244 in 1911, compared to a pre-famine peak of 422,923. The population of Galway city was little over 13,000 in 1907. The city's economy was suffering along with the rural economy that dominated the county. The fishing industry centred on the Claddagh Kelly knew as a boy was in decline as modern trawlers started to take over and one of the city's major employers, Presse's Distillery, was heading towards closure in the face of competition from the large whiskey producers in Dublin.

It wasn't all gloom. Clifden at the far western tip of the county had been chosen earlier in 1907 by Marconi as the base for its first transatlantic telegraph post and tourism was starting to establish a presence in Salthill just along Galway Bay from Galway itself. In 1895 Salthill had been linked to the centre of Galway by an extension of the horse-drawn tram service his father had worked hard to get off the ground in the 1870s. Plans were also being made for Galway to host an Irish industrial exhibition during 1908, a year in which the city received a major boost to its prestige with the passing of the Irish Universities Act which raised the college Morris was attending to the status of a university college (under Dublin University).

One consequence of this was that Morris completed his medical degree in Dublin in 1910-11 and spent his first seven years post-qualification working in Dublin hospitals, first for a year as house surgeon at Richmond Hospital and then for six years at the Coombe Hospital for women and infants. Denis

Above: The Marconi telegraph station at Clifden, one of the developments Kelly would have seen in 1907-08 on his first trip home in nearly 11 years.

Morris didn't return to Galway until 1918. This meant he was in Dublin during the bitter Lockout that lasted from August 1913 to January 1914 over workers' rights to join trades unions and for the Easter Rising in 1916. These events must have shaped the young Morris's political views as much as Kelly's father's battle with Parnell's Land League shaped his. Morris was a moderate nationalist for most of his life, a viewpoint that temporarily alienated him from his uncle. But that was all in the future.

Kelly bid Morris and his sister farewell as summer started to fade into autumn in 1908, setting off back to India via London by train, paying fleeting visits to a few European cities on the way, a frequent return route to India and one that would have appealed to a man now keen to see more of the world.

On arriving in India in October he was posted back to the 1st Bengal Lancers who he had already spent a year with after returning from Tibet and before being summoned to fight the plague in Persia. This was to be the start of his longest association with a single regiment and one of which he was especially proud, frequently referring to his time with Skinner's Horse later in life. IMS officers were not formally part of the regiments they were attached to so he would never have worn their famous yellow uniform but he definitely felt a great affinity to Skinner's Horse. Like all Indian regiments, it was commanded by British officers. They would have been his mess companions and also formed the frequent hunting parties that Kelly so adored.

By 1908 they were stationed in Lucknow, about 300 miles south east of Delhi, but were soon on the move. He was heading back to the North West Frontier. On 4 January 1909 the Lancers arrived in Dera Ismail Khan where they were to spend most of the next three years. In addition to the main depot, the Lancers also sent detachments to garrison outposts a Jatta, Drazinda, Jandola, Mullazi, Zam and Tank as part of their responsibilities for defending the North West Frontier.

As the only medical officer attached to the Lancers for most of this period he would have found himself travelling frequently by horse among the hills and mountain passes visiting these small outposts, constantly wary of the threat from snipers. Dera Ismail Khan itself was a large town with a substantial military presence as it was the winter headquarters of the entire Derajat Brigade, which Lord Kitchener had established in 1903 to defend the North West Frontier. As the brigade HQ the garrison usually consisted of a mountain battery, a regiment of Indian cavalry – the Bengal Lancers – and three regiments of Indian infantry. He wouldn't have had much time to settle in at Dera Ismail Khan that January as the Lancers were sent out on extended manoeuvres, an annual show of British strength in the region. At the end of the month he was at Murtaza, where his presence at a staff officers' rendezvous was recorded by Major (later Lt Col) Henry Tyndall in his diaries

Above: A Mashud Jarga (tribal meeting) taking place in Waziristan,
NW Frontier in 1909

Above: Kelly with Nibra, his Shikari (big game hunting guide),
and some of his trophies on the NW Frontier

(published in 2007 as *High Noon of Empire*). He probably got along with Tyndall as earlier in his diaries Tyndall had quite a lot to say about what we would today call the drinking culture of the typical officers' mess in India and he wasn't impressed.

> "I wish to record my aversion to the custom [of] offering one another drinks by way of hospitality. I am not in the least in favour of the temperance movement but I do object to having to swallow drinks at all times of the day and night when not inclined for it. If one were allowed by etiquette to refuse a drink sometimes when offered one I should not object, but this is out of the question, the matter has become a duty and has to be observed as such. Some individuals and some messes carry it altogether too far. The practice in vogue in our mess of sitting up till 2am on quiet nights when all you want to do is to go to bed is one I shall discountenance when I am C.O."

Kelly's teetotallism must have made him something of an outsider in some messes, compounding the distain that some British officers had for doctors in the Indian Medical Service.

His abstinence from alcohol would have played well with the Indian troops in his care, however, as the mixture of Hindus, Muslims and Sikhs rarely touched alcohol and many would have expressed a strong religious objection to it.

At the end of January 1909 he had his promotion to Major confirmed on completion of the standard 12 years' service and the three pips on his uniform were replaced by the single crown signifying his new rank. His routine for the next couple of years was running the main hospital for the regiment at Dera Ismail Khan with frequent visits to the various outposts its men were guarding. During the winter months life would have been busy and the officers' mess a bustling centre of activity as the brigade arrived for the winter and its annual manoeuvres. This annual demonstration of the might of the Indian Army obviously had the desired effect because the years before the Great War were unusually quiet on the North West Frontier, although quiet was a relative concept in that troublesome region with regular skirmishes with various tribes treated as routine and rarely reported outside of the region, as Major-General Sir George Younghusband, older brother of Francis, recalled in *A Soldier's Memories in Peace and War*, writing about his time there in those years before the Great War.

> "Year in and year out they live in a constant state of war, or preparation for war. Their vigilance must never relax, and in time grows into a habit of life. 'They are not easily taken aback in sudden emergency,' as Sir Harry Lumsden expressed it.

On one part of the Frontier on which the writer was recently stationed there were 165 raids made into British territory in the course of the year by the trans-border tribesmen; and each and all of these had to be met and dealt with. They were mostly small cattle-lifting raids, or to loot travellers or open villages, but they were made by armed marauders of desperate character and great hardihood, and required hard fighting and tremendous marching to deal with them.

Yet rarely do we hear of these outside the little circle on the Frontier, and medals and rewards rarely reach these hardy warriors. It is possible to serve for thirty years on the Frontier, it is possible to be in a dozen fights in as many months, and yet to leave the service without a single medal".

As the brigade left in mid-April with the arrival of the hot weather, returning to Peshawar, Dera Ismail Khan would have become quieter and he would have had a chance to catch up on the latest research in the medical journals he always subscribed to. In 1910 this period of relative relaxation was disturbed by the death of King Edward VII on 6 May, which necessitated attendance at solemn parades and services during a period of extended mourning. It also meant that within a year or so there would be a Coronation to celebrate with another Durbar along the lines of the one for the late King he had attended in Delhi in 1903.

The following year he was granted four months' leave in India at the end of the winter exercises which he most likely spent hunting game and travelling, possibly as far as Burma as he sent Annie some photographs from there around this time. A Lieutenant was appointed to be his assistant while he was away and remained with the regiment to the end of the following winter when the 1st Bengal Lancers found its headquarters moved almost 200 miles north to Peshawar, the summer base for the majority of the Derajat Brigade. It is unlikely that Kelly had much opportunity to enjoy the lighter workload having an assistant should have brought, because not long after returning from his leave towards the end of July 1911 he was packing his bags and heading for Delhi.

Above: Overview of the Delhi Durbar from *The Royal Visit to India* by John Fortescue.

Above: 1st Duke of York's Own Lancers (Skinner's Horse) with King George V (centre) at the Delhi Durbar in 1911. Kelly is in his IMS dress uniform in the back row, second from left. Although attached to the regiment as their medical officer he didn't wear their distinctive uniform.

As one of the elite and most loyal cavalry regiments in the Indian army, Skinner's Horse was originally selected to play a major part in the six-week visit to India by the new King George V and Queen Mary. This Royal tour was due to culminate in a spectacular Durbar in Delhi in mid-December to celebrate their Coronation, which had taken place at Westminster Abbey at the end of June. The summer of 1911 had been especially hot and dry in north west India, however, and a shortage of fodder for the horses meant Skinner's Horse's planned participation in the Durbar was cancelled.

The 400-page official directory (a monument to the meticulous efficiency of the British administration in India) for the Coronation Durbar was published with only token representation from the regiment. Captain R B C Raban (later killed on the Western Front) was appointed as an extra aide-de-camp to the King's party and Risaldar (a senior captain and the most senior rank that could be held by an Indian) Ismail Khan as one of the Indian orderly officers on the King's staff at Delhi. There were also five retired members of the regiment due to be presented to the King as part of a salute to the veterans of the Indian Mutiny and other major conflicts on the sub-continent in the previous 50 years.

There was clearly a last-minute change of heart, which may have been prompted by a cholera outbreak near Bombay, that prevented some other regiments due to appear at the Durbar from attending or it may have just been thought inappropriate for the most famous Indian cavalry regiment not

Above: A highly stylised watercolour by Major Alfred Crowdy Lovett of Skinner's Horse escorting King George V at the Durbar. There were only 24 members of the regiment at the Durbar.

to be better represented at the Durbar. Whatever the reason, a 22-strong detachment from Skinner's Horse hastened from the North West Frontier to Delhi accompanied by their medical officer, Major Kelly, as the Royal party sailed towards India. He had, of course, attended the 1903 Coronation Durbar so would have had a good idea of what to expect. The 1911 Durbar was the only one of these Imperial spectaculars attended by the monarch himself. Contemporary accounts say that for pomp, ceremony and grandeur there was little to choose between the two occasions, although the 1911 Durbar was larger and lasted for longer than the event eight years earlier. The scale of the whole enterprise was breathtaking and certainly impressed The Hon John Fortescue who travelled with the Royal party from England and published a detailed chronicle of the whole three-month long trip.

> "Certainly the first sight of the great canvas city, covering in all twenty-five square miles, was very wonderful, and all the more so when we saw the trim grass lawns which marked the camps of the greater officials, and remembered that a year ago this was a mere brown waste. The King-Emperor's camp lay at the extreme edge, being in the form of a huge semicircle, with the arc facing towards the remaining camps, and the base formed by the road to Delhi city. Opposite the central point of this arc was a large open space with a tall flag-staff, facing almost west, with the Viceroy's camp to the left or north, and the King-Emperor's on the right".

The official ceremonies lasted from 6 to 16 December with the Durbar itself, when Indian princes and maharajahs were presented to the King and Queen, taking place on Tuesday 12th December. That day more than 60,000 troops and civilians gathered in a vast temporary arena to witness the carefully choreographed proceedings that underpinned the might and prestige of the British Raj. As if to underline that it was the British who ruled India, King George announced the transfer of the capital of India from Calcutta to Delhi during the Durbar and laid the foundation stone of New Delhi three days later. The Durbar largely achieved its main purpose of cementing support for British rule among the ruling princes, as was demonstrated by the support given during the Great War, although, ultimately, it did not prevent the rise of Indian nationalism, a movement that was in its infancy in 1911.

The small detachment from Skinner's Horse was present at the Durbar itself on 12 December and the following day was accorded the privilege of being the Royal Escort for the huge military review when more than 50,000 British and Indian troops paraded before the King and Queen. During this review the 22-strong detachment along with Capt Radan and Risaldar Khan was photographed with the King, who was their Colonel-in-Chief. The British and Indian officers were in their striking dress uniforms with Kelly joining them in his rather more modest Indian Medical Service major's uniform. Kelly's copy of this photograph inevitably found its way back to Galway where it took pride of place at the front of one of Annie's albums.

The following day, 14 December, the Lancers were on duty again as part of the Royal Procession from the laying of the foundation stone for New Delhi to the military tournament taking place as part of the celebrations. This was captured in a rather romanticised watercolour by Alfred Lovett, an army major present at the Durbar.

The Durbar over, it was back to the North West Frontier with Skinner's Horse, moving between the two main bases at Dera Ismail Khan and Peshawar for the next two years. These were quiet years in India, although tensions were building elsewhere in the world and these were soon to intrude abruptly into Kelly's life.

He was granted a second long home leave – a year – in March 1914. This time he didn't head straight for Ireland. The only close family he had left in Ireland was his sister Annie in the Presentation Convent in Galway and the now qualified Denis Morris working as a junior doctor in Dublin so he decided it was time to see something of the world.

He travelled first via Singapore to Hong Kong, where on 30 April 1914 he boarded the *Empress of Japan* with around 700 other passengers bound for Vancouver, Canada. One of the attractions of this voyage was the planned stops in China (Shanghai) and Japan (Nagasaki and Yokohama) and he took full advantage of these to visit the sights, dispatching plenty of photographs back to the Presentation Convent for Annie to stick into one of her albums recording her brother's exotic and exciting life far away from the west coast of Ireland.

The *Empress of Japan* docked in Vancouver on 20 May. His final destination on the passenger list for that voyage is listed as London. His plan was probably to visit some Kelly cousins who had emigrated to Canada and eventually settled in Vancouver before travelling across Canada to the Great Lakes and Chicago where some Considine cousins from his mother's family had settled. From there he most likely headed to New York for a trans-Atlantic crossing.

He made it back to Ireland early that summer with one eye fixed on the gathering storm clouds over Europe, wondering what that would mean for him, now a senior officer in the Indian Medical Service. On 4 August Britain declared war on Germany and all serving military personnel were very quickly recalled which meant he had to hastily arrange travel back to London and then on to India. He was less than six months into his year-long leave and now had to hurry back to India.

Serving with the British forces was a sensitive issue in Ireland. The Irish Home Rule Bill was passing through its final stages in the House of Commons that summer and the leader of the large Irish Party at Westminster, John

Above: The *Empress of Japan*, on which Kelly was travelling, docked in Victoria, Canada in 1914 when he was returning to Ireland on a period of extended leave cut short by the outbreak of WW1

Redmond, was determined not to risk losing the best chance ever of bringing Home Rule to the whole of Ireland. He didn't shy away from addressing the sensitivities over serving in the war and, in particular, wanted to reassure the Protestant counties in the north – which were still looking for an opt out from rule from Dublin – that they had nothing to fear. Urging Irishmen to join up was a logical but controversial step in that campaign.

Redmond delivered a famous speech making clear his belief that Irishmen should join the British forces when he addressed the East Wicklow Volunteers (one of many nationalist paramilitary units in Ireland at the time) at Woodenbridge just two days after the Home Rule Act was passed.

"The interests of Ireland - of the whole of Ireland - are at stake in this war. This war is undertaken in the defence of the highest principles of religion and morality and right, and it would be a disgrace for ever to our country and a reproach to her manhood and a denial of the lessons of her history if young Ireland confined their efforts to remaining at home to defend the shores of Ireland from an unlikely invasion, and to shrinking from the duty of proving on the field of battle that gallantry and courage which has distinguished our race all through its history."

This was a deeply divisive speech among Irish nationalists but Redmond's support for the war and the need for Irishmen to join up didn't waver. His picture appeared on recruiting posters almost up the to Easter Rising in 1916, when his fellow nationalists made clear their allies were the Germans and the Turks. It was divisive in Kelly's remaining family too. Kelly was firmly convinced that Denis Morris's patriotic duty was to volunteer for the medical services and he urged him to become a ship's surgeon in the Royal Navy. But Morris was his own man by now. He had established himself as a gynaecologist in Dublin and had dreams of going back to Galway to run his own clinic specialising in that area of medicine. Kelly was firmly in the Redmond camp and did everything he could to persuade the 27-year-old Denis Morris to join up. It was to no avail. If his medical specialty didn't incline him towards war service he was also attracted to the moderate nationalist movement in Ireland, albeit always rejecting its more militant expressions. Serving the British Crown would therefore have held little appeal to him on either medical or political grounds.

By all accounts they parted on bad terms, leaving Annie to pick up the pieces, which she did with great patience over the next few years. She wasn't going to allow the remaining members of her diminished and fragmented family to become estranged over the small matter of a war. They were far from alone as many families were bitterly divided and remained so as turmoil and division raged across Ireland for the next decade.

With family conflict left festering and just five months into his year's leave, Kelly was heading back to India. Whether he believed the promises that the war would be over by Christmas or not he could not have imagined that it would be nearly another eight years before he was able to return to a very different Ireland – and that he would be a very different man too.

FIELD SERVICE

INDIA

POST **CARD**

ADDRESS ONLY.

Sister Columba

Presentation Convent.

Army Form A2042.

Nothing is to be written on this except the date and signature of the sender.

Sentences not required may be erased.

If anything else is added the post card will be destroyed.

_____

I am quite well.

~~I have been admitted into hospital.~~

~~Sick~~ ⎱ ~~and am going on well and hope to be~~
~~Wounded~~ ⎰ ~~discharged soon.~~

~~I am being sent down to the base.~~

I have received your ⎰ letter.
⎰ ~~telegram.~~
⎰ ~~parcel.~~

Letter follows at first opportunity.

~~I have received no~~ ⎰ ~~lately.~~
~~letter from you.~~ ⎰ ~~for a long time.~~

Date 7·2·15   Signature.

G. S. & Sons, Calcutta.

Above: Front and back of one of the many postcards from the frontline he sent to Annie, this one from Egypt.

Mobilisation
Defending the Suez Canal

Kelly returned to India as autumn approached in 1914 with no clear idea of what lay ahead.

Many Indian regiments, along with their own Indian Field Ambulances, were being prepared for fighting on the Western Front, while other regiments were being redeployed internally to ensure that India itself was adequately policed and defended. There was also the increasing likelihood of the Turks – then the fulcrum of the powerful Ottoman Empire – joining the conflict on the side of Germany. That would mean many of the British Empire's possessions and the increasingly important Middle East oilfields would be threatened.

Protecting the Indian home front is unlikely to have held much appeal for him, especially as the forces of Indian nationalism were beginning to stir. The Indian National Congress was starting to make its presence felt and, following a series of bombing incidents, there were genuine fears of widespread revolt in India with the mother country's attention focused on the conflict already raging in Europe. Many German propagandists were certainly predicting the fall of the British Raj.

Memories of his father's bitter battles with Parnell's nationalists in Galway had left deep scars and he was never sympathetic to any nationalist cause. His angry parting from Ireland over Denis Morris's refusal to contemplate joining the Royal Navy would have further reinforced his dislike of all things nationalist.

A posting back to the North West Frontier may have held attractions for him but he most likely arrived in India late that summer hoping for attachment to an active service brigade heading for Europe. As a Major he would have expected to be a second-in-command of one of the larger field ambulances being formed to accompany the troops in the large Indian regiments already being mobilised. These were substantial medical units. They varied in size but typically would have had eight to 10 officers (probably about half of whom would have been qualified doctors) and around 200 men. These would have included a large number of male Indian medical orderlies as there were no female nurses attached to Indian Field Ambulances at the outbreak of the war.

The title "ambulance" is rather misleading to modern readers. A field ambulance was a complete mobile front-line medical unit with operating theatres, wards and other facilities – rather like the hospital featured in M.A.S.H., the long-running US television series set in the Korean War.

Most were under command of a Division that usually had three Field Ambulances, a combination of British Field Ambulances staffed by Royal Army Medical Corps doctors and Indian Field Ambulances staffed by Indian Medical Service doctors. The treatment of British and Indian casualties was thus theoretically separated, a demarcation that was sometimes hard to sustain in the heat and chaos of battle. The nominal capacity of a typical field ambulance was 150 casualties, but in battle many would treat hundreds of casualties in a day.

A field ambulance was responsible for establishing and operating points along a casualty evacuation chain, from the Stretcher Bearer Relay Posts, which were usually around a quarter of a mile behind the frontline and ran shuttles to the Regimental First Aid Posts which took the casualties first and did little more than bandage wounds if that was possible. Behind them were Advanced Dressing Stations and a Main Dressing Station and then to the operating theatres and wards of the main sections of the field ambulance. It might also provide a Walking Wounded Collecting Station, as well as various rest areas and local sick rooms, especially in parts of the world where disease was as likely to be as much of a threat to the troops as bullets and shells. The ambulances were equipped and staffed to carry out major surgery so they could treat and stabilise all the casualties before sending them further behind the lines to the base hospitals.

The British ambulances were usually split into three sections and their Indian counterparts into four sections for ease of deployment and command. They would normally be supported by a Sanitary Section responsible for maintaining clean water, the latrines, delousing stations and providing laundry services, all so important in any hospital and vital for maintaining the health of thousands of troops.

The Indian Field Ambulances that were formed in India in the autumn of 1914 probably didn't expect to have many motorised vehicles, although some followed once they were deployed to the various combat zones where the roads and terrain allowed the rather basic and often unreliable vehicles to travel with reasonable efficiency. Otherwise they relied on horses and bullocks and needed teams of vets and specialist orderlies to look after them. In the desert camels were often the preferred method of transporting the wounded, dragging litters behind them across the sand or carrying the sitting wounded in specially constructed baskets (see picture on page 140).

Kelly was officially mobilised on 20 October 1914 in Peshawar and placed in command of the 105th Indian Field Ambulance with the rank of Acting Lieutenant Colonel "while commanding Medical units in the Field".

His ambulance was attached to the 28th Brigade, itself part of the 10th Indian Division, and was initially placed under Reserve Orders in Peshawar, with a section also based in Rawalpindi. During the next 10 days he was joined by four other IMS doctors, Majors Harry McKenzie and Francis Beit, and Captains Thomas Rutherford and Herbert Scott, the latter who was to stay with him for most of the war. He also started the daily task of completing an entry into an official war diary for the unit, always handwritten as IMS officers obviously didn't have access to secretaries and typewriters, a modest luxury many commanders on the Western Front and elsewhere clearly enjoyed judging by other war diaries from the period.

The diary provides a meticulous record of Kelly's involvement in the war over the next four years and is often typically forthright. Unlike many other field ambulance war diaries it isn't merely a record of the number of casualties in and the number leaving dead or healed – in fact there are very few such figures – but more of a commentary on the state of the ambulance, the conditions it was expected to cope with and the many challenges he and his team of doctors faced. A lot of it was clearly intended to be read by senior officers and was not always couched in terms that could be expected to enhance his popularity at headquarters.

It also differs from other field ambulance diaries in another respect. Although he was made an Acting Lieutenant Colonel he still signed himself as a Major right up until his promotion was made permanent in January 1917. Other war diaries from field ambulances that have survived in the National Archives show that many other similarly promoted IMS and RAMC officers were quick to use their new temporary rank whenever possible.

During late October and early November 1914 tensions with the Ottoman Empire were gradually racked up and British patience with the Turks finally snapped after a series of incidents and rebuffed ultimatums and war was declared on the Ottoman Empire on 5 November, immediately widening the scale and geographic scope of the war. It was now a global conflict.

It quickly became clear that cruisers from the German Mediterranean fleet already had plans laid to link up with the Turkish navy near the Suez Canal, threatening Britain's main sea route to India as well as the oilfields of the Middle East that were rapidly growing in importance as the world's first mechanised war gathered ominous momentum.

On 12 November the newly formed 105th Indian Field Ambulance was ordered to proceed to Karachi for embarkation to an "overseas destination" as part of the Indian Expeditionary Force 7, all that he felt able to record in the diary, or possibly all that he knew.

Moving his new unit the 700 miles down the Indus Valley to Karachi was a major logistical challenge. Even today the drive takes 17 hours, so moving the non-motorised unit by road was out of the question. Fortunately, Peshawar was the northern railhead for the North West Railway so men and supplies were loaded onto trains for the long journey south to the railway's southernmost station at Karachi. They arrived there at 6am on 16 November four days after receiving their orders to move and just three days later left on the *SS Devanha*, now designated Troopship No 5, with four other Indian field ambulances. Their destination was Egypt and the Suez Canal, now threatened from the land by a 70,000-strong Turkish army gathering in the Sinai Peninsula.

On paper, Egypt was still theoretically part of the Ottoman Empire but had been occupied and controlled by Britain since 1882. The Turkish Sultan in Constantinople moved quickly once war was declared and persuaded the Islamic clergy to back his proclamation of a Jihad (Holy War) against Britain and its allies. This had a dual intent. First, it was aimed at persuading the Egyptians – the majority of whom were Muslims – to back the Turks as they marched into Egypt. Second, it was aimed at adding to the unrest in India which would at the very least keep the British forces there fully occupied. At best they hoped it would provoke mutiny among the many Mohammedan regiments that made up a large part of the Indian Army, throwing India into the sort of bitter internal conflict it experienced during the Indian Mutiny of 1857. It failed on both counts.

In Egypt the British also moved quickly. The Khedive, Abbas Hilmi, nominally the Viceroy of Egypt but appointed by Turkey, was already in Turkey in August 1914. He was openly pro-Ottoman and he stayed in Turkey where he was used as a propaganda tool by the Central Powers. The British response was to proclaim Egypt a British Protectorate on 18 December 1914. Hilmi was deposed and his uncle, Prince Hussein Kamal Pasha, elevated to the Egyptian throne with the new title of Sultan. In a further attempt to reduce tensions in Egypt the Egyptians were told that they would not be pressed into fighting the Turks, thereby cleverly neutralising their concerns about being dragged into a Holy War against fellow Muslims. This reassurance didn't apply to the modest units of the Egyptian regular army that had been formed by Lord Kitchener while he was Consul-General prior to the war; they were required to fight alongside the British and Indian troops that soon arrived to repel the Turks.

One of the remarkable features of the First World War is the staunch loyalty of the Indian Army, including the Mohammedan (Muslim) regiments. The triumphal patriotism of the 1911 Delhi Durbar with its carefully orchestrated lauding of Indian princes still cast a warm glow across the Raj. The call to Holy War largely fell on deaf ears.

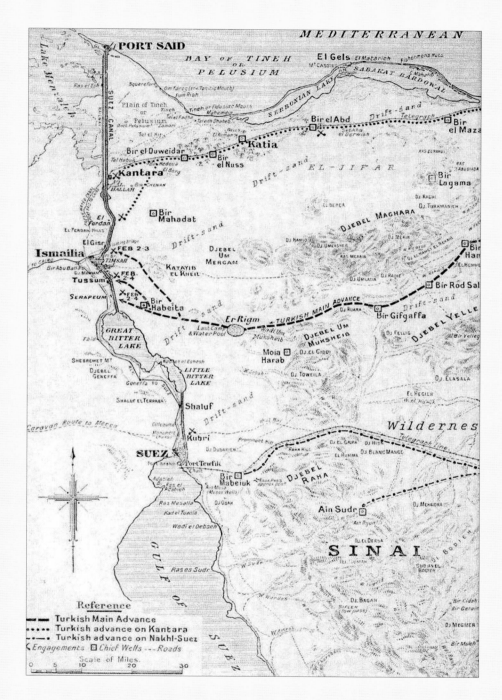

Above: Map of the attack on Ismailia where Kelly's field ambulance found itself in the front line

Above: Indian troops defending the Suez Canal from Turkish attack.

The immediate consequence of promising the Egyptians that they wouldn't be recruited in large numbers to fight was that the defences along the Suez Canal needed reinforcing as the Turkish forces started amassing to the south across the Sinai Desert. There was a British garrison already in Egypt made up of British troops but the War Office was keen to deploy these on the Western Front so it was to India that the British government turned.

Thus Acting Lieutenant Colonel Kelly and the 105th Indian Field Ambulance found themselves heading for Egypt as part of the 28th Indian Infantry Brigade, made up of Punjabi, Sikh and Gurkha regiments. This brigade was also known at the 28th Frontier Force Brigade, reflecting its formation and roots in the North West Frontier where most of the units, including Kelly, had been serving in the years running up to the war. The brigade was part of the 10th Indian Division, which was under the command of Major-General George Younghusband, the older brother of Francis Younghusband and not a name that Kelly would have been pleased to see near the top of his command structure. The overall Commanding Officer of Canal Defences, however, was another Major General just senior to Younghusband, Alex Wilson.

The *SS Devanha* arrived at Suez after a calm voyage during which Kelly created a routine that included daily physical drill on the upper deck for all the units on board. Suez is at the southern end of the Canal, so on 2

December the unit was moved up by train to the strategically important ferry post at Ismailia, roughly the mid-point of the canal, and where Major-General Wilson had decided to base his headquarters.

By 5 December Kelly had setup the basic hospital facilities, ready to receive the first patients the following day, quickly followed by several cases of mumps among the 1/5th Gurkha Rifles and 53rd Sikhs. Right across the Middle East throughout the war, heat, disease and sickness were major factors, accounting for thousands of deaths among British and Indian troops. Often the causes were poor sanitation, especially with the Indian regiments, and Kelly was to develop something of an obsession with highlighting this to senior officers. On 6 December he was already recording in his diaries the need for Brigade command to sort out the sanitation for the thousands of troops stationed around Ismailia.

During December he drilled the unit in the challenging tasks of moving casualties across open sand and coping with the heat and dust, even arranging a training exercise for Christmas Day 1914.

The Official History of the Great War describes the approach to deploying the British and Indian Field Ambulances in Egypt in those early months of the war:

> "The equipment of field ambulances depended on the character of the operations. Desert transport replaced the ambulance wagons and cars in operations in the desert, but ambulance cars were again given to them when roads were suitable. As a rule, especially in the operations of the Desert Column, the field ambulances were formed into mobile and immobile sections, the latter depending for their movements on any camel transport that might be required being provided at the time. The mobile sections were provided with camel cacolets, sand carts, sand sledges, and bicycle or wheeled stretcher carriers. These took the place of the normal ambulance car and wagon transport; but a modified scale of motor ambulance cars was allotted to divisions. In this way two of the three sections of a field ambulance were made mobile, and one immobile."

By mid-January the Turkish threat was getting nearer with some minor skirmishes taking place just 20 miles to the north of where the 105th IFA was based. The Turkish army had managed to cross the Sinai desert by marching

at night and now posed a significant threat to the Canal. The ambulance was reinforced with fresh animal transport – 23 camels and two mules with a range of litters for carrying the wounded. He also despatched Capt Scott to establish an advanced dressing station to deal with the expected casualties when the Turks finally attacked in force. He didn't have to wait long.

The first serious Turkish attack on the Canal came at El Ferdan on 1 February when they advanced to within a mile of the eastern bank and dug in, maintaining a steady stream of sniper fire on the British and Indian positions on the west bank. The casualties were evacuated from Capt Scott's dressing station by launch to the main field hospital five miles downstream, an arrangement that Kelly recorded worked well as it was quicker than going across the sand. At this stage the numbers coming in each day were relatively modest (2 Feb):

> "Five casualties in total from our side. Two from 21st M[ountain] Battery (one being serious) and three from 51st Rifles. All with bullet wounds.
> Evacuation arrangements worked satisfactory; all cases being dressed and in the clearing hospital by 11.15am. The newly enlisted IBC [Indian Bearer Corps] orderlies behaved exceedingly well under fire and did their work satisfactorily."

This was just a foretaste of what was to come over the next few days.

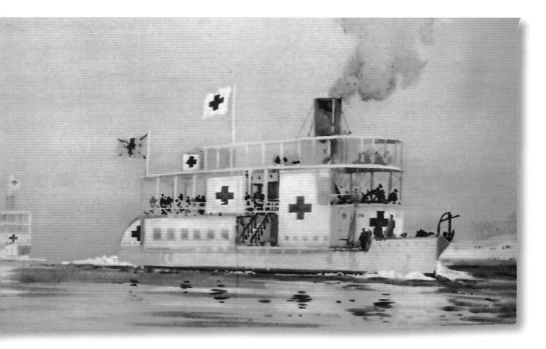

Above: Hospital ships on the Nile. These were used to transport the wounded away from the battle zones to Suez or to Cairo.

The Turks launched their main attack the following morning with an artillery bombardment that sent shrapnel tearing through the hospital tents, although he was able to record that there was "no injury to either personnel or animals – all of whom were sheltered under the high Canal bank".

Less fortunate was the Indian Marine Service ship *Hardinge*, which was moored near the ferry post at Ismailia. This was hit with small artillery fire and had to quickly move out of range, but not before several minor casualties among the Indian crew had been taken off and transported to the hospital for treatment. They were all on their way to a base hospital well behind the lines by the end of the day.

The main Turkish advance against the ferry post had been halted during the day but skirmishes continued throughout the night and into the following morning before the British launched a counter attack across the Canal to force the remaining Turkish units back from the Canal. The British and Indian causalities were relatively light at around 150 killed or wounded. The officer leading the main assault, Capt L F A Cochran from the 92nd Punjabis, was among those killed.

Eventually the Turks either retreated or surrendered with around 50 prisoners having to be treated before they could be moved back behind the British lines on the opposite side of the Canal.

Turkish assaults elsewhere along the Canal during those first few days of February were also rebuffed with a similar story of light British and Indian casualties and heavy Turkish losses, a pattern that was to be repeated across the region over the next three and half years. In total the Turks suffered around 700 casualties with a similar number taken prisoner.

There was no immediate rest for Kelly and the 105th IFA as on 5 February they were confronted by a severe infestation of lice in the main Ismailia camp and another outbreak of mumps. The lice were dealt with by ordering all clothing and bedding to be steamed over the next two days. The mumps were successful tackled by quickly isolating the infected soldiers.

He was quick to review his unit's first experiences of action and, while complimenting his fellow officers and men for the way they coped, he was not so impressed with some of the equipment they had at their disposal, especially the saddles and litters for carrying the injured by camel which he complained were inadequate and "inappropriate for camels".

He was busy tackling lice again at the beginning March, upping the measures to deal with it and petitioning his senior officers for better kit for the men – the Indian soldiers in his care – who had to keep suffering this unpleasant infestation:

> "Efforts are being made to reduce vermin by steam sterilisation of clothing and treatment of some with Izal & soap solution. The men are encouraged to bath regularly in lake & canal. The main cause seems to be the fact that the men have only one set of underclothing & until this is remedied there is little hope of eliminating lice completely."

Lice weren't his only problem that month. He was also tackling the reluctance of some men to be inoculated against enteric fever (typhoid) in a carefully measured entry clearly intended to be read and acted upon by his superior officers.

> "Regiments have submitted returns showing numbers inoculated against enteric fever. The 1/5th GR [Gurkha Rifles], 53rd Sikhs and 56th Rifles are all well protected. Practically all officers & men & followers having been recently inoculated. The 51st Sikhs have not adopted inoculation as four officers & 800 men declined to avail themselves of the protection afforded them by this system. Some recent literature on the subject – showing results obtained in British & American armies – has been supplied for information to the Regt authorities & it is hoped that the men will be inclined to fall in line with the other units of Brigade."

That he should be quoting from recent literature should come as no surprise as he rarely let himself fall behind with his reading of the latest medical journals, however remote and trying his circumstances.

He also found himself with the pleasant task of distributing the contents of 252 boxes of gifts for the troops from the Red Cross that he confessed to being rather surprised had survived the journey in remarkably good condition – only four boxes had been damaged.

By the end of March, the 105th IFA was on the move south to Suez where several Turkish units were still active, often working with local Bedouin tribesmen who, like most Arabs during the war, frequently switched sides depending on who they thought had the upper hand at the time. On 22 March he reported that the ambulance was supporting fighting across a wide front with Major Mackenzie commanding an advanced dressing station at Kubri, just north of Suez and Capt Scott receiving casualties from the 56th Rifles fighting at El Shatt at another advanced unit based in the town of Suez itself.

The fighting intensified the following day as the 51st and 53rd Sikhs and 5th Gurkha Rifles were drawn into the battle around Kubri. Kelly found himself working alongside the 135th IFA as their stretcher bearer resources were fully committed to evacuating casualties from the fighting north and south of Suez. Despite this the number of Indian casualties reaching the main hospital facilities were relatively few – around 20, of whom three died. They did treat quite a few Turks as well and had to find a way of holding them securely until the prisoner guard finally arrived late into the evening. It seems that the Turks were so grateful to receive decent medical care that they made no attempt to escape during the hours they were left more or less unguarded in the hospital tents.

By 11pm all the hospitalised casualties were safely in the main hospital wards of the 105th IFA and, as the Turks had either surrendered or fled back towards the Sinai Desert, he was able to pull back his advanced dressing stations to rejoin the main unit.

By the end of March he was back to arguing with the military commanders about their treatment of the men under their command.

A column of Indian troops arrived at Suez and, on being asked to inspect them, he quickly identified a mild type of colitis, an inflammation of the colon and bowel. He believed that the affected men needed to be hospitalised and treated but the Commanding Officer thought otherwise. He eventually compromised on treating the men on an out-patient basis but enforced a complete re-organisation of the sanitation system for the camp where they were based. He also made it clear to his superiors that he took a very dim view of establishing camps in swamp areas without much better protection from malaria-bearing mosquitoes and better drainage.

Above: A page from the War Diary of the 105th Indian Field Ambulance from 21 June 1915 showing how Kelly signed himself as a Major in the IMS despite being given the acting rank of Lieutenant Colonel

This argument went on for some weeks until he received confirmation that the Commanding Officer of the Canal, Maj Gen Wilson, had decided that all major sanitation issues should be placed under the supervision of a medical officer and not a military commander. For the next three years Kelly took full advantage of this important administrative victory and made better sanitation one of his top priorities.

Over the next month his resources became stretched out over a wide front. Major Mackenzie was commanding a dressing station and stretcher bearer section with the advanced units of the army column 100 miles south of Suez on the Gulf of Suez while the main hospital remained in Suez itself. The British decided to halt their pursuit of the retreating Turks across the Sinai Peninsula, however, unconvinced that they had sufficient logistical support. It was probably a wise decision as the Turks suffered terribly, losing many men to heat, dehydration and exhaustion as they struggled across the unforgiving desert.

Kelly still found he had plenty of problems to deal with in Suez, a further insight into how demanding the role of a commanding officer of a field ambulance was even when there was no fighting.

On 30 April he reported that several men from a detachment of sappers who had been vaccinated against enteric fever two days previously had died and that others vaccinated with the same type of vaccine the following day were also seriously ill. He immediately asked an RAMC officer to carry out an investigation and suspended the use of the vaccine. Satisfied that it wasn't his team's administration of the vaccine that was at fault he was winging another stiffly worded memo to Colonel William Robinson, the Principal Medical Officer of the Indian forces in Egypt, about the poor quality of the vaccine he had been supplied with.

Kelly's mood wouldn't have been improved the following day with arrival of a fresh detachment from the 128th Pioneers with several men suffering from flu. Fortunately, it was a "mild type of influenza" and quickly dealt with, but new units arriving with disease and illness were a constant problem. On 13 June the 9th Bhopal Infantry arrived from France and brought with them several bad cases of mumps, provoking another confrontation with a unit commander who was unsympathetic to his men's suffering. Kelly insisted the most severe cases should be hospitalised and isolated but it quickly became clear that his idea of who needed to be hospitalised and the commanding officer's were rather different.

All through May the temperature rose, causing severe problems with sanitary arrangements with the 51st Sikhs alone having 70 dysentery cases hospitalised at one stage. Dysentery was a major killer among the British and Indian forces in the Middle East throughout the war, with many deaths easily preventable by better sanitation, hence Kelly's constant focus on the sanitary arrangements. It seems that whenever he had an opportunity he used the new powers over sanitation he had negotiated to order inspections – usually visiting personally – frequently leaving military commanders with a long list of simple improvements to be made.

His view of the top brass was not improved a month later.

Owing to an obvious need for better co-ordination of medical administration following the ill-judged landings at Gallipoli, the Army Council appointed a Principal Director of Medical Services for the Mediterranean with headquarters in Egypt. This new post had overall responsibility for all medical services – British, Indian, Australian and New Zealand – in Egypt and the Dardanelles as well as in Malta and Gibraltar, and subsequently Macedonia. Surgeon-General William Babtie VC, up to that point Director of Medical Services in India, duly arrived in Egypt on 15 June 1915, but his initial tour of the hospital facilities in Egypt managed to bypass Kelly and the 105th Indian Field Ambulance. VC or no VC (Babtie won it in South Africa) Kelly made it very clear he was not impressed at being overlooked. Perhaps the staff officers thought it wise not to expose their new commanding officer to an outspoken Irishman, although he had met Kelly on an earlier inspection of the Indian medical facilities at the turn of the year and may even have decided to give him a miss himself.

They soon found something to keep Kelly occupied.

CHAPTER 10

Under fire in Aden
"An excellent improvised hospital"

In early July a large Ottoman force of Turks and Arabs marched south from Yemen towards the strategically important British port of Aden at the south-eastern corner of the Arabian Peninsula. On 4 July, as thousands of Arabs deserted the British, the town of Lahej fell to the Turkish-led forces. From there they marched towards Aden itself, digging in just two miles from the harbour. The port was defended by a relatively small permanent garrison, which the Official History confesses "had not been trained to fight under these trying conditions".

The British had to move quickly and the 28th Frontier Force and its field ambulances were sent on their way from Egypt on 12 July, arriving in Aden, now being shelled daily by the Turkish artillery, at 5am on 18 July.

This wasn't Kelly's first visit to Aden. He had stopped there back in March 1897 when the *Oceana* was carrying him and his fellow junior lieutenants to their first tour of duty in India.

He would have little time to reflect on his previous brief acquaintance with the place. While the men and animals were being disembarked, Kelly was informed that he would have to set up his main hospital alongside the Indian base hospital already operating in Aden. He was being asked to sort out some serious problems in double quick time, according to the Official History:

> "The medical arrangements [in Aden] had apparently not been carefully considered. The supply of such important items as water and ice had not been arranged for, and these were the first things that were urgently called for when the force became incapacitated during the advance and numerous cases of heat-stroke were occurring. The field ambulance sections have been hastily organised, and transport not authorised…The lack of previous arrangements for the supply of water and ice to the mobile column is all the more remarkable in view of the fact that everyone stationed in Aden had always been accustomed to a plentiful supply of both commodities. Extra medical assistance was

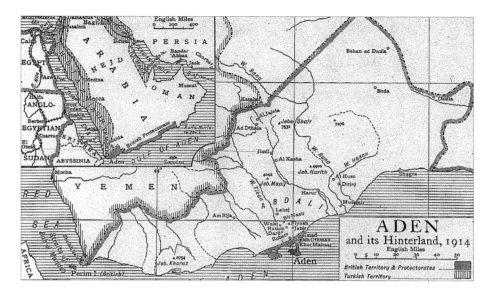

Above: Aden was considered strategically very important to British interests in the Middle East at the outbreak of WWI.

improvised, and local stretcher-bearers were enlisted to assist in the evacuation of casualties. The missionary doctors from Sheikh Othman [an oasis just outside Aden that fell to the Turks] were asked to take charge of the European hospital in Aden and to assist in the Indian infantry base hospital."

When Kelly found his way to the small 40-bed hospital it was already near to being overwhelmed as it had 96 casualties, many of them just lying on the verandah. The staff told him they had been warned to expect even more wounded men as the shelling intensified. On top of this, he was told that no time would be wasted in throwing the 28th Frontier Force into a counter-attack.

By the following morning he had expanded the facilities to 150 beds and established an Advanced Dressing Station on the outskirts of the town ready for the counter-attack. He had also been given command of a RAMC motorised ambulance unit, a foretaste of the reorganisation of the medical services that was to come the following year, when the often wasteful parallel services of Indian and British Field Ambulances were merged into combined units. The operating theatres had also been expanded and the team of surgeons fully briefed on what to expect.

The main attack to break out of Aden was launched just before dawn on 21 July and caught the Turks totally by surprise. The 53rd Sikhs attacked on the left and the 56th Rifles with the Aden Camel Troop attempted to outflank the Turkish line on the right. Kelly gives few details of the numbers of casualties they dealt with that day – the Official History says just 25 – but he is full of praise for his officers:

> "Advanced dressing station under Major [Francis] Beit IMS worked exceeding well – all cases being dealt with as they arrived, and Capt Scott IMS deserves much credit for the energy he displayed in establishing a practicable hospital at such short notice at Maala Wharf".

The Official History gives a rather more generous account of the role played by Kelly and his team:

> "The medical arrangements for this attack had been more carefully considered, owing probably to the fact that the field ambulance attached to the 28th Infantry Brigade has previously served with it in Egypt... It was decided that two sections of No. 105 Indian Field Ambulance would accompany the force, and that the remaining two sections, with the addition of some British personnel, would establish themselves at the Maala wharves in Aden. These latter sections were ordered to organise the large wharves into comfortable hospital wards to act as the main hospital for the reception of casualties evacuated from the area of operations. The officer commanding no. 105 Indian Field Ambulance [Kelly] at once set to work to obtain a supply of beds, mattresses, stretchers and feeding utensils. Suitable arrangements were made for the lighting of the hospital, and in the course of a few hours an excellent improvised hospital had been organised. In view of the anticipated operations, all the available ambulance transport, consisting of twelve ambulance tongas and a few motor cars, had been placed at the disposal of the senior medical officer accompanying the attacking force. The sick in Aden were retained in the section hospital, and the European Hospital was reserved for officers. All medical officers attached to units in Aden were forbidden to leave the precincts of their units."

It is hard to imagine how difficult it must have been to turn a dockside wharf into a serviceable hospital for 150 casualties almost overnight: it was a remarkable feat. The integration of Indian and British medical services under the command of an IMS officer was a radical move and was clearly successful, possibly influencing the review of medical arrangements across the Middle East theatre of war later that year.

The following day Major Beit found his dressing station being moved further up the line as the Turks were driven out of the nearby town of Shaikh Othman while Kelly struggled with an apparent contamination of the water supply coming into Aden. Initially the finger of suspicion was pointed at the Turks, but Kelly's analysis led him to conclude that it "does not appear to have been fouled by the Turks". New water channels and wells were rapidly dug in order to rectify the problem.

As the fighting died down on 23 July he faced a more conventional medical emergency as he was called to the Hospital Ship *Guildford Castle* where Captain Norman MacVean, an IMS doctor attached to the 62nd Punjabis, needed an emergency appendectomy. The operation went well but he recorded that his fellow doctor was suffering from other duodenal ailments, which might hamper his recovery.

For the rest of the month he treated a mixture of British and Indian casualties – sick and wounded – at the extended hospital he had taken over in Aden. It wasn't until 2 August that No 10 British Stationary Hospital opened in Aden and the British casualties were transferred. Before they left he had to cope with an outbreak of pneumonia and a rare autoimmune disorder called pemphigus which he saw first in a handful of Indian troops but soon spread to the British soldiers, infecting around 90 people in total, all of whom had to be treated in a special ward he set up alongside the hospital.

Pemphigus is characterised by very painful large blisters that often start in the mouth before spreading to the rest of the body: "The clusters vary in size, some being as big as half a good size walnut" he recorded. Nowadays it is treated with a combination of steroids and strong antibiotics, neither of which were available in 1915, so it was a matter of a careful treatment of the blisters to ensure they didn't burst and get infected and as good a diet as he could arrange. He and Capt Scott felt that the diets of the men were deficient in calcium salts and that this could have been a contributory factor in the outbreak.

At the beginning of August he heard that Major General Wilson had mentioned him in Dispatches for his services in Egypt. Obviously at least one senior officer appreciated that the frequent complaints from the commanding officer of the 105th IFA were well intentioned and often well targeted.

By now it was clear that the British wanted to push the Turks back further from Aden and that the next battles were likely to be fought across the desert. While he liked the new motorised ambulances he knew these would be no good on the sand. He was also having problems with the horse-drawn ambulance carts they had been using in Aden so he requested camels from Egypt. While he waited for those to arrive – 30 were sent – he set about adapting the horse-drawn carts so they were ready to be fitted to the camels.

At the end of August the British and Indian forces pushed northwards back towards Lahej but on 28 August 350 men of the 53rd Sikh Rifles advanced too far to a small town called Al-Waht and found themselves facing a counter-attack by around 2000 Turkish troops and Arabs. As they retreated back

Above: Kelly insisted that camels were sent from Egypt to Aden to transport the wounded across the desert.

towards the main force, Kelly was working alongside Capt Scott at the Advanced Dressing Station that was supporting the advance, treating the wounded as bullets tore through the fabric of their hospital tents: "caught in crossfire" he noted. He wasn't so sanguine about the performance of some of his unit under fire:

> "The men of IBC [Indian Bearer Corps] who accompanied this column under Major Beit IMS were very unsteady and could not be relied on to work under the somewhat arduous conditions of a retirement under heavy close range fire. The drivers of Ambulance Camels worked very well all through."

The casualties that day were three British officers wounded, 22 rank and file wounded, of whom one died, and two missing, two followers wounded and one follower from the IBC missing. "The enemy losses were very much heavier", he noted in the diary.

This reverse was soon rectified but not without cost; nothing to do with enemy action, as the Official History records:

"The march against Waht and subsequent attack on the Turkish force were remarkable for the number of cases of heat-stroke and exhaustion admitted to the field ambulance. To evacuate these cases all available transport was dispatched to the area of operations, and thenceforward two additional camels were allotted to the field ambulances to carry a supply of ice. The slabs of ice were covered with sacking and packed in sawdust in wooden boxes."

A further British push saw the Turks forced out of Lahej and safely back up the Arabian Peninsula, so the work of the 28th Frontier Force and its field ambulance in Aden was done. By 8 September Kelly was embarking with the 53rd Sikhs back to Egypt on *HT Chilka*, a ship he definitely approved of: "Excellent accommodation for the troops on the ship".

Back in Egypt the 105th IFA was posted to Kanlaia on the east bank of the Suez Canal where he was quickly noting that the nighttime temperatures were well below freezing. He kept up his regular inspections of sanitation, frequently recording that the arrangements for Indian troops were sub-standard. He also noted cases of scurvy and requested more vegetables for the Indian soldiers, initially more than a little displeased when all they managed to send were pumpkins.

He certainly cared for the troops and kept up an almost relentless campaign for better sanitation, diet and medical facilities for them but he was no soft touch if they stepped out of line.

When in early November 1915 he caught two Indian orderlies in his unit stealing he threw the proverbial book at them. They had clearly crossed his path before because to the charges of theft he added malingering, itself a serious charge in wartime, and held a Summary Court Martial on 9 November.

"Found guilty in both cases & sentenced to corporal punishment in presence of personnel of Field Ambulance".

Although such punishments were by 1915 rare in the British Army they were still common practice in the Indian Army and, having found the men guilty, it would have been seen as a sign of weakness had he imposed a less severe sentence. Judging by the lack of any qualification to his entry in the war diary he didn't see this as being anything exceptional and would have arranged for the punishment to be administered in front of a parade of the ambulance personnel.

Although casualties from Gallipoli had been arriving regularly at Alexandria on Egypt's northern Mediterranean coast since late April, none ever appear to have reached Kelly's hospitals down in the south of the country. He spent much of the last few months of 1915 and early 1916 being moved around with virtually the whole 28th Frontier Force to relatively little effect.

This clearly left him feeling more than a little disgruntled because when Robert Knox, an IMS Major six months his junior in service terms, was appointed Senior Medical Officer for the El Shatt region he complained vigorously, taking his grievance all the way to Major General Wilson, the Commanding Officer of the 10th Indian Infantry Division of which the 28th Frontier Force was a key element.

He never spells out any doubts in the war diaries over Major Knox's competence, but was clearly aggrieved not to have been considered for such a senior appointment himself.

The War of 1914–1918.

Indian Army
Maj. T.B. Kelly, F.R.C.S.E., I.M.S.

was mentioned in a Despatch from

General Sir Beauchamp Duff, G.C.B., G.C.S.I., K.C.V.O., C.I.E., A.D.C.

dated 9th March 1916.

for gallant and distinguished services in the Field.
I have it in command from the King to record His Majesty's
high appreciation of the services rendered.

Winston S. Churchill

War Office
Whitehall, S.W.
1st March 1919.

Secretary of State for War.

Above: Mentioned in Dispatches for his service in Aden

His complaint seems to have stopped with Maj Gen Wilson at the end of February. Possibly it was explained to him that the 10th Division was about to be broken up to reinforce other fronts, especially the Western Front and so he would soon be on the move. The Division was formally shut down on 7 March and Kelly started work on running down the 105th IFA. As he was doing so, he heard that, once again, he had been Mentioned in Dispatches, this time

Left: Kelly's 1914-15 Star awarded to those who served in any theatre of WWI before the introduction of conscription.

by Sir Beauchamp Duff, Commander-in-Chief of India, for his exploits in taking command of the medical arrangements in Aden. This was his third appearance in dispatches from commanding officers from Tibet onwards.

Family news continued to trickle through to him via Annie and while waiting to find out where he would be posted to next, he heard that his closest brother Denis, now 44, had volunteered for the Australian Imperial Force and would soon be on his way to France with the 28th Battalion. He would also have heard about the Easter Rising in Dublin that started on 24 April with the occupation of the General Post Office in O'Connell Street. Although this was quickly crushed by the British Army, the decision to execute the 15 leaders stirred up further resentment against British rule that was to have repercussions for Kelly's life a decade later.

At one stage during April he was told that the unit might be moved back to India rather than the Western Front. However, it wasn't just in France that the war was going badly.

900 miles to the east the British were facing disaster in Mesopotamia (modern day Iraq) where its forces had over-reached themselves in advancing to Baghdad. Initially the British had moved into southern Mesopotamia to secure the oilfields around Basra at the end of 1914. Having successfully done this, rather than consolidate, they decided to push northwards up the Tigris. There was no strategic objective behind this advance beyond a desire to take Baghdad from the Turks, a symbolic objective but no more than that. To start with the Turks retreated but when they fought back they caught the British and Indian forces by surprise, forcing them back to the town of Kut on a bend of the Tigris and surrounding them at the beginning of December 1915.

All attempts to relieve the 8000 troops trapped in Kut failed dismally and in one of the greatest British humiliations of the war the near starving garrison surrendered to the Turks on 29 April 1916. The casualties were heavy and the medical arrangements had broken down, rather like in Aden but on a grimly larger scale.

All thoughts of transferring Kelly and his unit back to India soon evaporated and by 13 May he was on board the *HT Bamora* heading for Basra. Mesopotamia was going to have a dramatic impact on his life.

CHAPTER 11

Mesopotamia
Hell, heat and chaos

The war in the Middle East was going badly. The ease with which a large Turkish force was pushed back from the Suez Canal in early 1915 was long forgotten as humiliation followed disaster.

Gallipoli is a name that has huge resonance across the present day Commonwealth. More than 56,000 troops from around the Empire, in particular Australia and New Zealand, died and another 124,000 were wounded during the disastrous attempts to land on the beaches on the north side of the Dardanelles Straits. The broad objective of the campaign was to reach the Turkish capital at Constantinople but the Allied forces never made it off a narrow beach head. The first landings there were in the middle of April 1915 but by early January 1916 the last Empire troops had been withdrawn and the landings declared a total failure.

In Mesopotamia initial easy success in securing the vital oilfields straddling Persia and Mesopotamia seduced the British into marching northwards to Baghdad only to end up besieged in the town of Kut-al-Amara [to give it its full name]. After nearly six months this too ended badly when the starving garrison surrendered at the end of April 1916.

This humiliation was made all the worse as the commanding officer at Kut was one of the heroes of the North West Frontier. Major-General Charles Townshend had been in a siege before – at Chitral in 1895. There he eventually broke out as the relief forces arrived and for a long time he believed he could repeat that feat at Kut, but he was in a far worse position.

He had pursued the Turks up the Tigris but had over-stretched his supply lines and, when the Turks attacked at Ctesiphon, he had no option but to retreat southwards to Kut where he found himself encircled.

Senior British officers outside the Middle East were in no doubt about what they thought of the mess: "A more mismanaged expedition never was – except Gallipoli", declared Lieutenant General Sir William Robertson, then Chief of the Imperial General Staff and the only man in the British Army ever to rise from being a Private to Field Marshall.

Increasingly desperate but badly planned attempts to lift the siege failed with significant casualties that completely overwhelmed the medical services, already struggling to cope with the heat and disease that made Mesopotamia one of the toughest places to fight in. An old Arab proverb sums up what many inhabitants of that part of the world thought of it: "When God Made Hell he didn't think it bad enough so he made Mesopotamia – and then added flies."

The chaos that followed the fall of Kut was still at its worse when Kelly arrived in Basra on 26 May, less than a month after the surrender. Casualties were still pouring in to ill-equipped and under-staffed hospitals, having taken weeks to move on slow, flat-bottomed boats down the Tigris, the only route available for evacuation down the flooded Tigris valley. Many had not been treated properly and were seriously ill by the time they were evacuated, a consequence of moving relief forces up to Kut without their field ambulances, an act of staggering negligence. On top of these there were more than 1500 sick and wounded captured at Kut, but handed over by the Turks before they marched the rest of the garrison north to long-term incarceration.

The conditions the poor wretches who escaped captivity travelled in were beyond appalling. A J Barker in *The First Iraq War* paints a grim picture of the conditions on the five-day journey back down the Tigris:

> "Even while the ships were still in midstream a sickening smell tainted the air and before the casualties were taken off, they could be seen lying in their own filth, crowded together on the iron decks. The wounds of many of the more serious cases were found to be in the advanced stages of septic poisoning and in some cases men with comparatively slight injuries were dying from huge bed sores. That was how things were and yet a report was cabled to India: 'General condition of the wounded very satisfactory. Medical arrangements, under circumstances of considerable difficulty, worked splendidly'."

The senior officers that sent that cable were based at Basra but one of their number, Major Robert Carter, was one of the few to complain – and threatened by the commanding officers for his trouble. He was able to speak freely to the Commission of Enquiry that a shocked British government quickly established once the news from the Mesopotamian front began to be widely reported in the British newspapers. He didn't spare anything in his description for that enquiry of what he saw as one boat arrived at Basra.

> "When the *Mejidieh* was about three hundred yards off, it looked as if she was festooned with ropes. The stench when she was close was quite definite, and I found that what I mistook for ropes were dried stalactites

of human faeces. The patients were so crowded and huddled together on the ship that they could not perform the offices of Nature clear of the ship's edge and the whole of the ship's side was covered."

By the time Kelly arrived all the old commanders had been replaced and a new, much more efficient regime was quickly being established under Lieutenant-General Sir Stanley Maude. Unlike his predecessors, he reported to the War Office in London and not to the Indian government in Simla. In future the operations in Mesopotamia were directed from London as they felt the Indian government was completely out of its depth in conducting major military operations well beyond its borders.

Sorting out the medical and wider transport arrangements was one of Maude's priorities and Kelly was immediately sent to Makina, a camp just outside Basra to help with organising and equipping hospitals capable of coping with the thousands of sick and wounded still to be repatriated from the battlefield areas. His first task was to deal with the casualties pouring off the ill-equipped shallow-bottomed boats coming down the Tigris.

One British officer serving with a Punjabi regiment who had trapped a sciatic nerve during the retreat from Kut years later recorded his memories of the journey and arrival at the hospital at Makina. He had lain on the deck next to an injured Seaforth Highlander who died on the five-day journey, his body just left where he died calling for his mother with his last breath. The officer had no access to any sanitation because he was immobile so all his bodily functions were performed as his lay on the deck.

"On arrival one's clothes were cut off. One was put into a hospital gown. It was all one blessed relief to be back to civilisation. You fell into the arms of the IMS and everything was so civilised from then on".

By early June Kelly was on one of those hospital boats heading up the Tigris, passing Querna where the two great rivers of Mesopotamia, the Tigris and the Euphrates, meet. The temperature was touching 115°F (46°C): high temperatures were to be a feature of his two years in Mesopotamia, which suffered consecutive heat waves that set records that still stand today. He stopped at Querna only long enough to note the terrible state of the latrines and cooking facilities.

Two days later – 14 June – he unloaded three sections of the 105th IFA at Sheikh Saad and started to collect the sick and wounded from the totally overwhelmed regimental first aid units and sparse hospital facilities. Within 24 hours Sections B & C of the ambulance had collected 400 Indian sick and wounded. Section A had 10 British officers and 170 British other ranks. A field ambulance designed to cope with around 150 patients in total was suddenly practically overwhelmed with nearly 600 men. Once again, the demands of

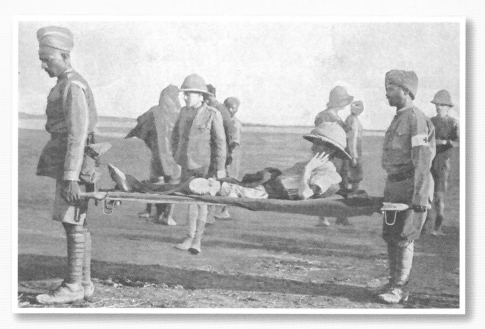

Above: British wounded from Kut being evacuated by Indian orderlies.

Above: Wounded from Kut arrive in Basra by boat.

the situation rendered the demarcation between British field ambulances and Indian field ambulances meaningless. The redoubtable Capt Scott was put in charge of the section treating the British casualties while Kelly took charge of the Indian sections.

Over the next week Kelly fought a constant battle to get the men on boats and down stream to the better-equipped hospitals at Amara and Basra.

At one stage he was told that the men with dysentery would be expected to march to "a hospital some considerable distance away". The nearest facility that he would have described as a hospital was at Amara, at least 30 miles march away. So he stood his ground and refused to send the men on a journey he felt many would not survive. He would rather cope with his over-crowded field ambulance until the hospital ships arrived, which they eventually did on 22 June. He took 23 British officers and 160 men on one boat all the way to Basra, arriving in considerably better state than the poor souls on the *Mejidieh* a few months earlier.

Above: Bellums in use by Kelly's hospital on the Tigris at Basra.

He did this journey at least three more times during June and July, experiencing frequent difficulties in transferring the more serious casualties and seriously ill from the river banks to the ships – usually old paddle steamers that had seen better days – without the benefit of any piers or jetties. Often they had to be transferred using bellums, small flat, open boats that would usually carry six to eight people: it was a slow, often painful, process.

The attrition rate among the troops was appalling. Although the fighting, apart from frequent skirmishes with the Marsh Arabs, had finished, the workload of the medical staff was immense.

General Hugh Keary, commanding officer of the 3rd Division, which was sent into the region south of Kut towards the end of May, had some clear views on some of the causes of the problems, including diet: "No extras to be bought anywhere in the way of food, eggs, milk, fowls, vegetables etc so food is very monotonous". It was actually worse than monotonous, according to Charles Townshend in *When God Made Hell*:

> "Thanks in part to sharp inequalities in rations – British troops were given one pound of fresh meat and of potatoes or vegetables daily, Indian troops a quarter of that amount – Indian troops were particularly prone to scurvy, which caused 11,000 of them to be evacuated in the second half of 1916."

It was not just the diet. The heat and lengthy catalogue of disease took a mighty toll on the troops too. Sun-stroke was a constant threat recorded Harry Philby, a British intelligence officer in his memoire, *Arabian Nights*:

> "The sun when he is strong, and one has no adequate defence against him, is the most relentless, untiring enemy a man can have. One's skin becomes an affliction, one's blood a curse, one's tongue and throat a torture."

A name familiar to Kelly from his time in Tibet, the journalist Edmund Candler, was also in Mesopotamia and had plenty to say about the climate.

> "I sampled the different types of heat and torment endured by that long suffering body of troops – the moist and tropical heat of the Tigris and Karun, the heavy-laden atmosphere of Bushire. Each variety had its attendant insects, its own particular plague. On the Karun you might be stricken with what its commonly known as 'dog-rot', the legacy of some poisonous fly. The water of the Tigris engendered colic."

At Basra he complained that "the very air seems to sweat. Strike a match and it will burn dully without a flicker as if the flame were choked". He went on to describe how flies would quickly cover everything, often making men standing out in the open during the day for any length of time look as if they were wearing a steely blue chain mail. At night the swarms of flies were replaced by malaria-carrying mosquitoes and sandflies.

Father C B Warren one of the Roman Catholic priests who served Kelly's hospitals also had plenty to say about the heat in his personal diary:

"In Mesopotamia there are sand storms, dust clouds and at times a density of atmosphere which is almost suffocating. How winds blow that make breathing difficult. The skin dries up and shrivels [sic] like parchment. With inexhaustable [sic] power and vigour, the sun glares down in fierce and relentless anger from its blue steel molton [sic] canopy above. Its blazing rays make day hellishly unbearable. To try to escape its scorching rays one makes a dug out, 10 or 12 feet down and erects a tent above it. It gives a few degrees less heat than on the surface."

The numbers who fell ill in these conditions were staggering. General Keary recorded in his diaries that the 82nd Punjabis were having a bad time with "cholera, bowel diseases of all sorts as well as jaundice and other things". Overall the sickness rate was horrendous, says Charles Townshend. During June and July as many as 2500 a week were being evacuated through the casualty clearing station Kelly established at Sheikh Saad.

The other hazard was the Marsh Arabs who constantly harassed the British and Indian forces – and the Turks. T E Lawrence, in early 1916 a British intelligence officer in Mesopotamia but soon to find fame as Lawrence of Arabia, was generally sympathetic to the Arabs, but held them in total contempt describing them as "impure savages without any code of manners or morals to restrain them" in a report he sent back to his superiors. "They cut up our wounded and the Turkish wounded, raid our convoys and the Turkish convoys, steal our rifles and the Turkish rifles," he added. The British developed a variation of the Butcher and Bolt tactics deployed on the North West Frontier to deal with the Marsh Arabs, stoking up resentment that lingered for many years after the war had ended.

At the end of July the 105th IFA was ordered to Nasariayh – a modest town on the River Euphrates and a little way upstream from Querna where the two great rivers of Mesopotamia met. The new command under Lt-Gen Maude had decided that Basra could no longer cope as the main centre for the reception of casualties and the increasing numbers going down with dysentery, cholera, scurvy and heat-stroke. He had identified Nasariyah as the best location for managing the overflow and decided that Kelly and his 105th IFA were needed to set up the sort of facilities he envisaged.

It was a relatively short river journey but one not without incident as the ship they were allocated ran out of coal not long after leaving Basra, requiring Kelly and his men to wade through the river bank mud to collect wood to keep the engines going. He found it hard to understand why the captain had left knowing he didn't have enough coal to complete the journey but was told such shortages were commonplace.

Once in Nasariyah on 29 July the 105th IFA started receiving sick and wounded still being repatriated from Querna.

On 2 August one of the first major changes following the change of command and the inquiry into the dreadful aftermath of the Siege of Kut was announced: all field ambulances and stationary hospitals were to be combined ending the inefficient – but often ignored – division between British and Indian medical facilities. His unit was renamed the 105th Combined Field Ambulance, still with Capt Scott at his side. It wasn't quite a full integration as British and Indian troops would still be separated within the ambulance and hospitals but it was a big step forward. In future it would be split into sections dedicated to the care of the different nationalities, catering for their different religious, cultural and dietary requirements but with much greater flexibility to allocate medical and nursing resources.

His first major task was to plan and oversee the building of proper hospital facilities in Nasariyah. On 10 August he was appointed senior medical officer for the area and the day after records that the first huts started to be built, while the tented sections of the ambulance continued to treat the steady flow of casualties – mainly sick rather than wounded – still arriving from the Tigris front.

By 18 October he was able to open a dedicated infections hospital for the Indian troops for whom cholera had become a major problem. This had six huts each capable of holding 24 beds, marking a significant expansion of his facilities:

"This brings hutting capacity of this ambulance up to 316 beds – allowing five feet of moving space per patient. The huts are semi-comfortable and well ventilated for dry weather but are not rain proof. Now understand that there is a prospect of tarpaulins being provided – this would suffice to keep rain out".

He also asked for some riding horses which were quickly supplied, enabling him to visit the sections of the field ambulance now being deployed further up the Euphrates as the British cautiously advanced, largely avoiding any direct confrontation with the Turks and too much additional work for Kelly's medical units.

Life in Nasariyah started to settle into a more ordered routine and, by late November, the enlarged unit was being supported by the 83rd Combined Stationary Hospital, which had arrived from France where it had been the Meerut Stationary Hospital based at Boulogne since late 1914. Under its commanding officer Lt Col Frank Wall – an IMS officer two years Kelly's senior – it established itself in old colonial buildings on the banks of the Euphrates. The 105th CFA was attached to this and the combined units continued to expand the facilities.

During December, life was sufficiently relaxed in Nasariyah for Kelly to organise swimming and fishing competitions for the medical staff and any

Above: Field hospital established up the line to evacuate the sick and wounded after the fall of Kut.

patients capable of joining in. He was a keen participant himself, proudly recording his own catch on 14 December in the war diaries: "108lb salmon caught. Length 5' 3", girth 36"" (see picture on page 165). That must had made a substantial meal for his fellow officers in a mood to celebrate the news that after months of re-organising and re-equipping, General Maude had the previously day started a fresh advance up the Tigris with the objective of re-capturing Kut and pressing onto Baghdad, this time with proper supply lines and support.

For the first time since the war started Kelly recorded that they were able to celebrate Christmas with some modest entertainment – improvised by themselves – and a Christmas lunch, albeit lacking anything that resembled a traditional Christmas meal back home. It was, however, a far cry from the horrors of the aftermath of the fall of Kut six months earlier.

He was also able to repatriate some sick and wounded officers and men back to Basra by one of the new ambulance trains able to run on the newly opened railway connecting the two major centres. He was clearly impressed with the new transport as he set out in detail in the war diaries how the train and its carriages were arranged and equipped (see page 160).

1917 dawned with the total capacity of the combined units at 960 beds, a substantial hospital by any standards. Lt Col Wall handed over the 83rd Combined Stationary Hospital to Lt Col Charles Watson, a familiar colleague from the IMS who Kelly had sat his exams with in 1896 and who travelled to India with him on the *Oceana* almost 20 years before. This was only a temporary change while confirmation of Kelly's own permanent promotion to Lt Col came through and the re-organisation of the medical resources along the Euphrates was completed, although Watson stayed with the hospital for just over two months.

He and Kelly must have spent many evenings together reflecting on their careers since they first met in London during the IMS examinations in the autumn of 1896. They must have mused on the fates of the 10 fresh-faced doctors who travelled with them to India. Five were still in India, two were serving with the Indian forces on the Western front, and one was in Egypt. Two had died, one in Bombay in January 1909 and the other, Andrew MacArdle, the top candidate in those first examinations for the newly re-organised Indian Medical Service, had died in Calcutta in October 1902.

While this transfer of responsibilities was going on Kelly decided to take up a few complaints about pay on behalf of his Indian staff, many of whom had now served with him for more than two years. On 21 February he wrote concerning the withdrawal of a series of allowances

> "Many complain very bitterly of the differential treatment of military and civil sub-assistant surgeons in FA [field ambulance] service as the latter, with no experience of camp work, are drawing about three times the pay of the former for performing the same work. Personally, I prefer the military sub-assist. surgeon in the field as he has experience of camp sanitation, transport, tent pitching, stretcher drill and the present discontent seems to be founded in very good reasons particularly as in peace time the military sub assist surgeon of the class quoted draws R35/- p.m. whilst the 4th class civil S.A.S. draws R30/- p.m."

He added some tables of comparative rates of pay for good measure and then did much the same for his ward orderlies and bearer corps. The records don't record what the response was when this missive arrived in the Assistant Director of Medical Service's office but he did arrange to make a full inspection in Nasariyah just over a month later, by which time Kelly had assumed a wide range of new responsibilities.

On 25 March he took over command of the 83rd CSH and bade farewell to his colleague, Lt Col Watson. But it was not to be a day of celebration. Another IMS doctor, Capt John Tackaberry, had been ill for some days and died that morning. Kelly's first duty as commanding officer was to arrange his funeral and burial that same afternoon. It was a reminder of how vulnerable the medical staff were to the rampant disease and illness that bedeviled the British and Indian forces in Mesopotamia. Kelly appears never to have had a day off sick the entire time he served during the war, as there are entries in the war diary covering every day and none of them suggest any lack of activity on his part. Only a few months later he learned that his colleague of 20 years,

Lt Col Watson, had been wounded and was being evacuated to India. He was awarded the Distinguished Service Order and survived his wounds, eventually retiring from the IMS in 1922. It was another reminder of their precarious lives.

During the first few days of his new command Kelly busied himself inspecting the various facilities, noting a wide range of defects that needed rectifying, especially the latrines for many of the Indian

Above: A flat-bottomed hospital boat on the Tigris, bound for Basra after the fall of Kut.

wards. He was rather more satisfied with the new kitchens that had been built for the wards housing British officers and other ranks, although not so happy that some of the ovens seemed to be faulty.

While all of this change was going on in Nasariyah Maude's forces were pressing on up the Tigris, re-taking Kut on 22 February and marching into Baghdad on 11 March. Maude resisted the temptation to pursue the Turks any further as he was worried that his supply lines were over-stretched and wanted to wait until the new railways the British were rapidly building could be enlarged and extended to Baghdad. He was also concerned that the onset of another fierce Mesopotamian summer would severely debilitate his men. Lessons had been learned.

The Turks retreated northwards all the way to Mosul where their remaining 30,000-strong force could be easily reinforced from neighbouring Turkey. It was the end of serious fighting in the country, although the Marsh Arabs remained a constant irritation and there was no escaping the climate, which was about to bite them very hard.

Early in April Kelly was struggling with one of the occasional failures in the vastly improved logistical support. A well-intentioned plan to modernise the ventilation and lighting in the hospital that now accommodated more than 1000 patients went wrong:

"A large consignment of electric fans & lights has arrived but engines & dynamos have not yet turned up & engineers consider that some time will elapse before fans are in working order. Have requested that specially selected wards be fitted up with ordinary hand pulled punkahs in meanwhile."

Above: Hospital ship at Basra ready to take casualties back to India.

Disciplinary problems kept crossing his desk too. On 7 April he held a Summary Court Martial for a British driver who had attempted to bribe one of the sub-assistant surgeons to sign him off to be invalided back home. He doesn't record what punishment was passed down but it certainly wouldn't have been a ticket home.

With the hospital now so large and its field ambulance stretched out up the Euphrates it was decided to split the role of Commanding Officer and Senior Medical Officer for the area so on 10 April Kelly handed over his SMO responsibilities to Lt Col O'Flaherty from the RAMC.

He was still constantly fighting battles on behalf of the Indian sick and wounded:

"Evacuated 100 cases to Basra by hospital train. As no accommodation for sleeping for a large number of these cases was provided the matter was reported for information to the G.O.C. [General Officer Commanding]. I am strongly of opinion that the men who are so debilitated that they will be finally evacuated to India should not be forced to travel sitting up all through the night."

Despite his constant stream of complaints and memos – or perhaps partially because of them – he found that when Lt Gen Maude's dispatch was published in the *London Gazette* on 10 April he had once again been Mentioned in Dispatches, this time for conduct during actions on the Tigris and Euphrates fronts between August 1916 and March 1917.

The other big change made in the medical arrangements that followed the initial inquiry into the catastrophe of the early Mesopotamian campaign, alongside the creation of the combined hospitals, was the decision to deploy female British nurses there.

At the start of the campaign, the policy was not to send women to serve in the fiercely hostile Mesopotamian climate, but appeals for British nurses from the medical officers – including Kelly – struggling to cope with overflowing wards brought about a change in policy. The War Office, now in charge of the campaign, therefore turned to the Queen Alexandra's Royal Army Nursing Corps to ask for volunteers to join the hard-pressed medical units on the Tigris and Euphrates. The first nurses arrived in August 1916 but initially they were allocated only to British hospitals, in particular those caring for officers. Their arrival had turned a few heads as one RAMC officer, Robert Campbell Begg explained in his post-war memoires *Surgery on Trestles* when the first contingent sailed up the Tigris from Basra:

> "Most of us hadn't seen a woman – black, white or brown – for the best part of a year. All the British troops who could wangle it converged on the Arab village and took up points of vantage as at a regatta; hundreds lined the banks as the P-boat passed slowly – I was one of them. Cheers resounded along the ranks when the uniforms of the QAIMNS appeared on deck. The sisters were middle-aged and capable-looking; any sex-appeal they had was damped down by their martial dress. But they wore the badge of femininity and they brought with them the aura of homes, and wives and children to the married men; and, to the rest of us, the nostalgic memory of an almost forgotten world which we scarcely hoped to see again."

Once the novelty of seeing female nurses had worn off these experienced sisters quickly proved their worth in caring for the sick and wounded, although they were constantly reminded of the need not to unduly excite the soldiers long-starved of any female presence. Having settled in and proved their value, their role was to be greatly extended as part of a controversial experiment to allow English nurses to care for Indians.

Indian medical units in the field had never had female nurses – they relied on male Indian nursing orderlies – but the Royal Army Medical Corps looking after the British medical units were accustomed to being supported by British nurses, a long tradition made famous back in the middle of the previous century by Florence Nightingale's exploits during the Crimean War, another conflict where the treatment of the sick and wounded fell far below what was expected. Now the doctors of both services – the RAMC and IMS – were pressing for the nurses to be allocated to all hospitals in Mesopotamia.

The question of deploying female British nurses in hospitals with Indian patients was a live and sensitive issue in the first few months of 1917. Kelly was among a group of IMS doctors who believed the addition of British trained female nurses to their staff would be hugely beneficial and had been involved in lobbying various authorities for some of the nurses arriving in

Mesopotamia to be allocated to the new generation of combined hospitals, of which the 83rd CSH was the largest at that time.

There was opposition from some of the senior military commanders. Even Lt Gen Maude argued against their general deployment in a lengthy memorandum sent to the Chief of the General Staff at Army HQ in India on 3 April.

"**1** I agree that theoretically it is desirable that female nurses should look after Indians in Hospital, but practically there are many obstacles. First and foremost the Indian will have to be educated up to the idea of permitting females in a public institution to attend to his needs.

2 In spite, however, of misgivings and warnings of those most favourably placed to judge, we have employed a certain number of trained women for duty in the operating room, and to dress serious surgical cases.

3 The experiment has proved that, with tact, common sense, and judicious firmness, the employment of European nurses in the operating theatre, and for dressing serious wounds, is possible, and this has been done with considerable success. Thereupon an attempt was made the [sic] extend the use of female nurses to nursing the

Below: Water purification, usually with chlorine tablets, was a constant chore in Mesopotamia.

Above: The remains of Kut after it was recaptured by General Maude.

seriously sick, etc., so that gradually the system existing in British Hospitals might be adopted, but from experience gained in MESOPOTAMIA it has been found that the time is not yet ripe for this innovation.

4 It does not at present appear practicable to obtain Indian women to attend on their countrymen owing to caste and other difficulties, and further to the fact that there are not sufficient trained women for this purpose among Indians.

5 Considerable difficulties are bound to arise with the class of hospital patients under treatment, owing to the fact that considerably more than half the Indian patients are followers, including coolies, Sonthalis [from a district of Rajastan and usually labourers], sweepers and men from Indian jails.

For a European female to perform certain offices for this class of patient, and then proceed direct to help an Indian soldier, is not calculated to raise the self-esteem of these highly sensitive men, as their whole life and breeding has ingrained in them the principles that find expression in caste prejudices. Neither is it calculated to raise the status of the white race in the eyes of those who look up to the Englishman as their rulers and leaders.

Much can be done by using selected wards for patients, etc., but the rush of sick and wounded, inevitable under war conditions, does not permit of this being carried into effect here.

6 Difficulties again arise because the Subordinate Medical Staff, who exercise control over the patients and menial personnel, must also give orders to the European Nurses, and this is apt to be resented and consequently the smooth working of the hospital is interfered with.

7 Lack of accommodation is a constant drawback in MESOPOTAMIA, and must always be borne in mind when considering the addition of female nurses to the existing hospital staff. The accommodation required by nurses is more elaborate than that of any other class of hospital personnel.

Further, the language difficulty is serious, as the usefulness of a nurse with patients is much impaired unless she can understand their wants.

8 It is necessary to have the most competent and efficient nurses: partially trained women in these circumstances are not a success, and most careful selection is essential in order to provide female nurses who will be a credit to the hospital staff, as tact and general behaviour are a sine qua non, and everyone is not competent to judge in this matter.

9 For the above reasons I do not consider that under War conditions in Mesopotamia we can assimilate more than two female nurses for every 500 beds of an Indian General Hospital, and I am of opinion that their work should be limited to operations and attention to surgical cases."

Above: Kelly, second from the right, shows a senior officer (possibly General Maude) around the wards at the 83rd CSH. The nurse in the picture is probably Phoebe Exshaw

Despite being the Commanding Officer of the forces in Mesopotamia he was over-ruled, probably by the War Office in London still smarting from the criticism levelled at the conduct of the war in Mesopotamia by the brief Parliamentary enquiry after the fall of Kut. Thus two weeks after Maude sent his memo a team of six nurses led by Matron Phoebe Exshaw was entrusted to Kelly to prove Maude's doubts unfounded. The precise details of how this new deployment might be managed were still being thrashed out as the nurses arrived, but it appears they settled in quickly and that the inspection the following week by the Acting Matron in Chief of the Army Medical Services passed off satisfactorily.

The summer started to gather ominous force as the nurses settled into their hastily arranged and furnished accommodation with just a basic kit consisting of a spare uniform and underclothes, a few possessions and a camp kit that came in a large green bag containing a bed, a canvas bath and basin and a small bucket.

Phoebe Exshaw and her team had been carefully chosen. She was a career army nurse with huge experience of India and its culture, having been born in Bengal when her father was serving in India, trained at Guy's Hospital, and then returned to India with the Queen Alexandra's Military Nursing Service (India).

Among their number was a 30-year-old nurse from Essex, Gertrude Agnes Fenn, who had volunteered in March 1915 and already seen service in Malta and on the Hospital Ship *Braemar Castle* treating casualties from Gallipoli before adding her name to the list of QA nurses prepared to serve in Mesopotamia.

She had arrived in Basra the previous August and been attached to the 40th British General Hospital as Matron-in-Chief before being admitted herself for three weeks in December 1916 suffering from dysentery. She was by no means alone among the nurses in falling ill as more than half were admitted at some stage during their time in Mesopotamia. She then served for four months at the Officers Hospital in Beit Naama before being posted to Kelly's hospital in Nasariyah.

Below: Kelly's detailed description of a layout of one of the new ambulance trains in the War Diary of the 83rd Combined Stationary Hospital.

Above: An ambulance convoy crossing the Euphrates near Nasariyah.

Above: An ambulance convoy ready to leave the 83rd CSH at
Nasariyah to collect casualties. Most are carts drawn by oxen but two
of the new motorised ambulances can be seen at the back

Kelly may have won his battle over nurses but less to his liking was the saga over the electric fans. His complaints about being sent fans without the generators to run them did not have the desired effect as the fans were suddenly taken back rather than the ancillary equipment supplied. "The Hospital would serve its purpose much better if provided with a good system of fans", he rather bluntly noted in the diaries.

He was now focused on the impending arrival of summer and the return of the blazing heat that he had seen was so deadly the previous year. His first concern was to get the patients lying in tented wards in the courtyard of the hospital into purpose built huts that could be ventilated better – the lack of electric fans nothwithstanding. This required requisitioning more land adjacent to the hospital and having the huts built, so he arranged for the General Officer Commanding and his staff to visit so he could show them the problem first hand. It had the desired effect and at the end of April he was given the go-ahead for the new huts, just in time as Nasariyah was hit by a succession of severe sandstorms at the end of the month.

The war diaries for May and June 1917 have been lost so little is known about the immediate impact of the heatwave that hit Mesopotamia that summer beyond the bare statistics of the numbers he evacuated back to Basra from his overflowing hospital. In June 16 British officers, 116 British other ranks and 281 Indians had to be evacuated. In July the figures jumped again with 25 British officers, 157 other ranks and 365 Indians being shipped out either by boat or on one of the new hospital trains. Many of these were so severely debilitated that they were soon returning to the UK or India.

With daily air temperatures frequently over 122°F (50°C) just taking temperatures was a challenge, as Campbell Begg explained in *Surgery on Trestles*.

> "The thermometers in use were graduated up to 110 degrees – the air was much hotter. The mercury of course always stood at the top of the scale; you couldn't shake it down in the ordinary way. The bowl had to be immersed in chagul water; the resulting evaporation combined with vigorous shaking brought the column down below 98.4°F, the normal mark. The instrument was then rapidly inserted under the tongue, and after a minute or so read while still in position; for as soon as it was removed the mercury chased up to the top again."

Ever more elaborate – and successful – treatments for heatstroke were being implemented and during July Kelly was able to report one particular success that set a new benchmark for what they could do: "One case was pulled through after temperature of 110.5°F in rectum", normally fatal. He was less successful in the case of the commanding officer of the 1/4th Somerset Light Infantry, Lt Col Openshaw who, he recorded, died of

Above: A ward in the main British hospital in Basra in 1917 when Gertrude Fenn was a nurse there.

heatstroke on 23 July. It didn't take much in the way of misjudging what to wear, especially covering the head and shoulders, how long to spend outside or how much water to drink to succumb to heatstroke in the ferocious temperatures that raged during June and July 1917.

To make life harder for Kelly some of the men under his command were getting homesick, a problem he had some sympathy with despite his own very rare visits to Ireland since leaving at the end of 1896. He reminded the HQ staff officers that many men in his unit hadn't had any leave since September 1914. Neither had he and his year-long home leave in 1914 had been cut short by seven months because of the outbreak of the war. He chose not to mention either of those things when pressing the case for his Indian staff to be granted some leave.

He also had to cope with a "slight earthquake" that struck at 7.05pm on 24 July and caused minor damage to some of the ward buildings. There may have been no battles raging nearby but life was far from quiet in Nasariyah.

By August the high temperatures began to relent and the hospital concert party – The Squeaks – was able to stage a concert for the staff and patients, the first of many as life became more relaxed.

Gertrude Fenn left Nasariyah at the end of that month, formally noted in the War Diaries: "Sister Fenn proceeded to Basra for onward passage to Baghdad".

She had made quite an impact on the 47-year-old Irishman in her four-and-half months in his hospital, something that Matron Exshaw had noticed. She went to some lengths to warn Sister Fenn off the idea of pursuing a relationship with him, labelling him a confirmed bachelor, a man who would never settle down.

Particulars Required for the Roll of Honour of Australia in the Memorial War Museum.

1. Name (in full) of Fallen Soldier _Denis Joseph Kelly_
2. Unit and Number (if known) _28th B. No 5384_
3. With what Town or District in Australia was he chiefly connected (under which his name ought to come on the Memorial)—
   Town (if any) _____ District _Broomehill_ State _W. Australia_
4. What was his Birthplace _High Street Galway Ireland_
5. Date of Death _October 4th 1977_
6. Place where Killed or Wounded _____

Particulars Required for the Nation's Histories.

1. What was his Calling _Mining_
2. Age at time of Death _49 years_
3. What was his School _St. Ignatius College Galway_
4. What was his other Training _____
5. If born in Britain or Abroad, at what age did he come to Australia _18 yrs_
6. Had he ever served in any Military or Naval Force before Enlisting in the A.I.F. (Please state particulars) _At the Boer War, where he retired as Sergeant_
7. Any other biographical details likely to be of interest to the Historian of the A.I.F., or of his Regiment—

8. Was he connected with any other Member of the A.I.F. who died or who distinguished himself. (Please state Relationship)— _Sgt. M. D. Kelly (Nephew) Bendigo_

9. Name and Address of the Parent or other person giving this information—
   Name _Mary Columba Kelly_
   Relationship to Soldier _Sister_
   Presentation Convent Galway Ireland

   any other persons to whom reference could be made by the Historian for further information—
   T. B. Kelly I.M.S. D.S.O.
   of Brief & Co Bombay India

   Secretary, Department of Defence, Melbourne. Please fold in four, and stick down gummed
   addressed portion is outside. The information is required urgently.

Left: His brother Denis Joseph Kelly in his Australian Imperial Force uniform shortly before departing for France where he died at Passchendaele.
Above: Record card detailing Denis Kelly's death and relatives.

Matron Exshaw stayed with the 83rd CSH until December and her departure was noted in the war diaries in some of the most affectionate language Kelly ever used in this official record: "The comfort of the patients has been very much improved during the period Miss Exshaw has been Matron here and we are very sad to lose her." She was Mentioned in Dispatches and received the Red Cross Medal, 1st Class for her work.

Above: Turkish prisoners unloading medical supplies.
Left: The fish Kelly caught in the angling competition he organised in December 1916.

With the sections of the 105th CFA – still under his ultimate command – spread out up the Euphrates to support the British occupation of Baghdad he had frequent cause to go out on inspections and visit Baghdad, an ideal opportunity to continue his relationship with Sister Fenn. She had another spell in hospital herself in early December suffering from laryngitis.

Just as this new happiness in his life was starting to flourish he received news that deeply saddened him. His brother Denis was killed serving with the Australian forces on 4 October during the Battle of Broodsiende, one of the many battles around the Third Ypres offensive, usually known simply as Passchendaele. Kelly was listed in his brother's papers as the next of kin so would have received official notification through army channels before the news reached Annie back in Galway. No mention is made in the war diaries of his brother's death but it must have caused him to reflect on their childhood in Galway and that moment 30 years earlier when he waved him goodbye as he sailed away to his new life in Australia, the last time he saw him. His brother's body was never recovered and he is commemorated on the Menim Gate.

Back in Nasariyah the list of diseases afflicting the troops continued to grow with an outbreak of amoebic dysentery among the British troops, cases of smallpox and cholera as well as beri-beri in the 1/4th Somerset Light Infantry.

All the time the hospital was being expanded with the addition of new convalescent wards and laundry facilities, the latter giving him an excuse for a rare slightly boastful entry in the war diaries on 15 November: "The results are very apparent as the linen comes back white instead of the cream colour usually seen in Mesopotamia".

A week before that he heard that Maude had once again mentioned him in dispatches for his conduct during actions on the Euphrates front and for his response to the abnormal heatwave and outbreaks of disease. Maude clearly didn't hold any grudge against Kelly for proving him wrong over the ability of British nurses to care for Indian soldiers. In return Kelly held Maude in high regard, one of the few military commanders he did so. He placed him alongside MacDonald, his commander in Tibet, as one of the few men whose methodical approach to logistics and organisation enabled the medical services to give of their best in supporting and caring for the fighting men.

Mesopotamia claimed Maude just two weeks after his final dispatch was published. He died of cholera on 18 November in Baghdad.

In wartime there are always men trying to find ways of getting themselves home, especially in a largely conscript army, and the lengths some went to in Mesopotamia are both startling and ingenious. At the end of November Kelly rumbled one such clever ruse.

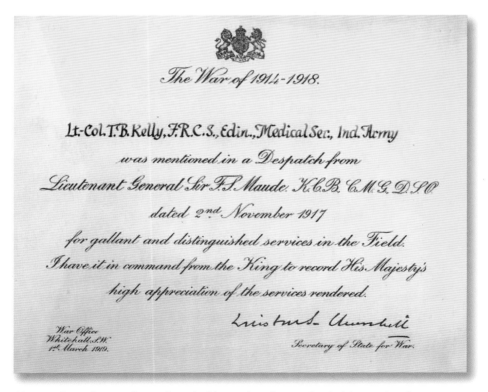

Above: One of several mentions in Dispatches for service in Mesopotamia

Above: Kelly in 1918 wearing his uniform showing
him as a Lieutenant Colonel.

George R.I.

George the Fifth, by the Grace of God
of the United Kingdom of Great Britain and
Ireland and of the British Dominions beyond
the Seas, King, Defender of the Faith, Emperor
of India, Sovereign of the Distinguished Service
Order, to our Trusty and Well beloved
Thomas Bernard Kelly Esquire.
F. R. C. S. Lieutenant - Colonel
in Our Indian Army.

Greeting

Whereas We have thought fit to
Nominate and Appoint you to be a Member
of our Distinguished Service Order We
do by these Presents Grant unto you the
Dignity of a Companion of Our said Order
And we do hereby authorize you to Have,
Hold and Enjoy the said Dignity as a
Member of Our said Order, together with
all and singular the Privileges thereunto
belonging or appertaining.

Given at Our Court at St James's
under Our Sign Manual this Seventh
day of February 1918 in the
Eighth Year of our Reign.

By The Sovereign's Command

Lieutenant - Colonel
T. B. Kelly F. R. C. S.
Indian Medical
Service.

The Principal Secretary of State
having the Department of War
for the time being.

Above: The formal citation for Kelly's DSO. The more detailed citation explaining
the reasons for the award was lost when the ship carrying the papers back to
England was sunk by a German submarine.

"Three sepoys admitted last evening from 12th Rajputs for venereal disease were found to be suffering from extensive abrasions of the glans penis with a corresponding abrasion (ie blistered surface) on inner surface of the foreskin.

"As the case did not appear to be venereal the Medical Officer of the unit was requested to make a thorough search in the kits of the company from which these cases came and he found a fair quantity of croton oil seeds and dhobi nuts.

"An experiment was carried out to see if these seeds could produce a similar lesion. A small amount of croton oil seed was placed under the foreskin and kept in position for three hours. On removal the corresponding surface of the glans penis and foreskin was red but the surface not broken. After 24 hours there was an extensive raw surface, much larger than the red area originally seen and resembling the lesions for which these men were admitted.

"The individual in whose kit the seeds were discovered as well as the three men referred to me will be sent up for Court Martial in due course."

What he doesn't say is how he selected the individual he experimented on with the seeds he discovered. Presumably it was some poor Indian orderly or follower who was asked to "volunteer".

Christmas Day 1917 was celebrated in some style with choice of curried chicken, duck or roast beef with Yorkshire pudding for all the staff and patients not on a special diet followed by plum pudding, stewed peaches with cream or fruit jellies. The Indian staff and patients were also offered an extended menu for the day, which finished with a concert in the evening. Life was clearly much more relaxed in the cool, damp winter weather with the Turkish forces no longer posing any threat.

New Year's Day 1918 was an opportunity for him to reflect on the hospital's workload during the previous year. Unlike many hospital and ambulance war diaries he provides few statistics about the numbers of patients his hospitals and field ambulances managed, but he provided a summary at the start of the final year of the war that showed the 83rd CSH had 4788 admissions during 1917, of which 3793 had been discharged back to their units and 926 evacuated to other hospitals or back home to Britain or India. He left a blank column on his table. Perhaps this was to record the death rate, which was a remarkably low 2% among inpatients. It didn't cover those who were declared dead before they reached Nasariyah from the outlying posts but it still suggests an impressive recovery rate among the patients in his care.

His achievements were about to receive further recognition.

Above: Gertrude Fenn as a nurse.

On 7 February *The London Gazette* announced that he had been awarded the Distinguished Service Order "in connection with Military Operations in Mesopotamia". The DSO was awarded for an act of meritorious or distinguished service in wartime and usually when under fire or in the presence of the enemy. Often, it would be awarded to commanding officers for their leadership over a sustained period and this was clearly the case with Kelly who already had four mentions in Dispatches during the war under his belt, two from Maude in Mesopotamia and a further one was in the pipeline from the new commander of the forces there, Lt Gen Sir William Marshall.

What isn't known is whether Maude or Marshall made the recommendation, as the citation and relevant papers from that period were lost when the ship carrying them back to the UK was sunk by a German submarine.

By February, the question of his future relationship with Gertrude Fenn had been settled, despite Matron Exshaw's warnings. From 2 to 11 February he was away from Nasariyah visiting frontline posts around Baghdad: it can't be mere co-incidence that on 12 February she handed in her resignation from the QAIMNS (Reserve) in order to get married to Kelly. In those days married women were not allowed to serve as either civilian or military nurses.

While this resignation was being processed, Kelly was observing how much quieter his hospital was: "This is the first day since I took over charge in March 1917 that the British officers' wards are quite unoccupied", he noted on returning to Nasariyah on 12 February.

The following month the defences around the hospital were significantly reduced, as the lower Euphrates was no longer considered under any sort of threat from the Turks who had now been pushed further north towards the border with Turkey.

He was clearly now planning for the time when he would be leaving the hospital and busied himself re-organising many of the services it provided, especially using the new X-ray equipment that had arrived and the extended ward facilities for managing infectious cases. He also wanted to look after

Above: His nephew, Robert (Roy) Denis Kelly served with the Australian Imperial Force in France where he was a sergeant and visited Galway in early 1919 before returning to Australia. He is pictured with Teresa O'Kelly (left) and Denis Morris (who she later married) and Annie.

some of the staff who had been with him since the 105th IFA was formed back in the autumn of 1914:

> "As I understand that Indian Ward Orderlies are eligible for appointment as nurses I am recommending several men who have been serving with the Hospital since 1914 for promotion to this grade as they are more suitable than some of the present incumbents".

On 15 April 1918 he handed over command of the 83rd Combined Stationary Hospital to Lt Col Bennett and learned that he had once again been mentioned in Dispatches by his commanding officer.

He departed from Nasariyah with an inscribed silver tray and tea service presented by the medical and nursing staff wishing him and Gertrude success for their forthcoming marriage. A new life was about to begin at the age of 48.

Above: Kelly's Victory Medal and British War Medal.
Together with the 1914-15 Star they were often referred to as
"Pip, Squeak and Wilfred" after popular comic characters.

CHAPTER 12

Gertrude Fenn
A Nurse and a Wife

Who was this woman about to commit herself to sharing her life with a 48-year-old doctor, an Irishman, a Roman Catholic and a man for whom the last 10 years especially had been one long adventure with the Indian Medical Service? A man, as Matron Exshaw warned, many saw as a confirmed bachelor unlikely to be given to settling down as a family man.

Gertrude Agnes Fenn was born just outside Ardleigh in rural north Essex at Good House, a large detached property still standing in its own grounds today, on 3 December 1886. She was the eighth of 13 children born to Cooper Fenn and Christina Wilhelmina Deane who had married just 10 years previously.

Cooper Fenn had inherited Good House and its associated farm from his father James when he died in 1872, along with £4000 (around £400,000 at today's prices). Soon after Gertrude was born he sold Good House and the farm, moving to Gould House, a large, well-appointed property with plenty of room for the family and servants in the centre of picturesque Dedham. Cooper Fenn had given up farming and become a land and Parliamentary agent. Her mother Christina for many years played the organ at the large Anglican church opposite their house in Dedham.

The children were educated at home by a governess and the family obviously lived comfortably for most of her childhood.

Some time during the first decade of the 20th century business must have taken a turn for the worse, or perhaps her father was never much good at it in the first place and the inherited money was starting to run out. The financial strain of supporting 13 children, living in a large house and maintaining governesses and servants had certainly taken its toll, because the Fenns moved twice, rather quickly, eventually settling into a relatively recently built but slightly gloomy semi-detached house at 96 London Road, Ipswich.

By that time most of Gertrude's brothers and sisters had left home. One brother was an Anglican clergyman and later taught for many years at Wellington School and others were building careers and families. She decided to train as a nurse and went to the Royal Berkshire Hospital at Reading after

Above: Good House, hear Ardleigh, where Gertrude Fenn was born.

doing some nursing work locally. Having qualified she moved to the East London Hospital for Children as a staff nurse. When the war broke out she moved back to East Anglia and was Sister-in-Charge at St Leonard's Hospital in Sudbury.

In April 1915 she decided to volunteer for war service with the Queen Alexandra Imperial Military Nursing Service (Reserve) and by mid-May was on her way to Malta. Shortly before she departed she heard that her 25-year-old younger brother Cecil had been killed at Ypres serving with Princess Patricia's Canadian Light Infantry, having emigrated to Canada in 1913 to establish a fruit farm. Cecil had been a keen sportsman and played for Ipswich Town for six seasons before departing for a new life in Canada and his loss was keenly felt in the family. Her own experience of losing a sibling must have helped her comfort Kelly when the news of his own brother's death at Passchendaele (the third Battle of Ypres) reached him in the autumn of 1917, especially as they died within a few miles of each other. Both are commemorated on the Menim Gate.

At Malta in May 1915 the casualties from Galipolli were pouring in and she was allocated to the British Hospital at Valetta. There she made a positive impact on many of the men she nursed – probably not difficult for a young

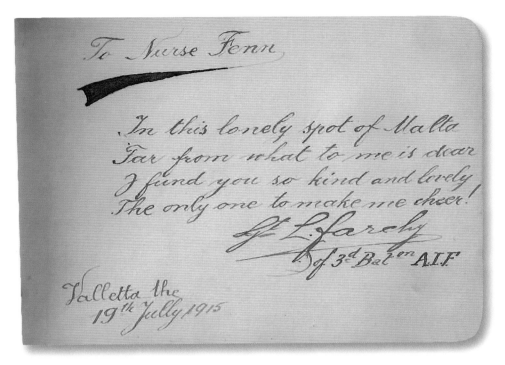

Above and overleaf: Pages from Gertrude's autograph books from her time in Malta, on the *Braemar Castle* and in Mesopotamia.

female nurse in a predominantly male environment – and she collected many affectionate messages and drawings by British and Australian troops in her autograph books. One written by Sergeant L Farely of the 3rd Battalion of the Australian Imperial Force on 19 July 1915 is typical of dozens and dozens of entries.

> "In the lonely spot of Malta
> Far from what to me is dear
> I find you so kind and lovely
> The only one to make me cheer!"

In the spring of 1916 she was serving on the Hospital Ship *Braemar Castle*, again dealing with casualties from Galipolli as they were moved from Alexandria to Malta. She was in Alexandria when the call came for QA nurses to volunteer for service in Mesopotamia following the debacle and breakdown of the medical services in the wake of the fall of Kut. She put her name forward and was accepted. She arrived in Basra and joined the staff at the 3rd British General Hospital there at the beginning of August 1916, moving to become Matron-in-Chief at the 40th British General Hospital at Basra in

November. Not long after arriving there she suffered a personal reminder of why Mesopotamia was such an unforgiving place to serve when on 1 December, two days before her 30th birthday, she was admitted with a bout of dysentery.

Gertrude Fenn wasn't going to let this put her off and she was back nursing on the wards just in time for Christmas. She was still at the 40th BGH in Basra when the decision to allow female British nurses to work on Indian wards in the new combined British and Indian hospitals was eventually made in April 1917. She was selected to be among the first six experienced nurses sent to Nasariyah to start the experiment under the leadership of Phoebe Exshaw and working alongside Lt Col Thomas Bernard Kelly in one of the new generation of large combined stationary hospitals.

Her patients in Basra thought every bit as highly of her as did those she cared for in Malta. Lance Corporal A Crisp from the Suffolk Regiment was clearly appreciative of her care:

> "In this book I write of Sister Fenn
> Who while in hospital on me did attend
> Her great kindness and goodness to us,
> Will remain dear in our memory from morn till dusk"

The drawings of her in her autograph books create an image of a woman of strong features and equally strong disposition. She is rarely shown with anything approaching a smile, usually looking slightly stern.

There are no comments from Indian patients in her books, presumably because very few of them could write in English – or maybe she just never asked them – but she was just as popular at the 83rd CSH as she was elsewhere, drawing a typically straightforward comment from one officer – officers were always inclined to be less flowery in their praise than men in the ranks: "There is no Hospital like Three and Eighty, & no Sister like Our Sister", wrote Capt Eric B Jardine of the 1/5th The Queen's Royal West Surrey Regiment in the midst of the ferocious heatwave of July 1917.

The "Three and Eighty" was held in high esteem from headquarters to the most lowly soldier who passed through its wards. It was also to hold a special place in the hearts of Thomas Kelly and Gertrude Fenn, although not all of her memories were entirely positive.

Gertrude believed right to the end of her life that Phoebe Exshaw, her Matron and superior officer, had designs on Kelly herself. When she was moved to Baghdad with Matron Exshaw still at the 83rd CSH she must have wondered whether her budding relationship with Kelly would be sustained over a distance of 250 miles (400km) and with all the restrictions that demanding military postings imposed on both of them.

Was he torn between the two women? Did he suddenly realise that this might be his last chance to marry and settle down after the war? The answers are not known. Matron Exshaw was 40, nearer to his age than the 30-year-old Gertrude Fenn, and she had a background of service in India that might have suggested she was more suited than a younger woman who had been brought up in rural north Essex. Whether he was weighing these thoughts in his mind as Phoebe Exshaw left the hospital some months after Gertrude Fenn isn't recorded, but clearly the Matron's attempts to deflect her interest in Kelly left her very suspicious. She was particularly resentful of the Red Cross Medal Matron Exshaw won and constantly grumbled about it whenever she had to put on her old uniform and campaign medals for Armistice Day events during the 1920s and 1930s.

Whatever the real truth of the story and whether there was ever a battle between the two women for his affections by April 1918, almost a year to the day after they first met in Nasariyah, Thomas and Gertrude were heading for India, her resignation from the QAs in order to get married having been accepted and processed.

CHAPTER 13

Return to India

War, children and 'retirement'

Just two weeks after he handed over command of the 83rd Combined Stationary Hospital in Nasariyah, Kelly married Gertrude Fenn in the Roman Catholic Church of the Holy Name in Bombay (now Bombay Cathedral) on 29 April 1918.

Bombay was the Indian port that received most of the troops leaving Mesopotamia and Egypt before posting them to new duties in India, sending them to France or, for the lucky ones, allowing them to return home to the UK. Many troops were held there for months, especially as the Indian

Above: The wedding party in Bombay. Standing l to r, Bernard Knobel, Kelly, Charles Fenn. Seated l to r, Elsie Little, Gertrude, unknown bridesmaid.

Above: Bride and groom outside the Holy Name Cathedral, Bombay.

Above: Honeymoon in the Jhelum valley in the Kashmir.

government was viewing events on the North West Frontier with growing concern and felt it might require reinforcements to deal with the increasingly rebellious tribes. One consequence of this was that the churches in Bombay were rather busy with weddings. The Church of the Holy Name was no exception and almost all the weddings held there during that period are listed as being conducted under Licence (rather than by the traditional Banns) with both bride and groom listing their places of residence as just Bombay as did Fenn and Kelly.

The witnesses at the Fenn-Kelly wedding were a Royal Army Medical Corps doctor, William Bernard Knobel, and Elsie Frances Little, a nurse who died in India in 1948, aged 48. Knobel joined the RAMC at the outbreak of war and served alongside Kelly for a while in Mesopotamia. He was probably in Bombay awaiting a new posting as it was by no means clear in April 1918 that the war against the Germans in Europe was going to conclude as tamely as that against their Turkish allies. Fortunately for Knobel the Armistice arrived before a new posting and he returned home to England at the end of 1918, resuming civilian life as a general practitioner.

There was also an unidentified nurse as bridesmaid who, presumably like Elsie Little had served with Fenn during the war. They weren't the only guests, however.

Charles Deane Fenn, Gertrude's younger brother by one year, was also at the wedding. He left England in March 1912 and emigrated to India where he worked for the Indian Civil Service during the war. He also joined the Indian Army Reserve of Officers, although was never required for active service.

His presence suggests that the Fenn family were supportive of the marriage; by no means a foregone conclusion given the couple's sharply contrasting backgrounds.

Kelly was an Irish Roman Catholic and Fenn was from a staunchly Anglican family. She would have converted to Roman Catholicism before the wedding, something that would have distanced many women from her background from their families in 1918. There was also the age gap to consider – 17 years – although a year was chopped off Kelly's age on the Marriage Certificate. On top of that there was the relative haste. He most likely formally proposed only in February 1918 when he visited her in Baghdad and here they were a little over two months later getting married in India. They would barely have had a chance to write to her family, let alone go through any of the then expected formalities of seeking her father's permission, although she may have softened them up with mentions of Kelly in earlier letters.

There was no prospect of any extended leave back to the UK after the wedding so the newly-weds headed off to the Jhelum valley in the Kashmir, a favourite spot of Kelly's.

Even on his honeymoon he couldn't help attracting attention. They were staying – camping Gertrude later described it and pictures confirm that – just on the outskirts of one small village when a group of Tibetans arrived trying to buy quinine and other medicines. It didn't take them long to find out there was a British doctor staying nearby so they headed off to plead with him to help one young boy – the son of one of the elders – who was in the grips of acute malaria. Kelly couldn't turn them away but with no access to western medicines he wasn't in the best position to help. Recalling the rudimentary Tibetan picked up nearly 15 years earlier he showed them how to boil wild herbs to make a solution to be given to the boy every few hours through the night. This the Tibetans duly administered as instructed.

The following morning he and Gertrude were awoken by the sound of the Tibetans celebrating because the boy had come through the acute stages of the fever. Before they left the village the two headmen presented him with their finest prayerwheel, an important symbol of Tibetan culture and religion. He refused to take it, explaining to them that it meant so much more to them than it ever would to him. This refusal to take money or gifts was a consistent feature of his career and one of the reasons he didn't retire from the Indian Medical Service as well off as many of his colleagues.

The one gift he did accept over all the years in India was a silver cigarette case from a maharaja who had ordered it from Mappin and Webb when Kelly's skill as an ophthalmic surgeon had saved his eyesight. It was a strange gift to give a man who never smoked but Kelly took the view that it would cause certain offence if he declined a personal gift from a man who could easily afford it. It was stolen in a burglary decades later.

On his return from honeymoon he was appointed as the Commanding Officer of the large Indian Stationary Hospital at Dehra Dun, in the Himalayan foothills about 150 miles to the north of Delhi, one of the politically calmer, more temperate parts of India with lush forests and valleys, although still ominously close to the North West Frontier. The posting carried with it the responsibilities of District Medical Officer and he frequently spent much of the week away from the spacious bungalow the couple had as their first home together. He made a point of inspecting the sanitation in the outlying villages, something close to an obsession wherever he went.

Their first home together was typical of the properties occupied by senior British officers and their families during the Raj. It was set back from the road within its own modest grounds with a thatched roof and an arcaded verandah. The rooms were large with high ceilings and plain walls allowing plenty of space for Kelly's many hunting trophies. There were several bedrooms, most leading onto the verandah and, of course, a generous retinue of servants, far more than might appear to be required for a modest household: "It is one of the social follies of Indian life that you

Above: Their first home together at Dehra Dun with Kelly at the wheel of their car.

must keep three servants to do the work of one", observed the anonymous writer of *Indian Outfits and Establishments* in 1882. The typical core of a household would have been a cook and a head bearer, possibly assisted by another bearer who acted as valet, the khitmutgar who waited at the table, the ayah (lady's or children's maid) and mehtar (a sweeper and general servant) and at least one gardener. All of these would have been accommodated in cramped but for many Indians desirable servants' quarters at the back of the property.

Comparatively calm and well appointed and staffed it might have been but for Gertrude being alone in the house wasn't without its potential hazards, so a soldier from the 7th Gurkhas, whose base was at Dehra Dun, used to sleep on the balcony "to protect the memsahib" in Gertrude's words. This arrangement worked well until one of the soldiers in the Gurkha regiment got himself into serious trouble. Having discovered his wife with another man, he killed her. Somehow he escaped execution but was sentenced to life imprisonment. His family didn't accept the punishment and sustained a campaign of arson against the hospital and other military buildings, many of which had thatched roofs. On one occasion they even managed to attack the bungalow, succeeding in setting fire to the roof. Although this was quickly extinguished, this experience left Gertrude with an acute fear of fire for the rest of her life.

The 7th Gurkha Rifles were removed from Dehra Dun after this incident and were replaced by the 2nd King Edward's Own Gurkha Rifles.

On February 17 1919 Kelly finally received his DSO from the Duke of Connaught – the same younger brother of Edward VII he had seen at the Coronation Durbar in 1903 – at a huge ceremony full of Imperial pomp in Rawalpindi.

By this time Gertrude was four months pregnant and beginning to settle into the routine of Indian army life. She was soon to be reminded that India was a volatile country with sudden demands made on its military and medical resources.

The North West Frontier was bubbling up as Afghan rulers sought to take advantage of what they perceived as the weakness of a war-weary British Raj.

Afghanistan had enjoyed almost 40 years of relative stability since the previous war between itself and the British in India in 1880, but the assassination of the Amir, Habibullah Khan, on 19 February 1919 ended all that.

Habibullah had kept his country neutral during the Great War, although he had entertained envoys from Germany, Turkey and Russia in Kabul during the war just to keep the British on their toes. His assassination unleashed a bitter family feud with both his brother Nasrullah Khan and his son Amanullah Khan proclaiming themselves Amir. By April, Amanullah had the upper hand with his uncle in prison and himself at least nominally in control. He still faced considerable internal opposition so he resorted to that well-worn tactic of leaders under pressure and started a war.

Things were not going well for the British in India as Indian nationalism was gathering momentum and the Indian government was struggling to come to terms with it, occasionally over-reacting in brutal fashion. One of the most savage and widely condemned examples of its heavy-handed response was the massacre of as many as 1000 unarmed protestors at Amritsar on 13 April 1919. Amanullah took this as a very visible manifestation of the instability and vulnerability of the Raj.

At the beginning of May he ordered a substantial force of Afghan regulars and tribesmen to attack through the Khyber Pass. They caught the defending forces ill-prepared and for a few weeks enjoyed several military successes while the British response was chaotic as the *New Statesman* reported at the time:

"There are two questions raised by this little war, to which the country must insist on getting an answer. What ails the Indian Army that it should have made such a mess of the operations? If there is one subject that the Indian Army ought to have studied, it is the defence of this frontier. Yet the Afghans, cut off as they are from communication with the outside world, showed themselves much more mobile troops than our own army. They penetrated the Khyber before we were ready to meet them: they out-manoeuvred us by the attack on

Above: The DSO presentation by the Duke of Connaught at Rawalpindi, February 1919, and (**top**) the medal presented.

Above: Kelly in his uniform as a Colonel in late-1923 or early-1924.

the Kuram, and, in addition, it would appear that some of the hospital scandals of the Mesopotamian campaign were repeated in this war. There was the same breakdown of transport, with far less excuse; the same shortage of hospital equipment; and the same (in kind, if not in amount) preventable disease and suffering."

The main medical units were 300-400km south of the initial fighting at Lahore and Peshawar with some units a little closer at Rawalpindi, just 155km away. Many of these were quickly moved up to the frontier regions with infantry, cavalry and artillery units, especially to Waziristan where some of the fiercest fighting occurred. When war was formally declared on Afghanistan on 6 May a plan was already being formed to create a force large enough to spare the Raj any further embarrassment. This included moving up other nearby units including the 2nd Gurkha Rifles at Dehra Dun and experienced medical staff. Lt Col T B Kelly now found himself running the large Indian General Hospital in Rawalpindi and organising the evacuation lines from the areas where the fighting was taking place, calling on his experience of stepping into a similar situation on his arrival in Mesopotamia three years previously.

Right: Kelly's India General Service Medal with Bar 'Afghanistan N. W. F. 1919'.

It was a short but bloody conflict. The British quickly regained control, deploying superior, better-equipped forces on the ground and, for the first time, in the air, an extension of modern warfare that was bitterly resented by the frontier tribes and the Afghans, much as they resent the use of drones nowadays. Amanullah wrote a letter of protest about the air attacks to the British government:

> "It is a matter of great regret that the throwing of bombs by Zeppelins on London was denounced as a most savage act and the bombardment of places of worship and sacred spots was considered a most abominable operation, while now we see with our own eyes that such operations were a habit which is prevalent amongst all civilized people of the West."

On the other side, the savagery of the tribesmen Kelly knew from his previous experience of the North West Frontier was once again in evidence and no less shocking for its awful familiarity. Walter Cumming, a British officer in the early days of his long service on the NW Frontier, experienced it first hand:

> "This was the first time in my service that I had witnessed battle and I must admit that I was shaken as stretcher after stretcher was carried past, where we stood, in an endless stream. On some were dead and others grievously wounded, groaning men and one or two British officers. Eventually the tired troops staggered back into camp under cover of dusk. Our casualties in that first battle could not have been less than sixty, many of whom were left out, the wounded to be slaughtered by the Mashuds who knew no mercy, and all to be stripped naked and mutilated. This was apparent to all the following morn when the battlefield was searched and the atrocities brought to light. Some bodies were minus their heads, others lacking hands and feet, many slashed open."

The same unspeakable brutality is still shocking western sensibilities today, especially in the parts of Syria and Iraq (Mesopotamia) controlled by Islamic State.

Above: The summer hill station at Naini Tal where Brigid was born while Kelly was back on the NW Frontier.

The Afghans were pushed back behind their borders and most of the tribes – apart from those in Waziristan – subdued sufficiently for this short, quickly forgotten war to be brought to a close with the signing of the Treaty of Rawalpindi on 8 August 1919.

While Kelly was away fighting another war, the heavily pregnant Gertrude moved with the other army wives and families to their summer hill station at Naini Tal, set in a valley containing a pear-shaped lake, approximately two miles in circumference, and surrounded by the foothills of the Himalayas. It was in this attractive, idyllic setting that Christine Brigid Margaret Kelly was born on 31 July.

Although the war was now over and his family growing, Kelly was not allowed to relax. His speedy response to the initial medical shortcomings of the war meant that he was confirmed as Commanding Officer of all the Indian hospitals in Rawalpindi and district at the beginning of October. Gertrude and Brigid (as she was always known) moved to Rawalpindi, one of the main provincial hubs of the Raj. They settled into a well-appointed town centre residence at 2 The Mall, not far from where Benazir Bhutto was assassinated 87 years later.

As the family were preparing to move from Dehra Dun to join him in Rawalpindi, Kelly received a chilling reminder of the danger that lurked a few hundred kilometers away in Waziristan when he heard that an IMS doctor within his command, Capt Henry Andrews, had been killed while evacuating casualties from a convoy that had been ambushed. His selfless action earned

Above: Brigid with the ayah
(mother's help).

Above: Family group in 1921. Brigid standing
with Kelly and baby Rosemary with Gertrude.

Above: Rosemary and Brigid in 1923.

Right: Brigid performing as Bo Beep
at one of the many shows the girls
appeared in in India and in Jersey.

him a posthumous Victoria Cross. It also ensured that a few years later when it was Kelly's turn to serve in Waziristan again he would not be taking his family with him.

For the next two and a half years Rawalpindi was to offer the Kellys a relatively settled life. As a senior and decorated medical officer, Kelly would have been invited to many of the most important celebrations and dinners that were such a feature of life in India at that time. By all accounts Gertrude enjoyed these events rather more than he did, although her attendance was soon curtailed by a second pregnancy.

Rosemary Anne Josephine was born on 14 January 1921 and, although her father was at least not away fighting a war this time, he wasn't thrilled at having a second daughter, something he all too readily communicated to the young Rosemary as she grew up. He was happy enough with one daughter but had ardently hoped his second child would be a son. Although Gertrude was still only in her mid-30s this was to be their last child.

The following year Rawalpindi received a royal visitor, something else that was not entirely to Kelly's liking.

David, Prince of Wales – later briefly Edward VIII – had arrived in India in November 1921 on part of one of several tours he made around the Empire after the Great War largely aimed at rehabilitating his already tarnished image as a playboy prince. By March 1922 he was on the last leg of his long Indian tour and heading for the north west of the country.

The original plans had included a spectacular military display at Rawalpindi but the cost of this proved controversial and it had been

Above: Gertrude and Brigid in hand drawn transport.

abandoned. It must have been much discussed in the officers' messes and at dinner parties in Rawalpindi in the months running up to the prince's arrival. Even without the big military show the Prince of Wales spent just over a week in the region including visiting some of the military hospitals in Peshawar and Rawalpindi for which Kelly was responsible as well as being the distinguished guest at various receptions, some of which Kelly also attended.

The royal visitor did not make a good impression on him: "He always said he was a drunkard and a womaniser after having to spend time with him in India," his daughter Rosemary recalled, views he forcefully aired at the time of the abdication crisis 14 years later. This may seem a harsh judgement but Kelly was both a Roman Catholic and a teetotaller and probably also resented having to parade some of the wounded soldiers in his care for a prince who had never seen active service.

By the time the Prince of Wales left India and moved on to the next leg of his trip, Kelly hadn't had a period of leave beyond that granted in India for his marriage and brief honeymoon in 1918 since he had to cut short his trip home in 1914 half way through as war was declared. It must have been with mixed feelings, however, that he left India at the beginning of April 1922 for eight months' home leave with his new family.

He would be meeting his new in-laws for the first time and introducing them to their two granddaughters, although the attendance of one of Gertrude's brothers at the wedding suggests that the family accepted what might have been a controversial marriage. He was also contemplating the challenge of visiting his home country of Ireland just as it was emerging from its war of independence but about to descend into a bitter year-long civil war.

He must have been keen to visit Annie, as he hadn't seen her for eight years. She had been steadily moving up through the ranks of the Presentation Sisters and was now the Bursar, the third most important nun at the large convent in Galway, as well as a senior teacher at the school next to the convent. He also wanted to heal the rift between himself and Denis Morris over the latter's refusal to join the British forces at the outbreak of the war and which they never resolved as Kelly rushed back to India in the summer of 1914. His sister Annie had been working hard during the previous eight

Left: Mother and daughters, Rosemary (left) and Brigid in 1923

years to bring them back together, especially once Morris moved back to Galway from Dublin in 1918 to take up the post of assistant professor of obstetrics and gynecology at Galway University.

Having spent time with Gertrude's family in Ipswich, the Kellys left the children in the care of their grandparents and headed to Ireland. It must have been a difficult trip with the need to be watchful and discreet about his long service in a British uniform, but it at least succeeded in breaking the ice in terms of his relationship with Morris, laying a foundation for them to build on later in the decade. It was a very gradual process as Morris was by now a moderate nationalist and a keen supporter of the progress being made towards Irish independence.

They were back in India by Christmas 1922 and contemplating another move, this time to Lahore where Kelly was to take up the post of Commanding Officer of the Indian hospitals in January the following year. His status and reputation also earned him an appointment as Honorary Surgeon to The Viceroy, by now Lord Reading, the former Rufus Issacs who had served as Attorney-General in the pre-war Liberal government. This would have taken him and Gertrude to many government functions at Delhi and Simla, especially after his promotion to full Colonel later that year.

1923 also brought some important news from back home in Galway – although how much he still thought of it as home after only three visits in a quarter of a century is an interesting point. With the

Left: Baby transport at the ready with one of his daughters being carried by the ayah.

Above: A photograph taken of Kelly in the grounds of their house in Lahore, 1923.

upheaval of independence, the partition and the civil war he must have viewed Ireland with a slight detachment.

What didn't weaken were his family ties and the news that Denis Morris had, like himself, married a nurse, Teresa O'Kelly, would have at least intrigued if not actually pleased him and given him another reason to look forward to his next visit to Galway.

He was now nearing retirement from the Indian Medical Service. On accepting his first commission back in January 1897 he would have expected to serve a maximum of 30 years in the IMS, probably retiring at 55, a landmark he was set to reach in March 1925. The pension arrangements had been significantly enhanced for long-serving senior officers in 1920, especially for those who had been on active service during the Great War so he was financially secure.

He and Gertrude returned to Lahore where he resumed his duties as Commanding Officer of the Indian hospitals. While he was contemplating his options, the IMS had one final appointment for him, one that he must have accepted with mixed feelings.

He was appointed as Assistant Director of Medical Services for the Waziristan region with his new headquarters at Dera Ismail Khan in the south-eastern corner of that volatile and violent region. Assistant Directors were the senior IMS officers for entire regions and among the most senior ranking medical officers in India. It was, in effect, an active service appointment, as Waziristan had never calmed down after the 1919 war. That would definitely

Above: Staff at the Indian Station Hospital,Lahore 1924.
Back row: Hav. Ghany Sham Dass, Q.M. Hav. Raja Ram, Subdr. Varyam Singh IMD, Jam. Hari Singh IMD, Jam. Gokal Singh IMD, Jam Milkhi Ram, Jam Balmokand Vaid IMD
Standing: Capt CSV Ramanar IMS, Capt BR Tandan IMS, Capt MA Singh IMS, Lt Karam Chand, Bahadur IMD, Capt PAC Davenport IMS, Jam. Ghulum Haidar IMD, Lt RS Varma IMS, Jam Moti Ram IMD, Lt SD Suri IMS, Jam. BN Lall IMD, Jam AD Gosain IMD, Jam. KC Varma IMD
Seated: Capt TR Khana IMS, Miss ED Buxton, Nursing Sister, Major AC Munro IMS, Mrs Kelly, Lt-Col Kelly DSO VHS, IMS, Officer Commanding, Miss E O'Sullivan, Matron, Capt PD Chopra IMS, Miss JD Rozario, Nursing Sisiter, Capt JC Pyper IMS
Seated on ground: Hav. Bhagat Ram, Jam. RS Mehra IMD, WO Gurbax Singh IMD, Jam. Mohd Sharif IOM, IMD, WO Harbhjan Singh IMD

have been more appealing to him than the more predictable routine of administrative and hospital work and accompanying dinners and receptions in Lahore.

The downside was his extreme reluctance to take his young family to a region where the threat of attack was never far away and where all the British officers lived in fortified, guarded compounds. Even the Prince of Wales had been taken aback by the amount of barbed wire protecting military buildings, houses and hospitals when he visited the region two years earlier.

So at the beginning of 1924 he and Gertrude agreed that he would take up the appointment but that she would return to England with the children to start planning for his retirement some time in the succeeding three years. Her father, now in his late 70s, was also ailing and having seen so little of her parents over the previous 10 years, Gertrude must have been anxious to be with them.

She eventually departed from Bombay on the *SS Domala* at the end of May, arriving in London on 16 June. This time she didn't head to her parents' house in Ipswich but to Suffolk and a hotel in Felixstowe. They stayed there for several months but, before long, tragedy intervened when her father died on 29 November. His illness was most likely the reason Gertrude and her daughters didn't stay at the house in London Road, Ipswich.

Gertrude left the children in the charge of a nanny at the hotel while she went to stay with her mother and help her with the funeral arrangements and adjustment to widowhood. Some time after Christmas 1924 she started the search for possible locations for their new life back in the British Isles. The children eventually moved in with her widowed mother at 96 London Road, Ipswich, a house that Rosemary remembers as being cramped and gloomy after the large, spacious homes she and Brigid enjoyed in India.

Kelly served 18 months in Waziristan and while he was there he received news from Australia that his sister Margaret had died towards the end of 1924, aged 75, another of his siblings whom he hadn't seen for over 40 years.

He took his fourth period of extended leave home – the standard IMS entitlement for someone serving as long as he did – in the summer of 1925. By then he had decided to retire from the IMS as he was entitled to a full pension the following year along with some enhancements for his seniority. His retirement date was fixed for 9 March 1926, conveniently coinciding with the final day of his eight-month leave, meaning that as he left India in July 1925 he closed the book on his life and adventures there for the final time.

Retirement now beckoned but he was only in his mid-50s and had known nothing but military routine, endless excitement and frequent danger for the previous 30 years. The prospect of years of relative inactivity quietly watching his children grow up held little or no appeal as he looked forward to the next chapter in his life. He had already thought about that as he and Gertrude headed home to be reunited with their children.

CHAPTER 14

New life
Jersey and ship's surgeon

Their first challenge as Thomas and Gertrude contemplated the transition to civilian life back home was to find somewhere to live as a family.

India had obviously been rejected. Why? He had been away from the British Isles for 30 years and may just have wanted to return home. Indian nationalism was on the rise and was making India a slightly less comfortable place for former officers of the Raj to live. The lifestyle possibly didn't appeal, as it would have revolved around British clubs with a heavy social life, not an environment Kelly ever felt entirely at ease in. It would also have entailed sending the children back to England to be educated. Gertrude in particular may not have relished the prospect of being parted from Brigid and Rosemary for long periods.

Presumably, another thought must have been Galway as this met the number one requirement which was to be by the sea in order to ease Kelly's malaria, but the instability in Ireland and the, at best ambivalent, attitude towards Irishmen who had served the British crown, especially during the Great War, made this a risky and uncertain option. Others managed to settle back in Ireland but perhaps they were more accommodating towards the new post-independence settlement. Kelly never relaxed his hostility to nationalism of any description.

Another possibility must have been the Essex/Suffolk coast as this was near to Gertrude's parents and some of her family but it never seriously figured in their plans.

The search eventually took them much further afield and ended in Jersey, in those days an easy place for a retired senior officer to settle and probably recommended by other officers with whom Kelly had served and who had already retired there. Its main town St Helier, much less developed than it is today, also had a similar feel to Galway with many buildings of stone construction and a nearby rugged coastline.

Kelly had developed a deep affection for the sea. Some of this must have dated back to his childhood in Galway which sits on the Atlantic coast of Ireland, and was subsequently reinforced by his experiences of being at sea

Above: Kelly with his daughters in the winter of 1926 outside their first house in Jersey in Raleigh Avenue. This was the first time the girls had seen snow.

on his return visits from India and his trip around the world in 1914. Indeed, his ocean voyages had sowed the seeds of how he was going to occupy himself once he left the IMS.

Kelly already knew some of his new neighbours on Jersey, giving him and Gertrude a ready-made social circle as they initially settled into a rented house in Raleigh Avenue. This was to be home for the first year in Jersey before they bought a larger property called Ellerslie at 8 Clarendon Road, St Helier. This was a large, imposing six-bedroomed detached house (which became a hotel for many years after World War 2) in the centre of the town and just a few minutes walk from the sea front.

Kelly didn't retire from the IMS as wealthy a man as some of his colleagues because of his refusal to accept gifts or money for treating non-military patients, something he often referred to with considerable distaste as bribes. He did have reasonable savings because for most of his career in India he had been single and posted to places where living expenses were minimal, if not non-existent. His commitment to support Denis Morris had ended when Morris qualified and started working in Dublin before the outbreak of war so, until he married and took on the responsibility of maintaining a household, he had little to spend his money on.

Above: The *RMS Orduna* on which Kelly served as the ship's surgeon on voyages to South America from the mid-1920s.

His IMS pension was generous, amounting to just under £1000 a year (around £54,000 at today's prices) and Gertrude had a small pension of her own, but Ellerslie must have been an expensive house to maintain, especially with a cook, a housekeeper and a gardener. On top of this there was the girls' education to consider with Brigid 7 and Rosemary 5 when they arrived in Jersey. Both attended the prestigious Jersey Ladies' College (now Jersey School for Girls) for their secondary education so incurring school fees was also part of the financial planning for the Kellys.

This need to maintain a high standard of living combined neatly with Kelly's desire to remain active and get back into uniform as quickly as possible. He had a solution.

He signed up as a ship's surgeon with the Royal Mail Steam Packet Company and by the summer of 1926 found himself on the 900-passenger liner *SS Orduna* for nearly two months on one of its regular voyages to the United States and South America. This was the start of a regular annual engagement with the shipping line (which was about to become the Pacific Steam Navigation Company - PSNC) and he spent two to three months every year for the next decade either on the *Orduna* or its sister ship the *Orbita*, increasing the number of voyages he undertook later in the 1930s so that he was then at sea for most of the year. The crew list for that first voyage records his height as 5' 10" and his weight as 175lbs (12st 7lbs or just over 79kg), one of the few such references to his stature in official records.

South America was an important continent for British commercial interests between the wars with substantial investments in mining, railways and commodities. All the major shipping lines had regular sailings there from the UK. PSNC was the only British shipping company to service the west coast of the continent, however. Its voyages usually left Liverpool calling at La Pallice (one of the Biscay ports), Bermuda, Nassau, Havana and Kingston, then through the Panama Canal to Callao and Iquique in Peru, finishing at the major Chilean port of Valparaiso. The outward and return journeys usually took around 10 weeks.

The late 20s also saw a succession of family chapters opening and closing alongside his retirement from the IMS.

Annie became Mother Columba in 1925 when she was elected Superior of the Presentation Convent. She was a popular Mother Superior and was re-elected by her fellow nuns for a second term in May 1928, which provided Kelly with an ideal excuse to take his family to Galway for an extended holiday. This visit provided the platform for a full reconciliation with Denis Morris, who by now had a young family of his own and was a well-established and popular figure in Galway. He had his own nursing home for women at Salthill and was heavily involved in the running of both the golf club and the town's racecourse.

Above: Brigid and Rosemary ready for one of their many dance performances in Jersey.

This connection with Galway and Annie in particular took on a greater meaning as the decade drew to a close. In the autumn of 1929 they heard that their one remaining sibling, Michael, had died in Bendigo, Australia, aged 76. Neither had seen him since he left for Australia in the mid-1880s but had remained in touch through letters and postcards. His son, Robert, had visited Galway towards the end of the Great War when he was serving as a sergeant in the Australian Imperial Force. Annie was 65 and Kelly was 59 and they were now the only surviving of 11 brothers and sisters.

Back at sea most of Kelly's voyages were routine with the usual mix of passenger illnesses, crew injuries and the occasional death – and at least one birth – on board but, inevitably, he wasn't capable of keeping a completely low profile all the time.

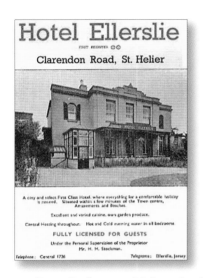

Hotel Ellerslie

FIRST REGISTER ⓖⓖ

Clarendon Road, St. Helier

A cosy and select First Class Hotel, where everything for a comfortable holiday is assured. Situated within a few minutes of the Town centre, Amusements and Beaches.

Excellent and varied cuisine, own garden produce.

Central Heating throughout. Hot and Cold running water in all bedrooms

FULLY LICENSED FOR GUESTS

Under the Personal Supervision of the Proprietor
Mr. H. H. Stockman.

Telephone: Central 1776   Telegrams: Ellerslie, Jersey

Left: The house the family lived in for most of their time in Jersey became a hotel after they left the Channel Islands.

In January 1932 he hit the headlines in newspapers around the world with his performance as a 'radio doctor' conducting operations on ships several hundred miles apart. The newswire report of his exploits was carried in newspapers in the UK, Singapore, Australia and Gibraltar and probably many more elsewhere.

"Sickness at Sea. Doctor Prescribes for Ships 300 Miles Away.

"Twice during the voyage of the P.S.N.C. liner *Orduna*, which arrived at Liverpool from South America in mail week, the liner's surgeon, Dr T.B. Kelly, gave medical advice to people travelling on other ships.

"On Nov. 26 the oil tanker *San Leonardo*, which had experienced rough weather during a voyage from the Gulf of Mexico, asked for advice concerning a woman passenger. Within twenty minutes Dr. Kelly's instructions were being sent by wireless to the San Leonardo, which was about three hundred miles away. Several messages were exchanged and further advice was given, and Dr. Kelly offered to continue to prescribe treatment throughout the voyage to Europe. But the master of the *San Leonardo* decided to land his passenger in Bermuda, at which port a special call was made, and the woman was taken to hospital. The latest information was that she was progressing satisfactorily.

"As the *Orduna* was steaming off the Welsh coast, a message was received from the steamer *Tilapa*, and advice was given as to the best method of stopping bleeding following the extraction of a tooth from the mouth of a steward."

Cargo ships do not usually carry a qualified doctor and first aid is normally left in the hands of the captain or the cook so it is easy to imagine the chain of events on the *Tilapa* that led to the desperate call for assistance. Similarly on the *San Leonardo*, the unfortunate woman being carried as a passenger on an oil tanker (probably for a little extra income or possibly the wife of one of the senior crew) found herself without access to a doctor.

Back in Jersey, the family was growing up and the two girls were frequent performers at school and local theatrical group shows. The Kellys were known as genial hosts for social evenings at which guests were always assured of a full glass despite his longstanding personal teetotalism. He was rather less keen on having to put in appearances as "the Colonel" at some of the island's more formal occasions and always made a point of turning down the official invitation to the annual Levée to celebrate the King's Official Birthday, although he kept his dress uniform and medals for some formal occasions until his death.

In general he enjoyed life in Jersey for the eight or nine months of the year he was there. He turned into a keen gardener, taking particular pride in growing Indian corn and serving it to visitors. He and Gertrude became highly skilled enthusiasts of bezique, a complex card game for two that was very popular between the wars and which filled many of their evenings.

Not surprisingly, he suffered periods of very dark moods. The previous 20 years must have taken a psychological toil on him as he had been through the expedition to Tibet, fought the plague in Persia, been on active service for almost the whole WW1 and then sent to the bloody horror of the NW Frontier. He was, according to his daughters, a stern man at the best of times but when these dark moods descended he wouldn't talk to them for days and

Above: Brigid in 1932.

it was only Gertrude that could bring him round. His malaria – most likely contracted in the early stages of the Tibet mission in 1904 – rarely surfaced and, when it did, the attacks were only mild so the sea air obviously did its trick.

He maintained his favouritism toward Brigid as the girls grew up, at least in Rosemary's eyes. She maintains that her constant desire to question things and try everything new frequently irritated him, although it occasionally seized his attention, she recalls:

"He was a very intellectual, forward thinking man and would sometimes surprise me. I was doing a school project on food and he offered to help. He told me about calories. Nobody talked about them then but he insisted that one day soon we would be measuring the food we eat in calories, and he was right."

He was never a family man, always uneasy with the children as they were growing up, although he brought back gifts from his trips to South America, many of which made them popular at school, such as a stuffed porcupine fish, which delighted their teachers when they took it in. Other presents were slightly more conventional and practical, including a fine crocodile skin handbag still in Rosemary's possession.

Galway was soon to tug at him once more.

In January 1937, Kelly received news from Galway that Morris's wife Teresa had died aged 39. He was at sea – and had missed the 1936 Christmas celebrations with the family as he left Liverpool on the *Orbita*, the sister ship to the *Orduna*, on 12 December, not returning until late February, suggesting an increasing detachment from day-to-day family life. He was almost immediately back on the *Orbita* but finally visited Denis in Galway in June that year and was sufficiently concerned with the way Denis was coping with his young family following his wife's death to ask Annie to keep him closely informed.

By the time the Kellys returned to Jersey later that month important decisions had been made about the family's future, which saw them end their decade-long stay in the Channel Islands. They remained at Ellerslie until the end of 1937 when they sold the house. Kelly moved to London briefly with Brigid so she could start a course at Mrs Hoster's secretarial college and he could look for somewhere for them to live. He soon returned to sea once his 18-year-old daughter had been found suitable accommodation, not being

Above: Kelly (centre) at a beach party in Jersey in the late-1930s.

Right: Kelly with Gertrude in the garden at Ellerslie, their house in Jersey, shortly before they left the island in late-1938.

inclined to hang around in London for too long. Initially, Gertrude remained behind in Jersey with Rosemary and they moved into the Royal Hotel for three months before she joined her elder daughter in London. Rosemary still had several months of schooling to complete and so she moved in with the family of one of her best friends in Jersey, Kaye Picot, until she finished school in April 1938.

Gertrude had never been as happy in Jersey as her husband. She found it all too parochial for her tastes and longed to live in London. Now was her opportunity. With the children's schooling finished she wasted little time in persuading a reluctant Thomas that it was to the capital city they should be heading. He recognised that it was time to let her choice dictate where life should take them next, especially as he was by now only at home for a few weeks each year, presumably happy to escape a house full of women, including two teenage daughters.

Money may also have played a part in their decisions both to move and for him to undertake up to four voyages a year. They had a large house to maintain in Jersey with a staff and private schooling to pay for. Although he was too careful ever to live beyond his means they may have been living close to the edge of those means by the late 30s. The voyages were earning him just over £50 a time (£3200 at today's prices), a more than handy supplement to his IMS pension.

He may also have been casting his eyes towards the storm clouds of Nazism gathering across Europe and wondering what another war might hold for him and his family, especially if they stayed in Jersey. Whether as 1937 drew to a close and they finally packed their bags he fully realised the threat to Jersey isn't known but it was a prescient move as the whole family – being non-Jersey born – would almost certainly have been sent to internment camps in Germany had they stayed when the Channel Islands were invaded after the fall of France in 1940.

The Kellys rented a three-bedroom flat at 36 St Mary's Mansions in Paddington and moved there in early 1938 when he was at home for six weeks, having this time spent their last Christmas in Jersey together as a family. Brigid was completing her secretarial studies and was soon to get a job as secretary

Above: The *RMS Orbita* on which Kelly was serving as ship's surgeon when Britain declared war on Germany in September 1939.

Right: Kelly (centre) on board the *Orbita* in August 1938 with the 2nd Officer Joseph Williams (left) and Wireless Officer Donald Sinclair (right).

to the matron of Guy's Hospital, making the Paddington home an ideal base for her. Rosemary was finishing her schooling and looking forward to pursuing her dream of a career on the stage by applying to the Central School of Speech and Drama in London.

By now the news from Galway and Denis Morris was not encouraging so he immediately arranged for the 17-year-old Rosemary to be dispatched to Ireland to look after Morris's four children, three girls and a boy ranging from four to 13 years old. She stayed there for several months and, as well as caring for the children until a suitable permanent nanny could be found, learnt to play golf and developed a life-long passion for horseracing. Denis Morris was by now a leading figure in Galway and influential in both golfing and horseracing circles. These pursuits must have seemed glamorous to a 17-year-old girl suddenly freed of tight parental control. By time she finished with the Morris family it was to London that she returned, not Jersey.

Kelly wasn't keen on staying in London for long periods so having found the flat in Paddington he signed up to serve as ship's surgeon on back on the *Orbita* for a succession of voyages that kept him at sea for almost the whole of 1938 and into 1939. He was a fit man and photographs from the late 1930s show he looked much younger than his age so few people would have found it strange that he was their ship's doctor. The crew lists show his age stubbornly stuck at 65 for the whole of 1937 and 1938, actually appearing as 56 for the last voyage of the year that left Liverpool in mid-October 1938 when he was half-way through his 69th year. Maybe it can be explained as a transcribing error – the crew lists are handwritten – but it does have his

Above: The family at the Presentation Convent in Galway in November 1939 to celebrate Annie's Golden Jubilee as a nun. *Standing:* Orla Morris, Denis Morris, Aileen Morris, Cecilie Morris, Gertrude, Kelly and Brigid. *Sitting*: Mother Alphonsus Brady (also celebrating her Golden Jubilee that day), Mother Bridget and Annie (Mother Columba). Rosemary was unable to leave wartime London because of her studies to become a radiographer. Orla, Aileen and Cecilie were Morris's daughters.

signature immediately adjacent to it. Perhaps he was getting conscious of his age even if he wasn't feeling it. Within a few months it was to become a bone of contention between him and the authorities.

The *Orbita* docked in Liverpool on Christmas Eve 1938 bringing Kelly home from a routine 10-week return voyage to South America. In those days trains ran on Christmas Eve and Christmas Day so there would have been plenty of opportunity for him to get back to London for a celebration with the whole family, Rosemary having left Jersey and now living with her mother and sister in St Mary's Mansions in Paddington.

The threat of war was, of course, getting closer month-by-month during 1938 and 1939 and he was starting to weigh up whether he could – or should in his late-60s – play a role in any conflict. Events were soon to open up another long chapter of danger and adventure for Thomas Bernard Kelly.

CHAPTER 15

'On the High Seas'

Evacuation, refugees and troopships in World War 2

Kelly was at home at the end of September 1938 when Prime Minister Neville Chamberlain returned from Munich flourishing his infamous piece of paper bearing Adolf Hitler's signature and confidently claiming it ensured "Peace for our time". Kelly was not impressed with Chamberlain's optimism and the almost desperate willingness of people to embrace it. He had taken the view for some time that war with Germany was virtually inevitable.

So convinced was Kelly of the certainty of war that he had already prevented Rosemary from taking up her place at the Central School of Speech and Drama. When she returned from caring for Denis Morris's children as autumn approached in 1938 she instead found herself heading for St George's Hospital in London as a trainee radiographer. "There was simply no discussion. He had decided that I had to do something useful because war was coming and had already arranged everything," Rosemary recalls. This further undermined her already fractured relationship with her father.

Kelly's attitude towards the impending conflict hardened as the shockwaves created by a brutally resurgent Germany began to be felt across Europe. It wasn't too long before he found himself close to a dismal demonstration of just how misplaced Chamberlain's hopes for peace with Germany were.

During 1938 the number of German Jews fleeing Europe steadily increased, especially after the horror of Kristallnacht left no-one in any doubt about the extent of the Nazi's hatred of the Jews. Like the British, many wealthy Germans had business interests in South America and Jewish refugees started to appear on the *Orbita* and *Orduna* during the late 1930s, culminating in the dramatic and desperate events surrounding the Voyage of the Dammed in May and June 1939.

More than 900 Jewish refugees were allowed to board the *SS St Louis* in Hamburg believing they had visas to enter Cuba. When they reached Havana they were refused entry. The German captain Gustav Schroder then headed

122 Leadenhall Street.
London.   5th July, 1940.
E.C.3.

Dear Mr. Kelly,

It was with much pleasure that we learned of the excellent performance on the part of the ship's personnel of the "MADURA" when carrying refugees from Bordeaux.

Captain Beatty has given us a very interesting account of the circumstances under which these services were rendered, in addition to which many of the passengers carried – including some of the East African travellers – have written expressing their appreciation and gratitude for the efforts which all on board the "MADURA" made to ensure their well-being, under extraordinarily difficult circumstances.

I would, therefore, take this opportunity of expressing our great appreciation to you personally for all that you, in conjunction with your colleagues on board, did under such difficult and harassing circumstances.

Yours sincerely,

Chairman.

Mr. T.B. Kelly,
        s.s. "MADURA",
        London.

Above: The letter of commendation Kelly received from the chairman of the British India Steamship Company for his part in the evacuation from Bordeaux.

to Florida where, on President Roosevelt's orders, they were again refused entry. Schroder moved on to Canada where they were also spurned. In desperation he returned to Cuba but entry was still barred. By this time the *Orduna* was in Havana, also with a small number of Jewish refugees on board and having similar problems. Captain Schroder felt he had no option but to return to Europe but not before he had arranged for as many refugees as possible to be transferred to other ships that would take them to countries where they would be accepted. The *Orduna* took some and eventually 233 were given asylum in the UK. Others went to France, Holland and Belgium as Schroder was not prepared to return any of them to Germany. After his death he was declared as Righteous among the Nations, a rarely given Israeli honour for non-Jews who helped save Jews from the Holocaust.

Kelly was at sea on the *Orbita* while this was happening and was closely in touch with these events, which were covered widely in the world's newspapers and broadcast media. They appalled him. He was very respectful of other people's religions and hated the stories of Nazi persecution he was now being acquainted with. By now he knew that he couldn't sit on the sidelines.

He arrived back in Liverpool from his final voyage on the *Orbita* at the end of September 1939, with war now official.

While he mulled over his next move family events intervened.

Gertrude's mother Christine died on 12 September, age 82. The funeral couldn't be delayed until the end of the month when he returned, but even with that out of the way this clearly wasn't the moment to rush back to sea, leaving the grieving Gertrude. He decided to stay at home for a while especially as he had a happier family celebration on the horizon. In November he headed to Galway to celebrate his sister's Golden Jubilee as a nun, accompanied by Gertrude and Brigid. Rosemary couldn't get time off from her studies to be a radiographer, now accelerated in the wartime conditions. Pictures of the celebrations on a cold November day appeared in most of the Galway papers, showing a large and majestic Mother Columba (as Annie was now known) seated in the centre of the group. She was often described as looking rather like a grand sailing ship in her flowing habit as she swirled down the corridors of the Presentation Convent.

The family spent the first Christmas of the war together in Paddington, but Kelly's mind was turning to the war and, in particular, how he could serve the British Crown once more. He initially volunteered for service with the Royal Navy.

Although his age was listed for that final voyage on the *Orbita* as 66 he was actually 69 and, not surprisingly, the Royal Navy declined to take someone soon to pass 70. Whether he attempted to lie about his age isn't recorded anywhere but he did feel the British Medical Association had a hand in the Navy's decision to reject him and promptly resigned in protest.

His attention now turned to the Merchant Navy and through a friend he applied to the British India Steam Navigation Company to be a ship's surgeon with them. These discussions quickly bore fruit as the merchant fleet was being rapidly mobilised in support of the war effort and experienced personnel were hard to come by.

By the end of February 1940 he was stepping on board the *SS Madura* in London, preparing to sail to Mombasa in east Africa via Gibraltar, Malta, Port Said and Dar-es-Salaam delivering and collecting a range of military, naval and intelligence personnel along the way, as well as collecting British and African civilians and their families for the return voyage. The merchant navy had no qualms about his age as it is correctly listed as 69 in the official crew list.

The outward voyage on this modest 9000-ton ship was relatively uneventful apart from an outbreak of German measles soon after they left Gibraltar that required the creation of a small isolation unit on the ship, not a major problem, as it was by no means full at that stage. Later in the voyage one of the Indian saloon staff died of heart failure and was buried at sea.

On the return voyage the *Madura* was forced into Freetown, Sierra Leone on the west African coast after the small convoy it was with was attacked by a German U-boat. While it was there the ship was fitted with the latest degaussing system to help protect against magnetic mines and also collected a Royal Navy contingent, filling it to its 280-passenger capacity. This delay meant that it was running over a week behind schedule when passing the French coast in mid-June, a crucial moment in the fall of France.

The evacuation of the British Expeditionary Force and a large number of French troops through the channel ports – codenamed Operation Dynamo – ended on 4 June when Dunkirk fell to the advancing Germans. By that time more than 338,000 men had been lifted from the beaches and the port. Many people assumed that marked the end of the war in France but a large part of the British Expeditionary Force had been cut off to the south of the German advance along the River Somme and were fighting their way to ports on the west coast. On 8 June these forces were actually reinforced with 8000 further British troops who were landed at Cherbourg as Prime Minister Winston Churchill responded to French pleas to help it establish a "Breton redoubt" in the hope that a foothold could be retained in France. This plan quickly evaporated but those troops now joined around 130,000 others still needing to be evacuated from France before it finally collapsed.

There were also many French units fighting on and nearly 30,000 Polish troops trapped south of the German lines, which had cut the Allied forces two. Alongside these retreating military forces were huge columns of refugees, including British diplomats, businessmen and the British press corps, all of whom had been told they wouldn't be evacuated through the channel ports and should head south to escape the advancing Nazi forces.

Above: Refugee vehicles in the centre of Bordeaux, June 1940.

On 10 June a small evacuation plan codenamed Operation Cycle was initiated and during the next three days managed to evacuate just over 11,000 more troops, mainly from Le Harve. This included the 8000, who had been hastily sent across the Channel a few days before in the hope of creating the Breton redoubt.

Two days later an even bigger evacuation plan, Operation Aerial, was launched and it was into this maelstrom that the *Madura* was sucked.

Operation Aerial focused initially on Cherbourg but quickly moved down the Biscay coast as port after port was captured by the Germans, who were determined not to let the British establish the sort of well-defended evacuation point that had held out for nine days at Dunkirk. After Cherbourg, Aerial moved to Brest, then Saint-Nazaire and when that fell to La Pallice Cla Rochelle before its focus moved further south to Le Verdon and Bordeaux in the Gironde estuary. This is where *Madura* was ordered on the night of 16 to 17 June.

Right: The *SS Madura* which was diverted into Bordeaux in June 1940 and returned to England with nearly 2000 people on board

By then the French government and the remnants of other Allied governments along with the British embassy staff from Paris, were all based in Bordeaux and thousands of British, French, Belgium and Czech military personnel were pouring in. Alongside them were huge numbers of bewildered, frightened refugees, not forgetting journalists of the world's press who were still reporting from the increasingly fragmented and shifting French war zone.

The *Madura*'s Captain John Beatty sailed into the Gironde estuary and was told to be ready to accept troops and civilians waiting for evacuation from the deepening chaos of Bordeaux where Marshall Pétain was gradually manoeuvering what remained of the French government into surrendering to the Germans. For nearly two days launches arrived with more and more people hoping to be conveyed to safety in England. During the morning of 18 June embarkation was suspended when Luftwaffe dive-bombers attacked the waiting ships. As bombs fell into the sea around the *Madura* her crew must have feared that she would share the same fate as the much larger *HMT Lancastria*, which the previous day had been sunk by dive-bombers just off St Nazaire with the estimated loss of 4000 men, the largest single death toll in Britain's long maritime history. Churchill instantly recognised that the *Lancastria* disaster would take the gloss off the "miracle of deliverance" as he had described Dunkirk and damage fragile public morale so he ordered all news of it to be suppressed. That disaster remained classified until the end of the war, which offers one explanation why Operation Aerial never received the same recognition as the earlier evacuations from Dunkirk.

Gradually, the *Madura* filled up with an extraordinary mix of passengers, nearly 1400 additional souls, bringing the total on board with the existing passengers and crew to almost 2000. Some on board were just civilians such as the 10-year-old Daphne Wall whose father was chief accountant for a French perfume company in Paris, one of many hundreds of British people working in France at that time. Years later Daphne Wall wrote down her memories of that day:

> "On board the most extraordinary sight met our eyes. Every square inch of the deck was covered with sleeping bodies wrapped in coats and blankets. They looked like ghostly corpses in the half-light, though some of them were beginning to stir and pour cups of tea out of thermos flasks. There were families with children like me, and I noticed some of them had dogs with them: so we could have brought Lucky with us after all. Now it was too late.
>
> "We were lying low in the water 'below the Plimsoll' line I heard someone say... The passenger list was an extraordinary mix of distinguished names like Baron Rothschild and Marie Curie's daughter Eve [sic], as well as just about every representative of the British press

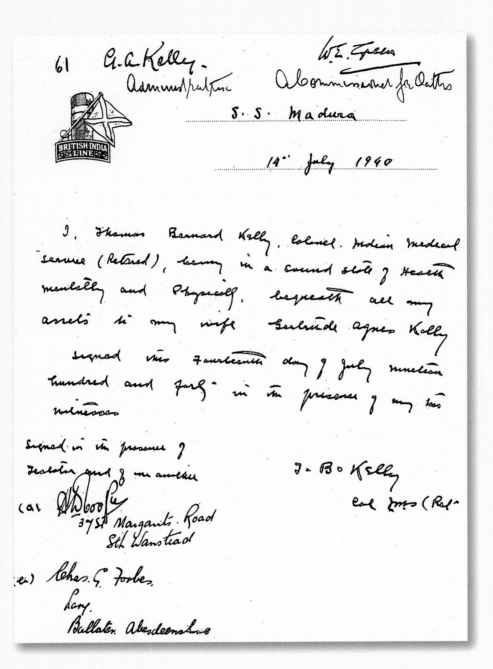

Above: Kelly's will – still valid at the time of his death in 1949 – was written on board the *Madura* in 1940.

that had been working in France. The journalists' view of the whole thing was different from mine; they all knew each other and as alcohol, unlike food, was plentiful, they seem to have partied most of the time, no doubt to forget the trauma they had just been through, and the uncertainty that lay ahead.

"Just before we sailed on the evening of the 18th June there was more screaming of aircraft and what sounded like a building crashing on deck. In the small cabin that my mother and I had been given there was only one life jacket, and as she strapped it onto me and we sat waiting for the ship to sink, my thought was that I could swim and she couldn't. But again, our luck held and we weren't hit. In fact the plane attacking us was brought down into the water by one of the last French fighter planes still in the air."

Eva Curie had been working with the French government and had decided she preferred the rallying call to the French flag issued by General Charles de Gaulle in London to the defeatist stance of Marshall Pétain in Bordeaux. She wasn't alone as some former French government ministers also found their way onto the *Madura*, along with Belgium and Czech ministers preferring to carry on the war from London rather than fall under German rule or even risk being thrown into captivity.

Baron Robert de Rothschild was one of the wealthiest men alive but as a Jew had a particular imperative to flee the Nazis. It was, in the words of one passenger, a "one class ship" and the Baron took his place on the deck with the other refugees as British graphic artist Aubrey Hammond wrote the day he landed in Britain:

"I shall never forget the voyage from France. The ship in reality surpassed anything vainly imagined in the wildest dreams. Beside me on the deck at night have lain millionaires and financiers, bank managers and bank clerks, middle aged ladies with comfortable villas in the south of France, French, Belgium and Czech refugees, an extraordinary collection of people.

"One sorted out amidst a maze of luggage and litter the recumbent figure of the Baron Robert de Rothschild minus a mattress or a covering. One saw near him M Henri Bernstein, the distinguished dramatist."

He later heard Baron Rothschild asking, after he had queued patiently for his food along with other passengers, if he may have half an extra potato as he hadn't eaten a proper meal for several days. The ability of the ship's crew to ensure that everyone was fed during the two-day voyage was much commented on by the many journalists who wrote their accounts of the voyage.

The partying press corps of nearly 60 journalists was certainly distinguished as it included all the leading war correspondents of the day – Hugh Carleton Greene (later Director-General of the BBC), Sefton Delmar, Virginia Cowles and Alexander Werth to name just a few.

Cowles wrote eloquently in *The Sunday Times* of the emotions that gripped the refugees as the ship eventually weighed anchor and left just before 6am on Friday 19 June:

> "…there were several hundred French people: many of them climbed on board weeping convulsively at the parting from their relatives and the uncertainty as to whether they would ever see their native land again. There in the harbour, with the sun streaming down and the peaceful outline of the French coast in the distance, it was hard to realise France had come to an end."

Kelly was busy. Among the last to be boarded before sailing out of the Gironde estuary was a launch carrying several wounded British airmen and many of the civilians had picked up injuries on their desperate journeys southwards. He found help among the refugees as some were nurses and he found more than enough work to keep them occupied.

The ship was directed to Falmouth in Cornwall where it had to sit outside the harbour for another day such was the crush of ships needing to dock with their vulnerable, battered human cargoes. Eventually, the *Madura* was able to land all those capable of walking ashore – the sick and wounded stayed on board and were taken on to London where this remarkable voyage ended on 25 June, just in time for its exhausted crew to pick up *The Daily Telegraph* and read its war correspondent Richard Capell's florid tribute to Captain Beatty and his crew:

> "What grand fellows! What a prodigious load they shouldered with great strength and uncomplainingly!
> "We, the Bordeaux refugees had no opportunity to thank them, the company of the good ship *Madura*; and if we had it we should not have known what to say. They had done for us too much for words.
> "Something that I think has not been said about the fantastic voyage of the *Madura* was the sheer generosity of it all. No questions were asked. It was enough that unfortunates had come down from Bordeaux to the mouth of the estuary for the *Madura* to take them on board to the very limit of possibility. No one was asked for his papers any more than if he had been escaping from a burning house.
> "There was no distinction shown between the British and the foreigners. It was madly quixotic, but it was sublime."

A few weeks later Kelly, back on board the *Madura* and heading for Africa once again, received a personal letter from the chairman of the shipping company commending him for his part in ensuring the wellbeing of everyone on board. He particularly mentioned that some of the east African travellers had written to express their gratitude, Kelly obviously having gone out of his way to ensure that the needs of these passengers so unexpectedly thrown into the mayhem of a European war were not overlooked.

Aerial was a huge success. It continued for some days after France surrendered on 25 June with the final evacuations taking place from the ports of Bayonne and Saint-Jean-de-Luz close to the Spanish border. More than 186,000 troops were brought home, including over 46,000 French, Polish and Czech soldiers. In addition, more than 20,000 civilian refugees made it to England.

Kelly spent the rest of 1940 on the *Madura*, which eventually returned to the UK from east Africa at the end of November, docking at Greenock on the River Clyde in Scotland. The vast convoys of troopships heading to the Middle East and north Africa – known as the Winston Specials – were starting to be dispatched from the Clyde ports and it was on these that Kelly was to serve for the next two years.

He handed over the ship's surgeon responsibilities on the *Madura* to a 50-year-old Scottish doctor, Peter Gorrie, who had served with the RAMC in the First World War on hospital ships in the Mediterranean and in the same hospitals in Malta that Kelly's wife Gertrude had served as a nurse. The *Madura* and its new surgeon would soon feature in another wartime drama.

While Kelly was on the *Madura* in 1940 Gertrude had been managing a refugee problem of her own back in Paddington. When France fell at the end June the Germans quickly invaded the Channel Islands, the only British home soil they took during the war and which Hitler looked upon as a major prize. The prospect of a German invasion prompted an exodus from the islands, especially those who weren't born there who – rightly it turned out – feared deportation to Germany. Among these were many of the Kellys' friends from Jersey.

Gertrude opened the doors of 36 St Mary's Mansions to them and during 1940 there was a stream of displaced friends staying there who she helped find accommodation. When the Blitz started Rosemary moved out to live in accommodation next to the hospital she was training at so there was a room to spare in the modest flat for these refugees.

Once her Jersey friends were settled in the UK, Gertrude volunteered at the shelters and kitchens run by St Martin-in-the-Fields, Trafalgar Square for Londoners who had lost their homes. She did this for most of the rest of the war, a demanding distraction from worrying about where her husband – who had celebrated his 70th birthday on the *Madura* in March 1940 – might be.

The first troopship to which Kelly was attached in 1941 after returning from his stint on the *Madura*, was the P&O liner *RMS Mooltan*, which had just finished serving two years as an armed merchant cruiser, mainly protecting convoys in the South Atlantic. She was now being converted at Tilbury to a troopship as the need to move tens of thousands of troops to north Africa was becoming increasingly urgent.

The war was going badly in the Mediterranean and Middle East in early 1941. Greece and Crete had fallen to the Axis forces and Rommel's Afrika Corps had advanced across the desert pushing the British back to the Egyptian border, leaving Tobruk under siege. It was a pivotal moment in the desert war and huge convoys of troops were being dispatched to reinforce the Eighth Army.

The *Mooltan* eventually joined convoy WS9A, which was taking nearly 22,000 personnel, mainly from the Northumbrian Division, to join the war in north Africa and the Middle East. There were around a dozen troopships in the convoy of which *Mooltan* was the largest with berths for 3200 troops, albeit very cramped. Into these squeezed the entire personnel of the 69th Infantry Brigade made up of battalions from the Green Howards and the East Yorks Regiment. They brought with them their own medical officers who had responsibility for the health of their troops while the ship's surgeon had responsibility for the crew and for running the medical facilities on board.

As the convoy formed up in the North Sea towards the end of May, Kelly would have noticed a familiar name among the ships joining the *Mooltan* as the *Orbita* on which he served as surgeon during many peacetime voyages to South America in the 1920s and 1930s, was also part of convoy WS9A. His former ship turned out to be a bit of a burden to the convoy as it was slower than the rest of the ships and they frequently had to slow down to ensure *Orbita* didn't get detached from the convoy.

The voyage to Freetown and then on to Durban was relatively uneventful with only one brief skirmish with enemy planes as the convoy was leaving the English Channel.

While there was plenty of routine sickness and occasional injuries to crew members, the medical teams were not unduly busy, so Kelly put on a series of lectures for the army doctors largely inexperienced in the conditions they would face once they arrived. Calling on all his years of experience of desert and tropical warfare he did as much as he could to prepare his fellow medics for the challenges ahead. These lectures were to become a familiar feature of the many voyages he was to make on troopships as part of the Winston Special convoys.

In Durban the troops were transferred to other, much larger ships running a shuttle service to Suez and the *Mooltan* loaded up with precious cargoes of food and raw materials needed to sustain the war effort at home.

Above: The SS *Mooltan*, one of the troopships on which Kelly served in 1941 taking the 8th Army to North Africa, in the Suez Canal. Note the troops swimming in the canal around the ship.

They also collected 56 Distressed British Seamen (DBS was an official term for sick and injured sailors) from Durban and Cape Town who were being repatriated. Many were malaria cases, while others had sustained severe injuries on board other ships and had no immediate prospect of returning to duty. It ensured Kelly had his hands full on the six-week return voyage. It was quite common for returning ships to repatriate seamen who had been classified DBS but it was usually just a few at a time: 56 was an exceptionally large number.

The return voyage took them out across the Atlantic on a tortuous route to avoid U-Boats with a refuelling stop in Trinidad, a day at Curacao, one of the Dutch Caribbean islands, for engine repairs and a stop at Bermuda to collect some additional passengers. Kelly's work wasn't finished when the *Mooltan* docked in Greenock on 22 August as he was required to attend and report on the sick and injured from the crews of two other ships that had recently docked, the *SS Pennland* and the *Kingston Hill*. This he did with his customary thoroughness, submitting a detailed typewritten report a few days later. He then headed for London where Gertrude was waiting to break some bad news from Galway.

Denis Valentine Morris had died of a heart attack on 3 July 1941 at the age of 54.

Annie had sent over all the cuttings from the Galway newspapers reporting on Morris's death and his funeral. Conflicting emotions of pride and grief must have swirled around the stern, restrained Kelly as he read the extensive reports of the death of the nephew he had mentored through medical college, had bitter arguments with over his refusal to join the Royal Navy in the Great War, found reconciliation with in the years after the war and for whom he sent his own youngest daughter to Galway to care for his children when his wife died so young.

> "Galwegians received a severe shock on this Thursday morning when it became known that Dr Denis Valentine Morris, brilliant local medical-man, had passed away in Seamount Private Nursing Home, Salthill, at 7.45am with tragic suddenness.
> "Dr Morris was seemingly in perfect health. He had attended patients at Seamount Home, which was his own property, on Wednesday afternoon and, feeling slightly unwell, was persuaded to pass the night there. Early on Thursday morning, he had a heart attack and passed away."

Galway mourned its loss. The town corporation, after some brief tributes, suspended its meeting. The golf club, the racecourse and the rugby club all paid effusive tributes. The report of the funeral and the list of mourners in the *Connacht Tribune* occupied six columns. Kelly found he merited a passing, tactful mention: "His uncle, Dr Kelly, was formerly a member of the Indian Medical Service, but he retired some years ago. When the present war broke out he joined the service again and is at present somewhere on the High Seas." Tact, of course, was required in strictly neutral Ireland when mentioning the war.

Kelly's war service went on pause for the next six months but that respite came to an end when news of another death reached him in February 1942. The *Madura* had found itself embroiled in another evacuation. This time the location was Singapore, about to fall into the hands of the Japanese, and the ship wasn't quite so lucky as it had been when he was on board at Bordeaux. On 3 February it was attacked by Japanese planes and five crew members were killed, including Peter Gorrie, the surgeon Kelly had handed over to 14 months earlier.

The following month the 72-year-old Kelly was back at sea but he had now developed a fatalistic attitude to the risks of war. He had decided that it was going to be his lot to join his fellow surgeon and die at sea, a belief that he didn't always keep to himself and which sometimes made other crew members slightly nervous of his presence on board. It is hardly surprising that he should be feeling that he had escaped death more times than the proverbial cat with its nine lives. Snipers on the NW Frontier, a chain-mailed assassin in Tibet, plague in Persia, bullets flying through operating tents in Aden, disease and intense heat in Mesopotamia, the savagery of Waziristan, bombed at Bordeaux: any human being would surely start to wonder how much more they could survive.

He now began a period of more than two years of almost continuous service on New Zealand Shipping Company ships that had been requisitioned by the Merchant Navy, starting on the *TSS Ruahine* which he joined at Cardiff in March 1942. This was heading to familiar ports in South America as part of a cargo convoy and, apart from a minor engine failure and grounding outside Montevideo, it was another relatively uneventful voyage in terms of military excitements. He did, however, have some unusual medical matters to deal with.

One of the ship's firemen thought he had found a way of getting out of the Merchant Navy. Fireman V Beckwith clearly knew little of Kelly's reputation for thoroughly investigating everything when he reported sick with dermatitis covering his hands. He was convinced it was due to one of the various oils he frequently came into contact with, probably Sperm Oil.

Kelly's report in the ship's log records that he carried out a series of patch tests using various substances, all of which proved negative. It wasn't, he concluded, a reaction to anything he had come into contact with on the ship: "Microscopic examination of scales of epidermis from the inflamed area shows growth of Fungus between the cells. The case is therefore due to Fungus infection and is **not** an occupational disease."

A month later his skills as an ophthalmic surgeon were called upon when assistant steward A Howes "whilst opening a bottle of beer with a knife sustained an incised puncture wound of the right eyeball caused through the

Above: The *TSS Ruahine*, the New Zealand Shipping Company ship he was surgeon on when it went to South America in 1942. It was on this ship that Kelly's skill as an ophthalmic surgeon was needed to save the sight of a steward who stabbed his eye with a penknife when opening a beer bottle.

Right :The *Rangitata*, the troopship which Kelly joined in the middle of 1942 and made several voyages on over the next two years.

knife slipping. The wound commenced in the lower and outer quadrant through the Sclerolic coat and Cornea tearing through the Iris and probably damaging the lens", records the entry in the ship's log for 11.15pm on 3 July signed by Kelly. By the time the ship docked three weeks later, Kelly felt confident that the unfortunate A Howes would recover most of his sight. He was fortunate his mishap with his beer bottle happened on a ship with a skilled ophthalmic surgeon serving as its doctor.

Back home Kelly's two daughters were by now both engaged to young doctors and weddings were being planned. The challenge was to fit the weddings in around the times when their father expected to be in the UK. This was only a partial success.

Both men, Tom Foot engaged to Brigid, now almost 22, and Adair Stuart Mason engaged Rosemary, 21, had trained at the London Hospital.

So at the end of July 1942 it was Brigid and Tom who married first at the Catholic church of Our Lady of the Rosary not far from St Mary's Mansions with a reception at Lord's Cricket Ground. Kelly was there, having returned to England on the *Ruahine* just 10 days earlier.

By mid-August he was bidding his family farewell again to join another New Zealand Shipping Company vessel, the *RMS Rangitata* at Liverpool, ready to sail to the Clyde to form part of convoy WS22 to take the 56th (London) Division to Iraq (the former Mesopotamia), a huge complement of 50,000 military and support personnel. For this voyage, unusually he had an assistant surgeon, W Carruthers, as well as the medical staff travelling with the 2600 troops on the largest of the New Zealand ships converted to troopships during the war. It was just as well he had additional help on this trip, because not long after they left UK waters there was a severe outbreak of venereal disease among the crew and the troops which necessitated setting up an isolation unit, no mean challenge on an already horrendously crowded troopship. Gradually, the crisis eased as the cases were dealt with and the men returned to duty so that by the time it reached Durban in early October the *Rangitata* was able to disembark a healthy contingent.

It had a routine return journey planned, crossing the Atlantic to collect food cargoes from Buenos Aires and La Plata, arriving back in the UK just in

time for Christmas 1942. More importantly for Kelly to be in good time for Rosemary's wedding now set for mid-January. Almost immediately the plans started to change. *Rangitata* was sent with additional troops to reinforce Diego Suarez on Madagascar, which had recently been seized from the Vichy French to prevent it being used as a base by the advancing Japanese forces. While there it collected a troop detachment to take to Mauritius, the only ship from any of the 30-plus Winston Special convoys – each consisting of dozens of ships – to visit Mauritius. Having done this it headed off to South America where it collected its cargo of meat but was diverted again, this time to New York where it was asked to pick up US troops coming to Europe. It docked in New York on 4 January 1943 and by then Kelly must have realised he wasn't going to make his younger daughter's wedding planned to take place on 11 January. Wartime secrecy meant that he was unable to send a message home to tell them of the delays.

Gertrude had been calmly reassuring her daughter that her father would be home in time for the wedding and even when Christmas came and went without any word from him she remained convinced he would arrive in time. He didn't.

On her wedding day Rosemary was accompanied down the aisle in the grand setting of St James's, Spanish Place by an uncle she hardly knew, convinced that her father couldn't be bothered to get to her wedding, a resentment that festered for more than 70 years until the research for this book revealed the truth of why he wasn't there. She never raised the matter with her father and saw relatively little of him after her marriage, not least because in early 1946 she followed her husband, by then serving with the

Above: Kelly's service medals from WWII. He also won the Atlantic Star, Africa Star and France-Germany Star but never got to wear them as they arrived a few weeks after his death and remained unused in the Post Office box.

RAMC, to India. Equally, he never made any attempt to explain what had happened: it was for him a simple matter of duty calls. He docked in England on 24 January, nearly two weeks after the wedding.

He was quickly back on the *Rangitata* this time to Algiers and Oran where it was attacked by German planes on 26 March. The ship was equipped with anti-aircraft guns and these quickly opened fire but not before the planes had launched two torpedoes: sharp evasive action ensured they missed the ship. 1700 German and Italian prisoners of war destined for captivity in the United States were embarked at the Algerian port of Oran requiring a long return voyage via Tristan da Chuna, Montevideo, New York and Gibraltar. This ensured he missed his 25th wedding anniversary at the end of April 1943. He consistently put duty before family throughout the war.

The prisoners-of-war on board offered an interesting contrast, according to Captain P B Clarke, the ship's master. He recalled in the company's official history that the Germans were "dour and tough" in sharp contrast to the Italians. They spent most of their time on deck singing and playing and when at 9pm every evening the Italians were required to return to their quarters they lined up on deck and sang "God Save the King!"

This voyage brought him home at the end of May and after a six-week break he was again on the *Rangitata* which had now been switched to a regular Liverpool to New York route, principally to collect US troops now being amassed in Britain for the expected invasion of Europe. This change in the course of the war was reflected by the addition of clauses in the standard crew agreements covering Mass Invasion of the Continent. All crew members were given the chance of opting out of the new obligation to stay with the ship should it suddenly be required to support an invasion. Needless to say, Kelly never opted out.

His fourth voyage on *Rangitata*.which was returning from New York in January 1944 with a mixture of US troops and RAF personnel and their families, was hit with a tragedy that must have touched even the battle-hardened Kelly.

There was clearly a problem with the quality of the drinking water on the ship as the ship's log records Kelly inspecting the tanks and insisting on them being cleaned. That was followed up by a direction from him that the water should be chlorinated, no doubt bringing back memories of his time in Mesopotamia when he drunk heavily chlorinated water pretty much constantly for two years.

Whether what followed was a consequence of poor-quality water isn't known but, whatever the cause, it ensured a sad end to the voyage. The ship's log records the event:

> "At 10.45pm 12.2.44 Dr Kelly, Ship's surgeon, was called in by the SMO (Troops) Capt V Candis for consultation in the case of Richard Ellis Pollard, age 6 months who had been under treatment for diarrhoea by the SMO (Troops). Despite treatment the child died @ 11.56pm 12.2.44. Cause of death, exhaustion resulting from diarrhoea."

Baby Richard was travelling with his parents, Harry, an RAF corporal, and his wife Miriam. As they were only two days from home they were permitted to take the baby's body home to be buried rather than see him buried at sea.

Kelly's fifth and final voyage on the *Rangitata* left from Liverpool to pick up more US troops on 26 February 1944, docking back in Liverpool in early April. It was a relatively straightforward voyage with the threat from U-boats and the Luftwaffe starting to recede. Kelly had the usual routine of minor injuries and illnesses to deal with apart from the case of one assistant steward who the log records as "suffering from persecution mania & has developed suicidal tendencies. He has been placed in the ship's hospital under restraint & constant supervision". Fortunately, they were only two weeks from home so he knew the round-the-clock watch wouldn't go on for too long.

When he stepped off the *Rangitata* on 9 April he fully expected to be assigned back to it or another ship within a few weeks. However, the Merchant Navy had other ideas and in early May he was told he was being placed in the Merchant Navy Reserve Pool (MNRP). He didn't take this well.

He was convinced that it was largely because of his age – he had celebrated his 74th birthday in March in mid-Atlantic on the *Rangitata* – but was adamant he was still fit and healthy enough to serve as a ship's surgeon. On all his ships during WW2 he was by several years the oldest crew member. From time to time there were some senior stewards, barbers, bookkeepers and chefs in their 60s but never anyone in their 70s.

His complaints fell on deaf ears.

With the invasion of Europe about to start and the thousands of US troops already in the UK ready to go, the losses on the Atlantic convoys rapidly declining and the need to move huge numbers of troops to other theatres of war also greatly diminished the merchant navy simply didn't need to have as many ships at sea. A doctor in his 75th year was probably an obvious choice to stand down from active service.

Being in the MNRP had one consolation: he was still paid. On the troopships he was paid £33 a month (£1350 at 2015 prices) and, although the rate was reduced for being in the reserve pool, it proved useful to the Kellys until he was formally discharged from the Merchant Navy the following year.

He had no choice but to return to London and sit out the rest of the war, his four years' service having earned him the Atlantic Star, Africa Star and France-Germany Star to add to his extensive collection from the Great War and his Empire adventures. His desire to die at sea was denied him.

By now he was a grandfather. Rosemary gave birth to a son, Alastair, at the end of March 1944, shortly followed by Brigid's first child, Deborah. Brigid and Tom had already moved to Golder's Green, not far from Paddington where Tom was a GP while Rosemary was living in a small flat in Romford, Essex. Rosemary's husband was serving with the RAMC in India and by the end of 1945 with the troops from Europe returning home she had had enough of being by herself with a baby and so took off – with baby – for India on a neutral Swedish ship, the *SS Drottningholm*. By the time they returned two years later, she was heavily pregnant with their second son and Britain was in the grip of its most severe winter for generations. Her concerned parents were waiting for them with armfuls of warm clothes as they disembarked at Tilbury, slightly to her surprise.

Right: Kelly with Deborah Foot, one of his grandchildren (Brigid's first child) after the war.

Left: Kelly with Gertrude shopping in Oxford Street in 1948, the last photograph of him.

Gertrude was for the first time in her married life enjoying an unbroken period with her husband. She was only in her mid-50s and life in post-war London was something she enjoyed. As well as the arrival of grandchildren there was the novelty of being together to celebrate a succession of landmarks in their lives: his 75th birthday in March 1945, her 60th the following year and their 30th wedding anniversary in April 1948.

This happy postlude came to an abrupt end on 29 January 1949.

While shaving at St Mary's Mansions, Kelly suffered a massive heart attack and died almost instantly. The curtain was thus lowered on a life of adventure, courage and service to country and his fellow human beings of many races.

Above: Service and adventure and, although Kelly would never say it, some heroism too. The medals he wore with pride (l to r); Distinguished Service Order (only the Victoria Cross took precedence over the DSO), Tibet Medal with Gyanste clasp, 1914-15 Star, Victory Medal, British War Medal with Oak Leaf, Indian General Service Medal with Afghanistan 1919 clasp.

CHAPTER 16

Postscript

Thomas Bernard Kelly DSO was laid to rest in St Mary's Roman Catholic Cemetery in Kensal Green following an unfussy funeral at Our Lady of the Rosary, Paddington on 2 February 1949. Gertrude briefly investigated the possibility of burying her husband at sea, a long expressed hope of his, but quickly dismissed the idea because of the expense and red tape involved. Instead he lies alongside many others who served their country in ways he would have appreciated including Mary Seacole and May Barrie, nurses from the Crimean War, and James Henry Reynolds, one of the recipients of the Victoria Cross at Rorke's Drift during the Zulu wars..

There were no great obituaries, even in Galway, although his death was noted in British and Irish medical journals. He passed quietly into history, many of his stories never even shared with his family.

Brigid had rushed from nearby Golders Green to be at her distraught mother's side, registering the death and taking care of the funeral arrangements – which took place just four days after his death, including time for a post-mortem. Her younger sister Rosemary was living in Essex with two small children to look after and a husband working flat out as a junior doctor at the London Hospital: she didn't attend her father's funeral.

Gertrude was left £1449 11s (£45,765) and now, just 62, had to work out what she was going to do as a widow. She soon gave up the flat in St Mary's Mansions, which was both too large for her and too expensive to maintain and moved to Hampshire to live with a cousin. In the early 1950s she briefly moved to Australia with Brigid and her family

Above: Kelly's grave in the Roman Catholic Cemetery at Kensal Green.

when Tom worked as a doctor just outside Melbourne in a practice run by John Cahill, married to one of Brigid's many cousins descended from the Irish emigration in the 19th century. Gertrude didn't take to Australians, considering them to be rude and uncouth, an attitude that probably contributed to the Foots' Australian adventure being cut short.

She remained with Brigid for some years after they returned to England before moving near to Rosemary in Gidea Park, Essex. It was there that she died in December 1979, age 83.

The connection with Galway was finally extinguished on 13 October 1954 when Kelly's beloved sister Annie died a few days short of her 90th birthday. She died at the Presentation Convent where she had lived without a break for 67 years since entering the convent as a novice in the autumn of 1887. A greater contrast with her younger brother's incident-packed life played out across the globe is harder to imagine.

Annie's death marked the final appearance of the Kelly family in the Galway papers, almost 80 years since their father had launched himself into local politics and the headlines in Galway.

"The death occurred on Wednesday at the Presentation Convent Galway of Mother Mary Columba Kelly. Mother Columba, who was born at High Street, Galway, was daughter of the late Mr and Mrs Denis Kelly, members of a well-known old Galway family.

"The late Mother Columba was educated at the Dominican Convent, Taylor's Hill, and at the Sacred Heart Convent, Roscrea. In 1950 she celebrated her Diamond Jubilee. She was sister of the late Col Thomas Kelly, Indian Medical Service, who died in England. She was aunt of the late Dr Denis Morris, Galway, and cousin of the late Monsignor Considine, St Patrick's, Galway." – *Connacht Tribune* October 16 1954.

Above: Annie is buried in the simple nun's cemetery in the garden of the Presentation Convent in Galway.

Bibliography

This bibliography contains the main sources relied on in the research for this book. It excludes items such as birth, death and marriage certificates and various incidental sources that merely confirmed something contained in one of the principal sources.

Ireland

Anon, Obituary of Mother M. Columba Kelly, Archives of the Presentation Convent, Galway

Cunningham, Jack, *Galway's Own* (Galway, Jack Cunningham, 1977)

Foster, R. F., *Modern Ireland 1600-1972* (London, Penguin Books, 1988)

Petty Sessions Order Books, 4th October 1880, CSPS 1/11533

Irish Petty Sessions Court Registers 1828-1912, CSPS 1/11495

The Galway Vindicator and Connaught Advertiser, Various editions 1883

Galway Express, Various editions 1883 to 1895

Connacht Tribune, Various editions from 1909 to 16 October 1954

Blake of Ballyglunin Park Papers, collection of miscellaneous papers relating to the Blake estate at Ballyglunin, County Galway, 1840-1920 (Complied by Catherine Fahy) MSS 26, 979-27,015. Accession No. 2471. National Library of Ireland

Diaries of Bishop Francis McCormack, 1887-1909, Diocese of Galway Archives

Census of Ireland, 1901 and 1911

Medical Register, 1911 and 1913

Slater's Commercial Directory of Ireland, 1881

Economy and Society in Galway in the early 20th Century, The National Archives of Ireland

Galway Town Commissioners, minute books of (1836-1899)

Griffiths Valuation 1855, South Ward, Parish of St. Nicholas

Galway and Salthill trams – Kennys Bookshop & Art Gallery

Local government and taxation inquiry commission (Ireland) part 3, Report and evidence

Irish Journal of Medical Science

Thom's Irish Almanac 1884

Local government and taxation of towns inquiry commission (Ireland) Part 3, Report and Evidence., House of Commons Parliamentary Papers, 1877

The Advertiser (Adelaide, SA: 1889-1931), 10th September 1901, page 5

Judgement of Mr Justice Keogh, Hansard 1803-2005, HC Deb 13 June 1872, Volume 211, cc1669-76

Clongowes Wood College archives

The Tuam Herald, Saturday, 2 September 1876

Royal Colleges of Physicians and Surgeons of Edinburgh, and the faculty of Physicians and surgeons of Glasgow; final examination schedule for the joint qualifications in medicine and surgery

Queen's College Calendar 1888

Queen's College Calendar 1890-91

Queen's College Calendar 1893

Queen's College Calendar 1907-08

India

Allen, Charles, Raj, *A Scrapbook of British India 1877-1947* (London, Andre

Deutsh, 1977)

Anon, *The Third Afghan War 1919 Official Account* (Calcutta, Government of India Central Publication Branch, 1926)

Baxter, Ian A., *Baxter's Guide, Biographical Sources in the India Office Records*

Beaumont, Roger, *Sword of the Raj, The British Army in India, 1747-1947* (New York, The Bobbs-Merrill Company, 1977)

Coughlin, Con, *Young Winston and the Fight against the Taliban, Churchill's First War* (London, Pan Books, 2013)

Crawford, Lieut-Colonel D. G., *Roll of the Indian Medical Service 1615-1930, Volume one 1615-1799* (London, W. Thacker & Co, 1930)

Crawford, Lieut-Colonel D. G., *Roll of the Indian Medical Service 1615-1930, Volume two 1800-1930* (London, W. Thacker & Co, 1930)

Fortescue, John; *Narrative of the visit to India of their Majesties King George V and Queen Mary.* Macmillian and Co, London, 1912

Goradia, Nayana; *The Delhi Durbar, 1911 Last Hurrah of the of the Raj.* India International centre, new Delhi

Hamilton, Angus; *Afghanistan*, J.B. Millet & Company Boston 1910

James, Lawrence, *Raj, The making and unmaking of British India* (London, Abacus, 1997)

Nevill, Captain H. L., *Campaigns on the North-West Frontier* (Uckfield, The Navel & Military Press, 2005)

O'Connor, Frederick, *On the frontier and beyond* (1931)

O'Meara, E. J., *I'd Live it Again* (London, Jonathan Cape, 1935)

Sidebotham, Herbert, Third Afghan War, New Statesman, 16th August 1916

Spawson, Maj Gen Sir Cuthbert Allan, unpublished autobiography, Liddell Hart Military Archives, GB 0099 KCLMA Sprawsona

Stewart, Jules, *Frontier Fighters on Active Service in Waziristan, The Memoirs of Major Walter James Cumming* (Barnsley,

Pen & Sword Military, 2010)

Tyndall, Henry, *High Noon of Empire, the Diary of Lieutenant Colonel Henry Tyndall 1895-1915* (Barnsley, Pen & Sword Military, 2007)

Rothero, Christopher, *Skinner's Horse* (London, Almark Publications, 1979)

Gazette of India 1907, 04/05/07 Foreign Departure Notifications

Passenger list: Oceana: 25th March 1897 (departure)

Quarterly Indian Army list; 1897-1926

Passenger list: Empress of Japan; 20 May 1914 (arrival)

Indian Medical Service successful candidates 1895-1896, British Library manuscript L/MIL/9/4/9

Wilkinson Sword blades: register of proof; infantry swords made 1894-1902

Coronation Durbar Delhi 1911, Official directory with maps, Superintendent Government Printing, India, 1911

The London Gazette, 23 May 1919

The London Gazette,17 October 1919

The London Gazette,23 May 1919

The London Gazette, 6 June 1924

The London Gazette, 26 March 1909

The London Gazette, 27 April 1900

The London Gazette, 19 March 1926

Marriages Solemnized at the Church of the Holy Name within the Arch Diocese of Bombay, 1918

UK Incoming Passenger lists, 1878-1960, record for Gertrude A Kelly

Passenger lists for Donala, Bombay, Via Beira to Plymouth and London 16/06/1924

Certificate of Baptism- Rosemary Anne Josephine Kelly, 3rd February 1921, St Joseph's Church, Clyde Road, Rawalpindi

The Prince of Wales Eastern Book – A pictorial record of the voyages of H.M.S. Renown 1921-1922, London, Hodder and Stoughton, 1922

A letter from the Military Secretary to his Excellency the Viceroy, 23rd April 1926

WO 100/400 Delhi Durbar 1911: medal rolls of Army in India and memorandum

WO 98/8/712 Victoria Cross details of Andrews, Henry John Rank: Temporary Captain

WO 95/5392 War Diary, Kohat-Kurram Force: 60 Infantry Brigade: 4/39 Battalion Garhwal Rifles

WO 95/5391 War Diray, North West Frontier Force

WO 106/57 Events and Operations regarding occupation of Waziristan

WO 106/156 Operations in Waziristan

WO 106/56 Lieutenant-Colonel G. L. Carter (106th Hazara Pioneers)

WO 95/5396 War Diary, General Staff

Tibet and Persia

Allen, Charles, *Duel in the Snow: The True story of the Younghusband Mission to Lhasa* (London, John Murray, 2004)

Brander, Lt-Col H., *32nd Sikh Pioneers: Regimental History; Vol 2, Sikkim and Tibet 1903- 04* (1905)

Candler, Edmund, *The Unveiling of Lhasa.* London, 1905

Fleming, Peter, *Bayonets to Lhasa. London,* Rupert Hart-Davis, 1961

Hedin, Sven Anders, *Overland to India.* London, Macmillan and Co, 1923

Hopkirk, Peter, *Trespassers on the Roof of the World, The Race for Lhasa* (London, John Murray, 1982)

Shakabpa, Tsepon W.D., *Tibet a Political History*; Potala publications, New York, 1984

Tousi, Re'za Rai'ss, British Encroachments in Seistan, Journal of J. Humanities (2006) Vol. 13

Younghusband, Sir Francis, *Memorandum on Our Relations with Tibet* (1903)

Younghusband, Sir Francis, *India and Tibet* (1910)

F197/145 Letters to his father. Younghusband Collection, British Library

F197/173-7. Letters to his wife May 1903 to September 1904. Younghusband Collection, British Library

F197/271. Lists of kit issued for Tibet. July 1903. Younghusband Collection,

British Library

Waddell, L. Austine, *Lhasa and its Mysteries with a Record of the British Tibetan Expedition of 1903-1904* (New York, Dover Publications, 1988)

Letters from T B Kelly to Sister Columba, Presentation Convent, Galway, July to September 1904

Gazette of India, Supp 20/01/06 v/11/173

Boston Evening Herald 02/04/06

Sydney Morning Herald, 03/04/06

British Library record 10R/V/27/281/34

British Library record 10R/L/MIL/17/13/119- Narrative

The Illustrated London News: NO. 3415- VOL. CXXV, Saturday October 1st,1904

Letters from Field Force to Lhasa 1903-4 from Captain Cecil Mainprise

The London Gazette, December 13, 1904

Bailey Collection: Tibet 1903-4. British Library'

Derby Daily Telegraph, 31 March 1906

Derby Daily Telegraph, 15 February 1906

Dundee Evening Telegraph, 15 February 1906

Edinburgh Evening News, 6 June 1906

FO 368138/18 Plague in Seistan; printed extracts from diaries of officers on plague duty in Persia, from India Office, sent November 1906, British Library

Bombay Plague Research Laboratory, British Medical Journal, 25 September 1904;

Plague Supplement to the Seistan consular diary, (No. 35, for the period 3rd to 9th September 1906)

FO 368/38 Folios 18-20. Plague in Seistan - note from the Persian government, British Library

Persia code 134, files 3202-32579

World War One

Arthur, Max, *Forgotten Voices of the Great War* (London, Ebury Press, 2003)

Barker, A. J., *The First Iraq War 1914-1918* (New York, Enigma Books, 2009)

Bondee Joanna, *Women and the Medical Services in World War 1*, Birkbeck College, University of London

Bruce, GR, Captain RAMC (SR) Malta Military Hospitals 1915-1917

Bruton, John. September 1914: John Redmond at Woodenbridge. Studies: An Irish Quarterly Review, Vol 101, no 402, Summer 2012

Caldwell, CE, *The Life of Sir Stanley Maude*, Coustut Co, London 1920

Campbell Begg, R., *Surgery on Trestles, A Saga of Suffering and Triumph* (Norwich, Jarrold & Sons, 1967)

Carver, Field Marshal Lord, *The National Army Museum Book of the Turkish Front 1914-18* (London, Pan Books, 2004)

Cohen, Susan, *Medical Services in the First World War* (Oxford, Shire Publications, 2014).

Connelly, Mark, *The British Campaign in Aden* 1914-1918

Cornish, Paul, *The First World War Galleries* (London, Imperial War Museum, 2014)

Crowley, Patrick, *Kut 1916, Courage and Failure in Iraq* (Gloucestershire, Spellmount, 2009)

Hallett, Christine E., *Containing Trauma, Nursing Work in the First World War* (Manchester, Manchester University Press, 2009)

Knight, Paul, *The British Army in Mesopotamia 1914-1918* (London, McFarland & Company, 2013)

Layton, Lieut-Col TB; Surgery next door to the front, The Lancet, September 29th 1917

Liddell Hart, B. H., *History of the First World War* (London, Book Club Associates, 1973)

Macpherson, Major-General Sir W.G., *Medical Services: History of the Great War based on Official Documents* (Uckfield, The Naval & Military Press,)

Mortlock, Michael J., *The Egyptian Expeditionary Force in World War I* (London, McFarland & Company, 1933/2011)

Rinaldi, Richard. *Order of Battle, British Army 1914*, Tiger Lilly Books, 2008

Townshend, Charles, *When God Made Hell, The British Invasion of Mesopotamia and the Creation of Iraq 1914-1921* (London, Faber and Faber, 2010)

White, Ian R., *Doctors in the Great War* (Barnsley, Pen and Sword Military, 2013)

Winter, J M, *The Experience of World War I* (London, Guild Publishing, 1988)

Woodward, David R., *Forgotten Soldiers of the First World War* (Kentucky, Tempus, 2007)

Casualties in the Medical Services, British Medical Journal, 1 July 1916

Medical notes in Parliament, British Medical Journal, November 1916

Service Papers for Robert Dennis Kelly, National Archives of Australia

Supplement to the London Gazette, 7th February, 1918

Sixth Supplement to the London Gazette, Tuesday 26th August 1918

Fourth Supplement to the London Gazette, Tuesday 8th January,1918

Fifth Supplement to the London Gazette, Friday 8th March 1918

Fourth Supplement to the London Gazette, Tuesday 10th October 1916

Second Supplement to the London Gazette, Tuesday 10th July 1917

Third Supplement to the London Gazette, Tuesday 14th August 1917

Supplement to the London Gazette, Tuesday 4th July, 1916

Supplement to the London Gazette, 21st June, 1916

British advance in Hinterland, The Times, July 26th 1915

A raid on Aden Hinterland, The Times, July 10th 1915

Hawkins, Edward A (Corporal) Collection, 1917, IWM PC476

Distribution of Mesopotamia Expeditionary Corps (Excluding Tigris Corps) 1st July 1916

WO 372 23 Service Card of Gertrude Fenn,

WO 399/2698 Service record for Gertrude Fenn

WO 95/5400 10 Indian Infantry Brigade:

125 Battalion Napier Rifles

WO 95/4421 Headquarters Branches and Services: Adjutant and Quarter-Master General

WO 106/915 Mesopotamian Expeditionary Force: Despatch on operations by Lt Gen Sir W.R. Marshall

WO 361/2082 Prisoners of war, Far East: Headquarters, 28th Indian Infantry Brigade

MH 106/1641 British Expeditionary Force in Mesopotamia

MH 106/1718 British Expeditionary Force to Mesopotamia - officers

MH 106/1895 British Expeditionary Force to Mesopotamia, officers

MT 23/632/16 Hospital River Craft. Whether hospital cots offered were suitable for the craft

WO 95/4421 War Diary Egyptian Expeditionary Force. 10th Indian Division. 105th Indian Field Ambulance

WO 95/5271 War Diary 140th Indian Stationary Hospital. 83rd Combined Stationary Hospital

WO 95/5254 War Diary Lines of Communication Troops: 3rd British General Hospital

WO 95/5273 War Diary Base Isolation Hospital (Basrah)

WO 95/5257 War Diary 65th British General Hospital

WO 95/5191 War Diary 105th Combined Field Ambulance

WO 95/5439 War Diary 26th Indian General Hospital

WO 32/5197 Operations, Narratives of: General (Code 46(A))

Private papers of Fr C B Warren OBW. IWM Doc 4201

Lemere-Goff, Eunice Winifred. IWM interview 9523

Macdonald, Ian Pendlebury. IWM interview 9149

Inter-war years

Crew List, Orduna, Arrival, New York, 13 September 1926

Singapore Free Press and Mercantile Advertiser (1884-1942) 19th February 1931, page 13

Official Log-Book and crew list 'Orbita' 11th March 1937- 23rd May 1937

Official Log-Book and crew list 'Orbita' 1st July 1937 – 15th September 1937

Official Log-Book and crew list 'Orbita' 14th July 1938 – 25th September 1938

Official Log-Book and crew list 'Orbita' 13th October 1938 – 24th December 1938

Official Log-Book and crew list 'Orbita' 30th September 1937 – 11th December 1937

Official Log-Book and crew list 'Orbita' 10th December 1936 – 21st February 1937

Official Log-Book and crew list 'Orbita' 22nd January 1938 – 4th April 1938

Official Log-Book and crew list 'Orbita' 22nd April 1938 – 3rd July 1938

Crew list for 'Orduna' arriving at New York 13th September 1926

World War Two

Bennett, G. H. & R., *Survivors, British Merchant Seamen in the Second World War* (London, The Hambledon Press, 1999)

Diamond, Hanna, *Fleeing Hitler France 1940* (New York, Oxford University Press, 2007)

De Marneffe, Francis, *Last Boat from Bordeaux: War Memoirs of Francis De Marneffe* (Cambridge, Coolidge Hill Press, 2001)

Freeman, C. Denis & Cooper, Douglas, *The Road to Bordeaux* (London, The Cresset Press, 1942)

Mould, Richard F. Eve Curie-Labouisse 1904-2007, Journal of Oncology 2008, Vol 58, no 1

Munro, Archie, *The Winston Specials, Troopships Via the Cape 1940-1943* (Liskeard, Maritime Books, 2006)

Raitan, Nicholas, *The story of 30 Assault Unit in WW2* Faber & Faber 2011

Saunders, Hilary St George, *A short history*

of the British India Steam Navigation Company in the Second World War 387. 50651 Brin

Sorel, Nancy Caldwell. *The Women who wrote the war*, 1999, Arcade Publishing

Waters, Sydney D., *Ordeal by sea: the New Zealand Shipping Company in the Second World War 1939-1945* (London, The New Zealand Shipping Company, 1949)

Port of Falmouth Harbour Masters Journal No 25, 1940

US Holocaust Memorial Museum, Holocaust Encyclopaedia- Seeking refuge in Cuba, 1939

A project by D. Hanna Diamond. Daphne Wall. 'Flight from France: from Bordeaux to London' www.fleeinghitler.org/ (accessed 05/04/2013)

Barvennon.com- Australian diary – Archives 07T, 12 November 2007 Refugees 1940

A letter to Mr T.B. Kelly from the chairman of the British India Steam Navigation Company

The West Australian (Perth, WA: 1879-1954), Saturday 7th September 1940, page 6

The Times, Saturday June 22 1940

The Western Morning News, Saturday June 22nd 1940

The Daily Mail- Saturday 22nd June 1940

Crew List, SS Madura, Arrival, London, 24 June 1940

Movements of Ruahine 1942

Names and descriptions of British passengers embarked at port of Liverpool on Drottringholm, 1946

Thomas Bernard Kelly's Merchant Navy Service Card

Medal card 1939-1949 Thomas Bernard Kelly R.268715

Western Morning News, Saturday, June 29, 1940

Cheltenham Chronicle, Saturday June 22 1940

Press and journal- 22 June 1940

Daily Telegraph 21 June 1940, front page

Daily Telegraph, 24 June 1940, article by

Richard Capell

Western Daily Press- June 21 1940

WO 106/1615 Evacuation of B.E.F. France; plan "Aerial"

WO 361/21 Information concerning vessels involved in the British Expeditionary Force (BEF)

BT 390/66 Kay E W to Kelly W S

BT 382/933 Kelly Thomas to Kelshaw W

BT 381/103 Registry of shipping and seamen: war of 1939-1945

BT 381/81 Registry of shipping and seamen: war of 1939-1945

BT 26/1191/86 London: SS Madura (British India Steam Navigation Company Ltd)

BT 381/2422 Registry of shipping and seamen: war of 1939-1945; Coast trade official Log books and crew agreements

BT 381/803 Registry of shipping and seamen: war of 1939-1945; Coast trade official Log books and crew agreements. Merchant and fishing vessels

BT 381/2901 Registry of shipping and seamen: war of 1939-1945; Coast trade official Log books and crew agreements. 149564.

BT 381/1773 Registry of shipping and seamen: war of 1939-1945; Coast trade official Log books and crew agreements. Merchant and fishing vessels

BT 381/1415 Registry of shipping and seamen: war of 1939-1945; Coast trade official Log books and crew agreements. Merchant and fishing vessels

BT 381/659 Registry of shipping and seamen: war of 1939-1945; Coast trade official Log books and crew agreements. Merchant and fishing vessels

BT 26/1195/8 Liverpool: MV Rangitata (The New Zealand Shipping Company Ltd)

BT 26/1200/113 Bristol: MV Rangitata (The New Zealand Shipping Company Ltd)

BT 26/1190/75 Liverpool: MV Rangitata (New Zealand Shipping Company Ltd) travelling from Wellington

BT 381/1985 Registry of shipping and seamen: war of 1939-1945; Coast trade official Log books and crew agreements. Merchant and fishing vessels

BT 381/925 Registry of shipping and seamen: war of 1939-1945; Coast trade official Log books and crew agreements. Merchant and fishing vessels

BT 381/1500 Registry of shipping and seamen: war of 1939-1945; Coast trade official Log books and crew agreements. Merchant and fishing vessels

BT 389/21/85 Ship Name: Mooltan Gross Tonnage: 20952, 21039

BT 26/1197/61 Liverpool: Mooltan (P & O Steam Navigation Company Ltd) travelling from Suez

General

Ed Barraclough, Geoffrey, *The Times Atlas of World History* (London, Times Books, 1978)

Ed Bayly, Dr Christopher, *Atlas of the British Empire* (London, Guild Publishing, 1989)

Cox, Jane & Padfield, Timothy, *Tracing your Ancestors in the Public Record Office* (London, Her Majesty's Stationary Office, 1981)

Duckers, Peter, *British Campaign Medals* (Risborough, Shire Books, 2000)

Mason, Mariette. Unpublished conversations with Gertrude Fenn. 1973.

Proceeding of the Royal Society of Medicine; Vol. 49; November 2, 1955

Births registered in January, February, March 1887- Gertrude, Agnes Tendring

1901 England census for Gertrude A. Fenn

1891 England census for Gertrude A. fenn

1911 census for Gertrude A Fenn

England & Wales, National Probate Calendar (index of wills and administrations), 1858-1966 record for Thomas Bernard Kelly

Certified copy of an entry of death- Thomas Bernard Kelly death 29/01/1949

England, Andrews Newspaper index card, 1790-1976 record for Thomas Bernard Kelly

England and Wales, National Probate Calendar (Index of Wills and Administrations),1949

Index

Picture Credits

Unless stated below, pictures with no credit are mostly from the family albums kept by his sister. Those credited below are from copyright sources. A few are from sources out of copyright although I have credited some anyway. The modern ones are taken by the author, except the medals which were photographed by Kelly's grandson, Martin Foot.

Chapter 1 Page 19 Shop Street, Galway, in the late 19th century. Lawrence Collection, National Library of Ireland. Page 20 St Ignatius College, Galway, Lawrence Collection, National Library of Ireland. Page 21 A horse drawn tram on the waterfront at Salthill. Lawrence Collection, National Library of Ireland. Page 23 The Claddagh. Lawrence Collection, National Library of Ireland.

Chapter 2 Page 31 Michael Kelly (1853-1929). Bendigo Historical Society. Page 34 The Presentation Convent, Galway. Lawrence Collection, National Library of Ireland.

Chapter 3 Page 37 Queen's College, Galway in the 1880s. Lawrence Collection, National Library of Ireland. Page 39 Entry in the Royal College of Surgeons of Edinburgh's register recording Kelly's success in 1891. Royal College of Surgeons of Edinburgh. Page 40 Detail of Kelly's successful completion of the Triple Diploma. Royal College of Surgeons of Edinburgh.

Chapter 4 Page 47 Passenger list from *Oceana*. The National Archives.

Chapter 5 Page 67 Tang La Pass. Younghusband 'India and Tibet'. Page 67 110th Indian Field Hospital in convoy. Bailey Collection, British Library Board. Page 68 Officers at Tuna. Bailey Collection, British Library Board. Page 71 The exposed fort at Tuna. Waddell 'Lhasa and its Mysteries'. Page 72 The forces leave Tuna. Younghusband 'India and Tibet'.

Chapter 6 Page 78 Gyantse Jong. Younghusband 'India and Tibet'. Page 86 The Mission quarters in Lhasa. Younghusband 'India and Tibet'.

Chapter 7 Page 103 The British consulate in Nasratabad. Sven Hedin 'Overland to India'. Page 107 The official plague diary. The National Archives.

Chapter 8 Page 111 The Marconi telegraph station at Clifden. Lawrence Collection, National Library of Ireland. Page 115 Overview of the Delhi Durbar from 'The Royal Visit to India' by John Fortescue. Page 117 Watercolour by Major Alfred Crowdy Lovett. National Army Museum.

Chapter 9 Page 128 Indian troops defending the Suez Canal. 'The Great War', part-work published by Amalgamated Press. Page 130 Hospital ships on the Nile. 'The Great War', part-work published by Amalgamated Press. Page 134 page of the War Diary of the 105th Indian Field Ambulance. The National Archives.

Chapter 11 Page 147 British wounded from Kut 'The Great War', part-work published by Amalgamated Press. Page 160 Kelly's detailed description of a layout of one of the new ambulance trains. The National Archives. Page 164 Record card detailing Denis Kelly's death and relatives. National Archives of Australia.

Chapter 13 Page 191 The Prince of Wales visits a medical college on his tour of India in 1921. 'The Prince of Wales' Eastern Book'.

Chapter 15 Page 217 The *SS Mooltan*. acidhistory https://acidhistory.wordpress.com/